Quoting Shakespeare

Quoting Shakespeare

Form and Culture in
Early Modern Drama

Douglas Bruster

University of Nebraska Press
Lincoln & London

Publication of this volume was assisted by a University
Cooperative Society Subvention Grant awarded by
The University of Texas at Austin.

Library of Congress Cataloging-in-Publication Data

Bruster, Douglas.

   Quoting Shakespeare : form and culture in early modern drama
/ Douglas Bruster.

      p.   cm.

   Includes bibliographical references (p.) and index.

   ISBN 0-8032-1303-4 (cl : alk. paper)

      1. English drama—Early modern and Elizabethan, 1500–
1600—History and criticism. 2. English drama—17th century—
History and criticism. 3. Shakespeare, William, 1564–1616—Criticism and interpretation. 4. Quotations in literature. 5. Intertextuality. 6. Literary form. I. Title.

PR655 .B78 2000

822'.309—dc21   00-024202

For Madeleine and Claire

CONTENTS

ACKNOWLEDGMENTS

I am indebted to a number of people for their help with this project. Christopher Cannon first showed me, through example, the possibilities of a historically oriented study of intertextuality. And along with Susan Baker, David Bevington, Edward Bonahue Jr., Heather Dubrow, Scott Gordon, Hugh Grady, Gerald Graff, Robin Gray, Elizabeth Helsinger, Kenneth Alan Hovey, J. Paul Hunter, Doran Larson, Eric Mallin, Janel Mueller, Michael Murrin, John G. Norman, David Riggs, Naseeb Shaheen, Stuart Sherman, Douglas Stewart, Richard Strier, and William Veeder, he has generously read and commented on parts of the manuscript. Gwynne Evans and John Tobin have earned my continual admiration and gratitude in demonstrating the value—as well as the methods—of solid scholarship. Their guidance and friendship have steered this book in its current direction. I would like to thank Constance Kuriyama and the members of the Marlowe Association for the opportunity to present a version of my Marlowe chapter at the Modern Language Association of America. Earlier versions of other chapters have been presented at the Renaissance Colloquium of Harvard University, at Washington University in Saint Louis, and at the University of Chicago; comments and suggestions by audience members in these venues have helped shape this project in productive ways. I am also deeply indebted to Roland Greene, the late S. K. Heninger Jr., Joshua Scodel, and Helen Vendler for reading and critiquing earlier drafts of chapter 2. Parts of chapters 1 through 5 have previously appeared as essays. Chapter 1 incorporates "New Light on the Old Historicism: Shakespeare and the Forms of Historicist Criticism," *Literature and History* 3rd ser., 5 (1996), 1–18; chapter 2, "'Come to the Tent Again': 'The Passionate Shepherd,' Dramatic Rape, and Lyric Time," *Crit-*

icism 33 (1991), 49–72; chapter 3, "Comedy and Control: Shakespeare and the Plautine Poeta," *Comparative Drama* 24 (1990), 217–31, used by permission of the editors of *Comparative Drama*; chapter 4, "Local *Tempest*: Shakespeare and the Work of the Early Modern Playhouse," *Journal of Medieval and Renaissance Studies* 25 (1995), 33–53; chapter 5, "The Jailer's Daughter and the Politics of Madwomen's Language," *Shakespeare Quarterly* 46 (1995), 277–300. I am grateful to these journals for permission to incorporate these materials and to their readers for thoughtful responses to the arguments presented therein.

The publication of this book was supported by a subvention from the University Cooperative Society of the University of Texas at Austin. I am grateful for this assistance.

I warmly thank Minna and Markku Salminen, who hosted three Americans at a time when the manuscript of this book was undergoing significant revisions. For assistance with Latin here, I am grateful to John Rundin. I also thank Lydia Cochrane for neighborly advice on translation and for the example of her wonderful family. Michelle Girard read the manuscript with care and sensitivity; her suggestions have improved nearly every page. *Quoting Shakespeare* was copyedited by Barbara Wojhoski; her assistance in the preparation of this book has been exemplary. It goes without saying that any errors that remain are my own. My greatest debt is to Elizabeth Scala, without whose support and companionship I would have been unable to write a book on indebtedness.

A NOTE ON TEXTS

Approximate dates for plays are provided the first time that the play is mentioned in a chapter; this holds through chapter 5. These dates, meant to serve as guides, are taken from *Annals of English Drama, 975–1700,* 3rd edition, ed. Alfred Harbage, revised by S. Schoenbaum and Sylvia Stoler Wagonheim (London: Routledge, 1989). Unless otherwise noted, all references to Shakespeare in this book draw on *The Riverside Shakespeare,* 2nd edition, ed. G. Blakemore Evans et al. (Boston: Houghton Mifflin, 1997), and all references to Jonson are to *Ben Jonson,* ed. C. H. Herford, Percy Simpson, and Evelyn Simpson, 11 vols. (Oxford: Clarendon Press, 1925–52). I have silently modernized the spelling and punctuation of many of the early modern texts quoted in this book.

Our debt to tradition through reading and conversation is so massive, our protest or private addition so rare and insignificant—and this commonly on the ground of other reading or hearing—that, in a large sense, one would say there is no pure originality. All minds quote. Old and new make the warp and woof of every moment. There is no thread that is not a twist of these two strands. By necessity, by proclivity, and by delight, we all quote. We quote not only books and proverbs, but arts, sciences, religion, customs, and laws; nay, we quote temples and houses, tables and chairs by imitation. The Patent-Office Commissioner knows that all machines in use have been invented and re-invented over and over; that the mariner's compass, the boat, the pendulum, glass, movable types, the kaleidoscope, the railway, the power-loom, etc., have been many times found and lost, from Egypt, China, and Pompei down.

RALPH WALDO EMERSON, "Quotation and Originality"

Introduction

It is a commonplace observation that writers make their works out of borrowed materials, but apparently ordinary instances of borrowing can tell us extraordinary things about texts and authors. Focusing on the plays of Shakespeare and his dramatic contemporaries, this study seeks to enhance our current understanding of early modern England and its texts by proving that such *bricolage* can give us valuable insight into the cultural, historical, and political positions of writers and their works. I should say at the outset that I mean my title, *Quoting Shakespeare,* to be read two ways—a Shakespeare both quoting and quoted—for how a text is dispersed into later texts can often illuminate not only the work in question but also the authors, works, and cultures that borrow from it. So where the following pages advance a way of reading that stresses the "thickness" of intertextuality in early modern plays, intertextuality is also seen here as tethering works to the future as well as the past. By tracing such lines of appropriation, we can situate early modern texts and their elements in and after their time and culture.

Doing so, however, confronts us with several problems raised by recent trends in critical approaches to early modern literature. Among these approaches is the New Historicism, a critical methodology that examines literature in the context of social and cultural history. New historicist critics often accomplish this task by reading the relations among texts, broadly conceived. But these critics' "return" to History has just as often left out both the history of books themselves and the details of historical change. Ironically, New Historicism has left us *less* conscious of the fact that literature itself has a history, that it speaks with others' words, talks back to them, and manifests authors' own histories of reading and writing. Partly

responsible for this oversight is New Historicism's dependence on historical conjuncture—a synchronic or "sideways" alignment of objects—that
effectively excludes earlier and later texts related to the work in question.
We need to consider instead how literature exists in and over time, for we
can better appreciate the historicity of works, including the historical
changes they may signal, by examining their overlap with texts, events,
and individuals outside New Historicism's often limited windows of inquiry.

Whether called source, borrowing, appropriation, or intertextuality,
this overlap can reveal a mosaic-like textuality. For reasons that this study
will explore, such overlap is especially evident in the patchwork of early
modern plays—among the most thoroughly social of all literary texts, and
ones that have assumed a special place in our understanding of early modern England. In what follows, I will call this overlap "quotation," drawing
on a meaning current in the early modern era better to show the intensively composite nature of its dramatic works. By quotation I understand
the textual incorporation of such discrete components as words, events,
and identities, a process that links texts to specific elements in the world
outside them. Quotation in this sense stands midway between imitation
and citation, and refers to both the borrowed matter of texts and the activity of borrowing itself. The tension between our sense of quotation as
attributed borrowing and the tendency of these plays to "quote" without
attribution will ask us to consider how well our notions of property, language, and textuality apply to early modern drama. Seeing the parts of
texts we examine as quotation also prompts us to examine how we analyze
these texts. In conventional source study, for instance, these quotations
sometimes seem ends in themselves, borrowings predestined to appear as
notes at the bottom of a page or in a scholarly journal. New Historicism,
in contrast, takes these quotations as the beginning of a thick description
of the text's place in a complex cultural milieu.

New Historicism commonly focuses on markedly resonant points of
contact among texts, on borrowing and contiguity that point to provocative elements in the surrounding culture: a riot, a transvestite marriage, an
exorcism, an erotic dream. The sometimes dazzling results of this practice
have clearly changed not only how we write literary criticism but also how
we read and conceive literature. Yet, as I argue here, we can learn more
about texts and the history they incorporate if we look beyond the provoc-

ative material that New Historicism commonly employs, for the *positions* of texts and authors—their orientations, habits, and inclinations—often appear most clearly in otherwise ordinary borrowings. By acknowledging that we use quotations to read the worldly thickness of these plays, we may also place ourselves in a better position to confront the synecdochic problem of *pars pro toto,* or "part for the whole," endemic to new historicist readings. Typically using a work's quotation of an exterior text, an event, or person to sketch the outlines of a larger cultural text, New Historicism often begs the question of representativeness. That is, granting that early modern plays have many quotations, which among them should we focus on and why?

We can begin to answer this question by probing the heterogeneous makeup of these dramatic texts. How, and what, early modern plays signify depend greatly on how playwrights made them: the various materials in these plays have an important role in producing their meanings. We need to understand more fully the range of material in the books that New Historicism analyzes before we judge its success as a methodology. Unfortunately, many evaluations of New Historicism have taken place on an abstract plane, as though the validity of this approach depended more on its relation to a universal standard than on its "fit" with certain texts written in specific times and places. Indeed, critiques of New Historicism devoted to early modern texts come as often from specialists in nineteenth- and twentieth-century literature as from those who have worked closely with the primary texts at issue. Perhaps this practice is encouraged by the lack of attention to formal specificity in new historicist criticism itself, for too rarely do new historicists consider how writers made these plays and what that process of writing may imply for our interpretations. As I argue in the following pages, New Historicism found its earliest and most marked success with plays of the early modern era because these plays are materially fragmented in a way that proves crucial to historicist inquiry concerned with texts' worldliness—what we could call their quotation of the world.

Criticism interested in how texts quote usually relies on the modern term "intertextuality" and attendant ways of reading. However, current theories of intertextuality and criticism devoted to exploring intertextual relations have serious shortcomings. Critics have made "intertextuality" less relevant, for instance, by separating it from historical process and by shifting it from author to reader. It no longer seems important to know which books authors used to produce their own—something that can leave us with a very vague, and even misleading, sense of the past. We therefore need a criticism that pays attention to what authors read and to how they used and replied to precursors and their texts. Reading quotations can enhance our understanding of literary works, authors, and cultures by foregrounding the positions in texts, and of texts, over time.

Along with "quotation," then, the word "position" has a pivotal role in what follows. Where I define quotation as a material unit, positions are relational, involving orientations, directions, assumptions, and points of view. While recognizing that a quotation is a formalistic endeavor, analyzing how quotations are positioned relative to other texts and authors calls for a variety of explanatory languages, from those of ethics, historical study, and feminism to those of anthropology and political thought. Reading in this way will help us address significant problems raised by intertextual criticism and by New Historicism—in particular, the former's shift to what I call a readerly intertextuality and the latter's penchant for the synchronic and for *pars pro toto* readings. To read quotations and the positions of texts means attending to how authors fabricate texts—by itself an expansion of the picture that intertextual criticism conventionally provides. We can also begin to see that these plays have numerous quotations from texts of various eras and that they are replete with contradictory positions that often discredit synecdochic interpretations. Reading single parts of a dramatic work, even beside provocative materials from outside it, can blind us both to divergent matter and to larger patterns of orientation in that work. Although we are beyond searching for organic unity in literary texts, we cannot afford to overlook the significance of these texts' organization and patterns.

It is precisely to establish a way of reading these patterns that chapters 2 through 6 analyze the worldly intertextuality of specific literary works from early modern England. These chapters follow chronological order, beginning in the late 1580s of Elizabeth's England and ending, in a retrospective chapter, with an examination of the intensive quotation of Elizabethan literature in the 1930s and 1940s of FDR's America. Although I will highlight significant variations in the intertextuality examined, my primary goal lies more in illuminating literature historically than in making unverified (and perhaps practically unverifiable) claims about the shapes of intertextuality over time.

My second chapter focuses on the cultural afterlife of Christopher Marlowe's famous lyric, "The Passionate Shepherd." This chapter seeks to enrich our understanding of this poem, its many contexts, and the positions it was seen to take. Initially, Marlowe's poem would appear to concern anything but "positions." In advocating a turn toward pleasure and delightful objects—a turn, by implication, away from the *negotium* of political life—his inviting shepherd appears to eschew active positions, giving us instead a beautiful catalog of delights. As couched in Marlowe's sensuous lines, the appeal of this catalog stretched well beyond the fictional world of the poem. "The Passionate Shepherd" was among the best-known secular poems of the English Renaissance, proving so popular that dozens of writers incorporated its words into their works and otherwise responded to it. We immediately recall polemical responses, such "answer poetry" as Ralegh's "The Nymph's Reply" (commonly printed in anthologies as a kind of companion piece to Marlowe's) and Donne's "The Bait." These poems qualify the Marlovian invitation; had Marlowe's lyric not been so popular, either of them might suggest that something in "The Passionate Shepherd" struck contemporary readers as begging a reply.

But these canonical rejoinders were far from the only responses to "The Passionate Shepherd" in that period, for playwrights like Shakespeare frequently incorporated versions of Marlowe's invitation in their works. Concentrating on these responses to "The Passionate Shepherd," on what happened when the lyric was in effect *staged,* one can see that playwrights almost invariably connected this poem with sexual aggression, even violence. In many plays, characters attempt to seduce others with the Marlovian lyric, then threaten—and sometimes perform—violence if the listener refuses the invitation. So frequently does this occur when early modern plays quote "The Passionate Shepherd" that the relation between this poem and the violence following the invitation seems more than arbitrary. It suggests, I argue, how Marlowe's contemporaries and successors saw the poem *positioned*—what they felt about the poem's orientations toward power, gender, and authority. Other ways of reading Marlowe's poem do little to help us see this. One could "close read" this twenty-four line poem dozens of times, for instance, and never guess at its potential for such a meaning. Similarly one could, in new historicist fashion, look for a "representative anecdote" close to its time of composition to explain the poem. But an attempt to historicize "The Passionate Shepherd" synchronically would not help us discover what becomes apparent when examining the poem's borrowings and its effects on other writers. Only by recognizing the constituent elements of Marlowe's poem and, especially, how it was dispersed through other works can we sense the weight and shape of "The Passionate Shepherd" in the early modern era.

My reading of Marlowe stresses the dramatic reception of a contemporary poem by Shakespeare and other early modern playwrights. Chapter 3 takes up a pressing issue for Shakespeare criticism while examining Shakespeare's relation to the plays he quoted in fabricating his own. Many of Marlowe's readers saw his Passionate Shepherd as a suspicious figure, his invitation a dangerously seductive bid for control. I show in this chapter that Shakespeare's dramaturgy would, in effect, legitimate a similar model of power relations by giving agency to aristocratic controlling characters responsible for governing their playworlds' societies. This tendency gives us insight into a fiercely debated issue in Shakespeare studies: the nature of Shakespeare's politics as represented in his dramatic practice. Traditionally, critics have made contradictory claims about the political orientations of his dramas, a situation exacerbated, of course, by the obliging *copia* of his plays. This *copia* ensures that the same play supports Shakespeares of various inclinations, often in firm agreement with each critic's own beliefs. Chapter 3 shows that we can see the general politics of Shakespeare's dramatic practice, and the general inclinations of his plays, by examining a central pattern in his dramas, paying attention to how he changed, repeatedly and significantly, the power relations of one of his earliest and most influential sources.

Rewriting the Plautine comedies standard in the Elizabethan grammar schools, Shakespeare articulated a political bias—perhaps his own, perhaps that of his culture—by consistently pushing agency upward in the hierarchy of political power. The Plautine "maker" or "producer," always a slave figure, becomes in Shakespeare an aristocrat—often a governor or monarch. The resulting master/servant relations in plays like *A Midsummer Night's Dream* (1596) depend on a model of dramatic and social agency that prefers that power lie in the hands of an aristocrat. There exist, of course, significant departures from this tendency. *All's Well That Ends Well* (1602), for instance, offers a notable exception, with Helena a controlling figure from the lower orders. And every play, again, contains moments that work against the tendencies I have described. Yet the pattern that emerges from reading all of Shakespeare's plays, especially in relation to those he borrowed from, makes it hard to dismiss their consistent habit of authority, a habit visible in Shakespeare's aristocratic controllers.

This manipulative controller figures importantly in chapter 4, which establishes *The Tempest* (1611) as a strongly "local" text that quotes more than the well-known Bermuda narratives often used to support colonialist readings of the play. If during the last two decades critical orthodoxy has painted *The Tempest* as the bible of European colonialism, it has done so through too selective a treatment of the play's quotations. Critics read the play's borrowings from Bermuda narratives like Strachey's "True Repertory" and Jourdain's *Discovery of the Bermudas* beside its indebtedness to Montaigne's "Of Cannibals" as prima facie indications of Shakespeare's intent to address European exploration of the New World—despite the play's Mediterranean setting. The way critics have taken *The Tempest*'s quotation *of* these documents as indication of an identity *with* them simplifies the play's meanings. For as much as *The Tempest* uses the theater to talk about issues involved in these New World narratives, it uses these narratives to talk about the theater—in particular, about Shakespeare's lived history of work in the Globe and Blackfriars playhouses. Intertextuality crucial to Shakespeare's romance, then, lies not merely in the familiar links among *The Tempest* and the travel narratives it quotes but in Shakespeare's more homely resources.

While it remains a commonplace that *The Tempest* concerns the theater, Shakespeare wrote for and acted in real theaters, and with collaborating writers and actors. *The Tempest* is Shakespeare's fullest meditation on a life of collaboration in two playhouses of early modern London. Although Prospero traditionally has been described as a playwright-like double for Shakespeare, too rarely have we taken the resemblance seriously. A theatrical as well as a political character, Prospero embodies the controlling figures examined in the preceding chapter of this study. *The Tempest*'s picture of playhouse relations includes not only Prospero as a playwright/director but Miranda as a figure of an idealized spectatorship and Ariel as boy actor. Further, Shakespeare's portrait of the unscriptable Caliban seems to draw on memories of Will Kemp—the improvising, often obscene clown who had helped make Shakespeare's theater successful and appears once to have threatened his idea of what plays should be. *The Tempest* is thus in part a history of Shakespeare's repertory, inflected by the playwright's memories of Kemp and the anarchic folk energy Kemp represented. By elaborating the material sources of *The Tempest,* this chapter shows that early modern plays quoted more than books; it also shows that we unduly limit our understanding of these texts if we restrict our definition of informing "source" to printed matter. History in and for *The Tempest* is as much Shakespeare's theatrical experiences as it is England's exploration of the New World.

Whereas *The Tempest* asks us to think about the thoroughly collaborative nature of Shakespeare's theatrical career, his late collaboration with John Fletcher, *The Two Noble Kinsmen* (1613), features a special pattern of quotation—a pattern that, in gathering various cultural fragments, serves as a metaphor for the quoting tendencies of early modern drama itself. Chapter 5 examines the speech patterns of the Jailer's Daughter in *The Two Noble Kinsmen,* a character from the play's lower orders who, finding her love unrequited, goes mad in a series of pathetic but largely unscrutinized scenes. Like that of Ophelia, the mad language of the Jailer's Daughter initially seems a random assortment of cultural themes and tags: snatches of ballads, the outlines of familiar stories, remnants of traditional practices. But when read in light of her character's status and interests, of the plot's social fictions, and of the play's cultural and historical contexts, the quotations of her mad language take on a meaningful coherence. Indeed, if such mad language has commonly been seen as literary decoration, a close examination of its patterns indicates that it has a strong link to the realities of life both inside and outside the theaters of Jacobean England. Grounded in a pathetic madness, the Jailer's Daughter stands apart from the play's definition of the social and is not recognized as politically significant by any character in the drama. As this chapter demonstrates, however, it is precisely in the "mad" quotations of the Jailer's Daughter—an otherwise disempowered character—that we get the richest picture of the arrangements of power in the play, of the social relations in the early modern playhouse, and of the transformations in the Jacobean culture that produced *The Two Noble Kinsmen.* By foregrounding the process of quotation that everywhere characterizes early modern drama, the speech of this "madwoman" also advances her as a strong rival to Prospero as Shakespeare's portrait of the dramatic artist.

A more pointed kind of quotation occupies the core of the final, retrospective chapter of this study. Chapter 6 extends my critique of New Historicism's generally synchronic model of literature-and-history by showing how *The Tempest*'s "New World"—in the form of FDR's America—would come to quote works from the early modern era, effectively inventing an English Renaissance as necessary prologue to an American one. In this chapter my methodological and historical arguments converge, for here I hold that a clearer understanding of the fashioning of the English Renaissance earlier in the twentieth century gives us reason to approach early modern texts differently. During the 1920s and 1930s, America canonized texts of early modern England at an increased pace, making them what we now receive as English Renaissance literature. This translation had important consequences for the shape of literary criticism: invoking the Renaissance, for instance, encouraged the employment of the paradigm of *imitatio,* which, in its tendency to emphasize singular rather than multiple orientations, can have a limited explanatory value in relation to the patchwork dramas written for the public theaters of early modern England. We need, therefore, to approach early modern plays not only—perhaps not primarily—in terms of Renaissance *imitatio* but also with a strong concern for the *bricolage* by which they were originally fabricated. Where much of this study historicizes quotations in early modern texts, my final chapter shows how America's quotation of early modern works differed strikingly from patterns of borrowing in these works themselves.

This chapter takes up the "Thirties Renaissance" in America: that is, the profusion of references to and borrowings from the early modern era between 1925 and 1940. Obviously Shakespeare and early modern English literature have long been important to American culture. But from the "Negro Renaissance" of the mid-1920s and the lecture of Gene Tunney (ex-heavyweight champion of the world) on Shakespeare at Yale in 1928 through Ernest Hemingway's quoting Donne in titling *For Whom the Bell Tolls* in 1940, Americans alluded to, quoted, and used the early modern era as source of (and setting for) their stories with increasing purpose and dedication. Scholars would figure importantly in this new emphasis, joining imaginative writers and artists in contributing to a larger, generational project. The generation of artists and scholars who made this Renaissance came into the world in and after 1888, the birth year of both T. S. Eliot and Maxwell Anderson, and included Raymond Chandler, Philip Barry, William Faulkner, Thomas Wolfe, Langston Hughes, John Steinbeck, Ralph Ellison, Willard Thorp, and F. O. Matthiessen. Although we rarely consider Eliot and Anderson together—they form, between them, something like the poles of literary Modernism—their shared affection for the English Renaissance speaks to a larger American investment in the literature and culture of Elizabethan England. When one considers that the first work of Americanist scholars like Matthiessen and Thorp concerned Elizabethan literature, their later success at creating an "American Renaissance" takes on a new significance. But this creation meant, for them, more than domesticating a foreign Renaissance, for until this time it was not usual anywhere to speak of an English Renaissance. Before America could have a Renaissance of its own, it needed to invent one for England. Americans invented this Renaissance through a conscious pattern of engagement that made quotation work like advertisement. What they advertised was a culture they felt they were heirs to—yet needed, somehow, to earn through devotion.

That we have inherited a Renaissance that Shakespeare and his dramatic contemporaries could not have envisioned stands as more than a curiosity in the following pages. For too long, I believe, we have idealized works from this era; similarly, we have perhaps too seldom cared how they were made by real individuals in specific times and places and from to-hand material. *Quoting Shakespeare* addresses this problem by insisting on the realities of literary making; it stresses the importance of literary history to the historical study of literature and to readings that use literature to shed light on culture and politics. An argument running throughout this study concerns the authority of words, from the challenged authority of Marlowe's lyric invitation and the controlling authority of Shakespeare's playwright figures to the struggle for authority between Prospero-as-playwright and his acting repertory and the paradoxical authority of mad language in *The Two Noble Kinsmen*. My concluding chapter suggests how the force of such words can be conceived on a larger scale. That the period of American history examined in this chapter virtually invented the English Renaissance we know speaks to the larger cultural authority that literature has gained. The authority that Renaissance works often located in characters' words was increasingly ascribed, in the American emphasis on Tudor and Stuart literature during this period, to the Renaissance itself. In contrast, it is with regard for what remains the most expressive form of early modern authority—for the hard facts of plays and their composition—that this study advances its argument.

CHAPTER I

Quoting Shakespeare

All cometh to this pass, that what heretofore hath been served in several dishes for a feast is now minced in a charger for a gallimaufry. If
we present a mingle-mangle, our fault is to be excused, because the
whole world is become an hodgepodge.

JOHN LYLY, Prologue to *Midas* (1589)

The last two decades of the twentieth century witnessed a flurry
of critical activity relating to early modern drama. Much of this activity
concerned the relation of plays to the larger culture surrounding them.
Often reading plays alongside, and in light of, elements drawn from other
texts, methodologies such as Feminist criticism, Cultural Materialism, and
New Historicism created impressive vistas for those interested in these
dramas and the issues they raise. It is no exaggeration to say that these
methodologies contributed to a critical revolution that has changed how
we read. Like all revolutions, though, this one has ended, and the excite-
ment that surrounded these newer ways of reading has largely subsided.[1] If
it is inaccurate to say that the study of Shakespeare and his contemporary
dramatists has reached a still point, it is primarily because approaches are
being reshuffled rather than rethought, leaving the field busy but without
the direction it once had.

This book offers no magic solution. However, it does try to rethink
some of our basic assumptions about reading early modern plays. As part
of this attempt, it argues for a particular way of reading, and, in the chapters that follow this one, it gives practical demonstrations of this way of
reading. Put briefly, this mode of reading pays attention to the materials
that authors used in composing their works; it focuses on what these authors retained, what they changed, and, importantly, on their patterns and
habits of doing so. It is certainly not my claim, of course, that no one has

ever read books in this way before—such would run contrary to this study's emphasis on the thorough indebtedness of all texts, and of all writers, to texts and writers who came before them. It *is* my claim here that by reading this way we may better address questions raised, though left largely unanswered, by current critical methodologies.

By retaining an interest in the cultural significance of literature at the same time that we concentrate on the materials that authors chose for their works—materials demonstrably available to and employed by them, hence demonstrably a part of their culture—we can add a meaningful focus to our criticism. Such focus may seem to take attention away from the "cultural" as currently received. When examined in relation to their habits of making, for instance, such authors as Shakespeare, Marlowe, Jonson, and Middleton look surprisingly different from one another. They look like individuals with personal visions and tendencies, ones that, owing to these figures' shared historical moment, often coincided but remained in many ways idiosyncratic. At first, such idiosyncrasy may seem to lift them out of their time and place. But to notice these authors' differences is not to deny that they were part of a larger group or that they shared practices, beliefs, and habits. Nor is it to forget that they collaborated with others. On the contrary, to see the differences among such authors is to begin to sense the range and complexity of their culture, a culture in every way deserving of the most supple critical paradigms we can offer.

This last point is one that might be extrapolated for literary criticism generally. However relentlessly its theorists have claimed for postmodernism such phenomena as collage, fragmentation, pastiche, and compilation, none of these phenomena is peculiar to postmodern texts.[2] It is in the nature of texts to overlap with many others. A foundational belief of this study is that early modern drama did so to a tremendous extent. The compositional material of these plays included an amazing variety of things specific to their time and place, and to the individuals who wrote for and worked in the theaters of early modern London. A concern for such material returns us to basic questions that can help us understand these texts and their cultural context. Readers of these plays will benefit from asking not only "What is it I am reading?" but also "What is it made of?" For asking the latter about a text may help us address the question "What does this mean?" And while these questions clearly have relevance outside the period emphasized by this book, the ways they are answered here in relation to works of early modern England may sharpen our picture of their time and place and of those who labored to produce them.

A World of Quotations

If drama is among the most heterogeneous of literary modes, then plays of early modern England seem especially full of sights, sounds, forms, objects, and events. The placard traditionally imagined for the Globe Theater—Hercules bearing the earth on his shoulders, accompanied by the motto *Totus mundus agit histrionem* ("All the world plays the actor")[3]—thus not only recalls the *theatrum mundi* trope so prevalent in early modern drama but also visually embodies what John Lyly implied in more homely words: that plays of the era held the world's "hodgepodge" in remarkable ways. Reasons for this well-known heterogeneity are perhaps themselves not far to seek. Playwrights wrote for diverse audiences and for many venues, from the domestic to the Continental, the urban to the rural, for public as well as private theaters, and for courts and courtyards alike. These playwrights also wrote when a love of *copia* found expression in an altogether malleable English language, producing rich, even "golden" poetry.[4] And importantly, professional dramatists worked during an unprecedented expansion of print culture. As Robert Weimann has indicated, "a vigorous impetus had been given by the Reformation with popularized Bible reading, but this was soon absorbed in an expanded and secularized context and—helped along largely by printing—the social scope for discursive activities of all kinds was greatly enlarged."[5] Writers in the later sixteenth century frequently expressed wonder at how much printed material was available. By 1591, the Epistle Dedicatory of *Martin Mar-Sixtus* believed itself justified in saying "We live in a printing age," and seven years later John Florio would lament what he called "this our paper-sea."[6] It was in and with this abundance of texts that playwrights constructed their plays. As much as diversity of audience, venue, and language prompted the variety of early modern drama, this new sea of printed matter formed the most tangible source of its heterogeneity. Shakespeare and his dramatic contemporaries were voracious readers, and collected words and phrases from what they read. Patching together their plays from a variety of sources, they were among the least "original" writers in history.[7]

From the chronicle histories of the late 1580s and their dense weave of verbal interrelations through the poetic fragments of Webster's tragedies, the borrowed words in many of these dramatic works remain among their most characteristic features.[8] The apparatus of a scholarly edition of one of Shakespeare's plays, for example, typically reveals its links to a host of other works. So sustained is this appropriation that we might with fairness invert the old joke about someone reading *Hamlet* (1601) for the first time and announcing that it seemed nothing but quotations. That is, while this jest depends on the historical diffusion of Shakespeare's plays through quotations, acknowledging that others' words and phrases entered plays like *Hamlet* first makes it harder to laugh at the reader in this apocryphal story. In fact, by revising an earlier *Hamlet* play, Shakespeare's tragedy structurally as well as internally "quotes."

This generalized, even anonymous sense of the word would have been immediately understood by early modern writers, for to quote (sometimes spelled "cote" or "coat") commonly meant the recording—in or out of writing—of words, phrases, actions, thoughts, or feelings. In *Microcynicon* (1599) Thomas Middleton speaks of a velvet-gowned Madam who "quotes her paces in Characters down, | Valuing each step that she had made that day" and Ben Jonson's Sir Politic Would-be in *Volpone* (1606) swears "I do slip | No action of my life, thus, but I quote it."[9] Here "to quote" means "to record." We should ourselves notice that what these characters quote begins not as words but as actions. The heterogeneity of early modern plays owed its diversity to borrowings from many sources, from the textual to the historical and the personal; plays quoted these sources in ways not dissimilar to the recording described in the preceding passages.[10] Other senses of "quote" in early modern usage involved "giving reference to (a passage in a book) by specifying the page, chapter, etc. where it is to be found," "to mention in speaking," and to "bring forward for having done something."[11] "To record," "to refer," "to mention," and "to bring forward": it is with such verbs that this study seeks to explain the shape and function of quotations in early modern drama. We might provisionally define quotation as the incorporation, in a text, of discrete elements from outside that text, with or without acknowledgment.

To modern readers, of course, "quotation" implies the reduplication, typically *with* acknowledgment, of others' words—a phenomenon for which we have both cultural protocols and an array of punctuation. When we think of quotations today, we perhaps typically think of well-known figures and their sententious remarks on important subjects. Powerful and recognizable, quotations introduce past to present, and quoter to quoted, like conspicuously dressed ambassadors. Quotations often strike us as important and unmistakable; in the words of Walter Benjamin, during the twentieth century quotations have come to possess a "transcendent force"—perhaps the best gloss for the shape of quotation in Modernist poetry, where borrowed words and phrases seldom risk being mistaken for the author's "own."[12] Yet borrowing often reveals the irrational character of linguistic power. For instance, the uncanny feelings that borrowed words can produce lead Marjorie Garber to define a quotation as "a ghost: a revenant taken out of context, making an unexpected, often disconcerting appearance." To Garber, "A quotation is *always* 'in quotation,' always *in*appropriate for its proper place."[13] The truth of this claim is perhaps magnified for us because we see quotation largely in terms of deeply held convictions about property and are made uncomfortable by changes in ownership without payment. Quotation is thus "transcendent" not only through the agency of psychology but through legal support as well. Quotation dictionaries, databases, copyright restrictions, assumptions concerning "fair use" and attribution: all contribute to an environment that respects verbal property.

To be sure, we live in an era when there are academic suspicions about literary authority, about the role of authors, and about originality.[14] However, these suspicions respond to a comparatively recent solidification of copyright and authorship and rarely affect feelings about quotation in the larger culture: such is the typical resonance of quotation in our time that most readers believe, with Garber and Benjamin, in quotations' intrinsic force and authority. So natural do quotations seem that it is becoming more and more common to hear speakers refer to the resonant words and sentences of others as "quotes," even before they are quoted—as in "I will read the quote from X's editorial," when what such speakers might mean to say is "I will quote X's editorial." That is, in popular speech now, "quotes" seem to be self-defining if not self-evident.

But the force and authority we ascribe to quotations—even in this casual way—can prevent us from seeing the prevalence of ordinary borrowing in the early modern era. Works of this period quoted in such a regular fashion that neither transcendence nor the uncanny adequately explains how they incorporated their materials. To understand early modern quotation, then, we need to unlearn the associations we currently bring to the term. During the early modern era, many of our notions of literary authority and property were just being constructed; many more had yet to be imagined. The relations among words, ownership, and typographical demarcation had not begun to resemble our current system.[15] As one critic put it in an observation from the Cold War period, although in the Elizabethan era "the sense of property in land, material and money was strong . . . in literature and drama there was a Communist attitude to available goods."[16] The unaffected anachronism of this statement need not prevent us from conceding the familiar paradox it addresses: the early modern literary properties that we revere took form in an era with decidedly less reverence for literature as property.

Perhaps it was partly for this reason that early modern plays seldom attributed their quotations. A notable exception is Jonson's *Sejanus* (1603), published in quarto in 1605 by Thomas Thorpe (who would, four years later, bring out Shakespeare's *Sonnets*). Because Jonson's play proves such an exception to the standard practice of contemporary dramatists, it bears our examination here. Jonson's "Roman" play, a grim panorama of the *realpolitik* marking the reign of Tiberius, had obvious implications for his own day's courtiers and politicians, whose excesses under Elizabeth promised only to increase in the Jacobean court. After *Sejanus* was performed at this very court during the Christmas season of 1603–4, Lord Henry Howard, the Earl of Northampton, called Jonson before the Privy Council, where the playwright was accused of treason—apparently because *Sejanus* seemed to comment openly on the political affairs of the day. Jonson therefore had every reason to be chary of publishing it the year following. He appears to have solved his dilemma by carefully annotating the play, flagging the origins of various passages with hundreds of marginal citations to his sources in such writers as Suetonius, Tacitus, Seneca, and Dio Cassius.

In his "Letter to the Readers," Jonson explains this peculiar feature in a defensive way:

> lest in some nice nostril the *Quotations* might savor affected, I do let you know that I abhor nothing more, and have only done it to shew my integrity in the *Story*, and save myself in those common Torturers, that bring all wit to the Rack: whose Noses are ever like Swine spoiling and rooting up the *Muses* Gardens, and their whole Bodies, like Moles, as blindly working under Earth to cast any, the least, hills upon *Virtue*.

18

Whereas they are in *Latin* and the work in *English,* it was presupposed none
but the Learned would take the pains to confer them, the Authors themselves
being all in the learned *Tongues,* save one, with whose English side I have had
little to do. To which it may be required, since I have quoted the Page, to name
what Edition I followed. *Tacit. Lips.* in 4. *Antuerp. edit. 600. Dio. Folio Hen.
Step. 92.* For the rest, as *Sueton. Seneca.* &c. the Chapter doth sufficiently direct, or the Edition is not varied. (vol. 4, 350–51, lines 26–42)

Jonson argues (with, it may seem, some irony) that his *Sejanus* has an "integrity" evident through the quarto's marginal citations, thereby foiling
meddlesome readers who scrutinize fictions in an unseemly manner. The
implication is that these "common Torturers" read historical fictions for
their contemporary applications. Jonson's quotations, then, offer his story
its alibi even as they parade his learning. When, a half decade earlier, John
Hayward had offended Elizabeth with his putatively topical *The First Part
of the Life and Raigne of King Henrie IIII* (1599), Francis Bacon jokingly re-
assured the Queen that Hayward stood guilty not of treason—that is, for
any pro-Essex material in the *Life*—but of felony: "I told her, the author
had committed very apparent theft: for he had taken most of the sentences
of Cornelius Tacitus, and translated them into English, and put them into
his text."[17] Jonson may have borrowed Bacon's logic in his epistle prefacing
Sejanus: each marginal reference to the sources of his "*Quotations*" comes
not merely as testament to his pedantry (providing the date, edition, and
place of publication of his sources is a touch we might expect only from
Jonson) but also as an assertive bid for preservation of story and self. Even
as the Lord Chamberlain's Men may have felt some protection against
prosecution, owing to the forty-shilling bonus for their special performance of *Richard II* on the eve of Essex's rebellion in February of 1601—
making them mercenary rather than political players—so does Jonson
point here to something he feels should absolve his work of any contemporary political import. Like the forty shillings, his marginal citations
inoculate the body politic and the body Jonson from any harm people
might see in "his" story: the quotations prove the story is not his.

The thoroughness with which the quarto *Sejanus* documents its quotations offers the exception to the rule; the intensive borrowing it manifests
is absolutely typical of playwriting in the early modern era. Nowhere, of
course, was it so pedantic. John Marston would seem to have spoken for
most of the period's dramatists when, in a chide of Jonson's Roman his-

tory, he proclaimed to the "general reader" of *Sophonisba* (1605, printed 1606) that "To transcribe authors, quote authorities, and translate latin prose orations into English blank verse, hath, in this subject, been the least aim of my studies."[18] But while Marston contrasts his method of writing with Jonson's, in *Sophonisba* he nonetheless borrows from such sources as Livy, Appian, Lucan, Montaigne (in the Florio translation), and perhaps Seneca, Machiavelli, and Nicolas de Montreux as well. The primary difference between his quarto and Jonson's is that Jonson takes pains to annotate his story. As Marston's preface epistle might indicate, other playwrights did not.

Among the most quoted of authors, Shakespeare himself "quoted"—in the modern sense of the word—very rarely. The sacred and secular texts most influential to his work are, arguably, the Bible and Ovid's *Metamorphoses,* but his representation of this debt is less than forthcoming. Only twice in his works, for instance, does Shakespeare have a character cite a biblical book by name. And while Lucentio recites Ovid in the language lesson of *The Taming of the Shrew* (1592), in just one of Shakespeare's plays does a character directly credit this major resource of his. And in *The Merchant of Venice* (1596), Lorenzo only hints at Ovid in noting that "the poet | Did feign that Orpheus drew trees, stones, and floods" (5.1.79–80). Other examples of this reluctance abound. Cicero appears as a character in *Julius Caesar* (1599), for instance, and *Titus Andronicus* (1594) mentions his books, but nowhere does Shakespeare attribute Cicero's words *to* him. And when Shakespeare does directly quote Christopher Marlowe in *As You Like It* (1599), he ascribes the words only to the "Dead Shepherd." Thus, we can see something like a Shakespearean pattern of divorcing borrowed words from authors' names when Feste "quotes" an imaginary authority in *Twelfth Night* (1601)—"What says Quinapalus?"—as well as when Hamlet summarizes the invective of "the satirical rogue" whose observations on the infirmities of old age have relevance for Polonius. In fact, of the two citations of biblical texts in Shakespeare's plays, each refers to a "nameless" book—Numbers, and Psalms—rather than to an "authored" book. And when, in *2 Henry IV* (1597), Shallow names the writer of the Psalms, Shakespeare has Shallow refer to "the Psalmist" rather than to "Holy David" or even "Ethan the Ezrahite."[19] These examples show us that, when it came to quotation, Shakespeare practiced a strangely aggressive anonymity. So it was that indirect speech, proverbs, and songs formed the bulk of what his audiences and readers might have recognized as borrowed, as what we would call "quotation." But an even greater part of Shakespeare's works quote without appearing to, retaining borrowings without identifying them *as* borrowings. In this, Shakespeare well represented the practice of writing plays in his day.

When early modern playwrights quoted this way, they extended a humanist emphasis on adopting others' words, sentences, and sayings. We have heard Middleton's Madam and Jonson's Sir Politic Would-be testify that commonplace books, both printed and manuscript alike, enjoyed great popularity during the period. These books also strongly shaped literary composition. As Ann Moss relates, the printed Renaissance commonplace book "worked as a memory store of quotations, which could be activated to verbalize present experience in the language of familiar moral paradigms and with reference to a cultural history shared by writer and reader; it marshalled excerpts from sources invested with the necessary degree of authority to 'back up your argument or point of view'; and it was arranged by headed sections in such a way as to ensure maximum ease and efficiency in retrieving the information it contained."[20] Such forms as florilegia, miscellanies, proverb collections, and encyclopedias contributed to a rich genre of "Renaissance compilation literature."[21] Observing that "renaissance authors speak the language of the commonplace-book," Moss acknowledges that "[t]he most informative place of all to look for the influence of the commonplace-book on vernacular production would be in vernacular works themselves."[22]

This is precisely the method that informs one of the most compelling studies of composition practices in early modern England, Mary Thomas Crane's *Framing Authority*. In contrast to Moss's focus on the *printed* commonplace book, Crane takes up the larger habit of compilation as expressed in the "notebook method" of writing, the informal habit of recording interesting words, phrases, and larger units of writing in private notebooks. Crane shows that this notebook method of writing formed "a central mode of transaction with classical antiquity and provided an influential model for authorial practice and for authoritative self-fashioning."[23] Closely joined to memorization, the commonplace book indicated a way of thinking about literature as "a space containing textual fragments"; correspondingly, authors "imagined their interaction with that literature as the collection and redeployment of those fragments and not, in many cases, as the assimilation and imitation of whole works."[24] While this method offered a way of engaging with antiquity, however, writers did not limit their handling of fragments to those of classical texts. Sometimes even the simple notebook seems too formal an instrument for grasping how readers gathered attractive words and phrases. For instance, in his copy of John Leland's *Principum in Anglia Virorum Encomia* (1589), Thomas Nashe jotted on the final two leaves "Faustus: Che sara sara devinynitie adieu," "Faustus studie in indian silke," and "devynitie adieu"—quotations from Marlowe's *Doctor Faustus* (1592).[25] We see Nashe "quoting" Marlowe, collecting sensuous images and sounds like a buyer in a bazaar: of the thirteen words Nashe recorded here, seven—over half—either come from foreign languages ("Che sara sara," "adieu") or refer to a foreign land and its (nonverbal) goods ("indian silke"). We might not recognize in this the Nashe who made one of the most extravagant claims of the era in saying, "This I will proudly boast . . . that the vein which I have (be it a *median* vein, or a mad [vein]) is of my own begetting, and calls no man father in England but myself, neither *Euphues*, nor *Tarlton*, nor *Greene*." Yet we *would* identify him as the same Nashe who himself collaborated with Marlowe on *Dido, Queen of Carthage* (1586). The same Nashe who displayed his deep engagement with antagonists when he famously quoted (in order to refute) Martin Marprelate and Gabriel Harvey. And the same Nashe—as J. J. M. Tobin has shown us—whose manuscripts and printed works Shakespeare must have had before him when he composed many of his dramas, methodically borrowing (in and out of context) particular words and phrases to weave into his plays.[26]

Far from producing words in a vacuum, playwrights borrowed their material in a way that makes terms like "mingle-mangle" and "hodgepodge" entirely appropriate for describing plays of this era. Such terms characterize making as fabrication rather than as creation and ask us to see that dramatic texts were *bricolage*—a pastiche of various to-hand materials, sometimes by a handyman or *bricoleur*. These French terms actually overlap with those of Lyly, for the more familiar one with which they are connected, bric-a-brac, is a word whose varied reduplication (as in "mingle-mangle" and "hodgepodge") helps signal what it describes. The word *bricolage* was used, influentially, by Claude Lévi-Strauss in *The Savage Mind* (*La Pensée Sauvage*) to describe the ad hoc construction of cultural myths and rituals.[27] To Lévi-Strauss, mythical thought is analogous to the at-hand, everyday construction of *bricolage*; its opposite, the methodical engineering of science—with its forward-looking, seemingly limitless potential—forms the other pole between which "artistic creation lies." Science can be seen as creating new products; *bricolage* puts together things already produced (even used) and circulating in a culture. A *bricoleur* is a professional "handyman" or "do-it-yourselfer" who makes do with any odds and ends (compare bric-a-brac) at hand to complete a task of construction or repair. Lévi-Strauss uses the *bricoleur* as a metaphor for how cultures produce myths and rituals. We can take the *bricoleur* as a figure for how artists produce texts.

Quotation has few better synonyms than *bricolage*, for the incorporation of worldly elements into plays—part of their fabrication—was a thoroughly material practice. One senses that it struck people in early modern England as such: those who criticized the writing of plays often described playwriting in terms that resemble *bricolage*.[28] Stephen Gosson did so early on, alleging in his *Plays Confuted in Five Actions* (1582): "I may boldly say it, because I have seen it, that the Palace of pleasure, the Golden Ass, the Æthiopian history, Amadis of Fraunce, the Round Table, bawdy Comedies in Latin, French, Italian, and Spanish, have been throughly ransacked, to furnish the Play houses in London."[29] Gosson, himself once a playwright, calls these dramatists "our *playmakers*," and implies that not only was making plays work but that this work could involve an aggressive, highly unoriginal relation to others' books. It seems significant that the first notice we have of Shakespeare's activities in the playhouses of early modern London calls him a "*Johannes fac totum*," which might be translated as "John Mend-all" or "Jack-of-all-trades," the former an anglicized version of the *bricoleur*.[30] The fabricated texture of early modern plays found its most memorable expression perhaps in Middleton's preface to the readers of *The Roaring Girl* (1611):

> The fashion of play-making I can properly compare to nothing so naturally as the alteration in apparel: for in the time of the great-crop doublet, your huge bombasted plays, quilted with mighty words to lean purpose, was only then in fashion; and as the doublet fell, neater inventions began to set up. Now in the time of spruceness, our plays follow the niceness of our garments: single plots, quaint conceits, lecherous jests, dressed up in hanging sleeves; and those are fit for the times and the termers. Such a kind of light-colour summer stuff, mingled with diverse colours, you shall find this published comedy.[31]

Plays of the early modern era perhaps most resembled the quilted motley of a fool's coat, with its varied fabrics and "diverse colours" representing the words and phrases of the playwrights' materials.

In comparing playmakers to tailors, Middleton's conceit had a basis both in what playwrights did and in where they originated, since many professional playwrights came from families engaged in "mechanical" trades. For every Francis Beaumont—the son of a judge—there were many dramatists from backgrounds of manual labor and crafts: Henry Chettle was the son of a dyer; Robert Greene, a saddler; Jonson's stepfather was a bricklayer—as was Middleton's own father; Kyd was the son of a scrivener; Marlowe was fathered by a shoemaker, Munday by a draper, Shakespeare by a sometime glover and whittawer, and Webster by a cartwright. If we add to these professions the unrecorded household labor (and, possibly, various commercial activities) of these playwrights' mothers, a picture emerges of commonplace handiwork. The fabrication of plays must have seemed, to these sons of "mechanical" men and women, different work. Yet it may not have seemed different in kind.

Significantly, contemporary sneers at dramatists' origins in the lower orders sometimes involve aspersions on their writing as mechanical endeavor. In an epigram of 1617, Henry Fitzjeffrey, a contemporary of Webster's, calls him "The playwright-cartwright (whether either!)," and returns to this image of writing as manual labor in mocking Webster: "Strike Vulcan, with thy hammer once again."[32] In this vein the university satire *The Return from Parnassus, Part Two* (1603) calls Jonson "The wittiest fellow of a Bricklayer in England," and mocks him with language that slips between how Jonson wrote and his earlier labor: "so slow an Inventor, that he were better betake himself to his old trade of Bricklaying; a bold whoreson, as confident now in making of a book, as he was in times past in laying of a brick."[33] To their contemporaries, such dramatists were, as Paul Yachnin reminds us (quoting Jonson himself), "stage-wrights."[34] One might sense a developing vocabulary, in fact, by comparing two phrases: "throughly ransacked" (Gosson) and "laying of a brick" (*Return from Parnassus*). While Gosson had described the work of playmaking with terms from romance (where "ransack" and plunder is what thieves and armies do), the contemporaries of Jonson and Webster are content to see it as ordinary, mechanical labor.

They were right to do so, of course, not only because playmaking had become a more regular craft in the decades following Gosson's diatribe but also because writing *is* labor. And as labor it invariably confesses one's dependence on audience and materials, invariably reveals self-begetting a fantasy. Anyone who has written realizes that writing involves physical objects that the end product may only hint at. Among the many materialist accounts of literary composition, a version that usefully affirms the role of such objects is that of the Russian poet and critic Vladimir Mayakovsky. Mayakovsky described writing as kind of *bricolage* when he wrote in *How to Make Verse* (1926) that, in addition to skill, knowledge, and a social purpose, a poet needs both material (words) and equipment to write poetry. This equipment could include "Pen, pencil, typewriter, telephone . . . a bicycle for riding to editorial offices, a well-arranged table, an umbrella to write under in the rain . . . and even a pipe and cigarettes."[35] Here literature, like Lévi-Strauss's myth and ritual, is seen as production instead of as creation, its requisite materials part of the tool kit of the artist as *bricoleur*. Obviously, Nashe's claim of literary independence would prove specious in any era, not only because writers need physical equipment to write (books, paper, pens, ink) but also because language itself implies community, literature an inherited, shared body of words, motifs, and forms. Everyone quotes, as the epigraph to this book holds, and everything we make is quotation. Yet if we choose a meaning for this term that falls between imitation and citation—the former awkward in its generality, the latter limited by its specificity—literary "quotation" reveals more than the structural dependence of all writers on materials and audience. Involving themselves to various degrees with what lies beyond their margins, literary texts speak to a *worldly* dependence legible in, with, and through what they borrow.

As we have seen, early modern playwrights quoted with remarkable frequency, weaving their plays from many other "texts." Such texts, again, were not always printed, for these playwrights quoted a wide variety of materials, events, and persons. Their plays drew on such works as Holinshed's *Chronicles* and the Book of Common Prayer, on such events as the defeat of the Spanish Armada and the Gunpowder Plot, on such institutions as Parliament, and also on such individuals as the Earl of Essex and Queen Elizabeth. However important printed matter was to their composition, then, however much they appropriated their worldly hodge-podge from the pages of other printed works, these plays regularly borrowed from the world itself. Like verbal borrowing, this quotation ranged from the brief to the extensive, from allusion to whole-cloth adoption. Calling these worldly borrowings "quotation" risks implying to the modern ear that they have the same shape as words, phrases, and sentences. Obviously they differ. But as the following chapters seek to demonstrate, worldly borrowings in early modern plays are, like verbal borrowings, invariably partial in nature. Unlike Hercules in the mythical placard, dramas bore in the world by parts. A person might be "quoted" in a character and scene, that is, but not so extensively that one should use symbols for equivalency to describe their relation across a play: Hamlet = Essex; Holofernes = Florio. Likewise, an event can be quoted in a play without suggesting the identity of play and event.

Using quotation as a descriptive as well as analytical unit will therefore help us solve one of the structural problems of "Old" Historicism—which, in its topical and à clef forms, commonly required plays to be consistent allegories of their political backgrounds.[36] Most readers are willing to concede that certain events and individuals contributed to the actions and characters of various plays. Yet these same readers are unpersuaded by critical arguments that ask them to see plays as thorough, and consistent, allegories of the external world. Even as an early modern sense of "quotation" compels us to question our assumptions concerning linguistic property, realizing that playwrights quoted events and individuals (rather than represented them) will better help us discern what these plays are and how they held the world.

Our interest in these plays' worldliness begs for a heightened attention to their quotations and, correspondingly, for a more careful approach to the relations between text and context. Plays were formally fragmented, and they incorporated the world in these fragments. Reading quotations will help us comprehend the partiality of these plays' incorporation of other texts, people, and events. The focus that "quotation" gives us will also help us address some shortcomings in current ways of reading these parts. In seeking to restore agency to authors, this method of reading addresses problems of intertextual criticism and responds to New Historicism by attempting to restore a meaningful diachrony to the historical analysis of literature. When we move, for instance, from quotation as a material unit to "position" as a political one, we more closely approach New Historicism's interest in issues of power and authority in these dramatic texts. Yet New Historicism typically uses quotations without much consideration of them *as* quotations—as borrowings from the world, that is, among many such borrowings. Early modern plays are too heterogeneous for us to rely on single quotations as representative of a text's positions. One solution offered here involves looking for patterns of positions, for repeated orientations. By finding such patterns, we can begin to account more responsibly for what these plays mean. Before we turn to the reading of patterns, however, we need to examine the role of quotation in what is still the most influential critical paradigm in the study of early modern drama.

Quotation and New Historicism

If we grant the worldliness I have claimed for these plays, significant interpretive and methodological questions remain. How may we grasp what these quotations mean and how they mean it? How are we to describe them? How, that is, should we interpret the *bricolage* of early modern drama? These questions, of course, have ready-made answers in a variety of established ways of reading. Source study comes immediately to mind, for it has traditionally shaped the interpretation of literary *bricolage*. Sometimes phrased in terms of "influence," source study perhaps more often attempts to find out what writers have used to construct their texts, explaining what a text is by identifying its materials. This material, again, ranges from language to events and people. These persons, texts, and events, source study holds, have an a priori claim on our interpretations of the plays that use them: we can best perceive what plays are by identifying what they are made of. But to many critics, the positivistic assumptions behind this way of reading seem questionable. Many scholars believe that by implying a direct correspondence between a text and a source, source study simplifies literature and the complexities of writing.

Accordingly, critics in the latter half of the twentieth century gave the study of literary relations new directions. We can describe this as a general shift from "source" to "intertextuality." As Jay Clayton and Eric Rothstein have pointed out, during the twentieth century, criticism interested in literary *bricolage* moved gradually from "source" to "influence" to "intertextuality," the latter involving an "impersonal field of crossing texts."[37] Robert Miola summarizes the beliefs behind this movement in speaking of a new model of literary relations that remains "plural rather than singular, encompassing and allowing for a wide range of possible interactions between sources, intermediaries, and texts."[38] He catalogs some synonyms for "source" in criticism today: "deep source, resource, influence, confluence, tradition, heritage, origin, antecedent, precursor, background, milieu, subtext, context, intertext, affinity, and analogue."[39] Embracing multiple relations among texts and authors, the approaches these terms represent have offered attractive alternatives to what often appears a constricting, even forensic way of reading.

If source study has evolved or even been replaced through this move to intertextuality, the most conspicuous way of reading literary quotation is New Historicism. Like source study—from which it draws many of its interpretive materials—New Historicism sets out to describe the relations among "texts," both loosely and strictly conceived. Yet, eschewing what it sees as the critical tradition's overly formalist accent on the relations among books, New Historicism takes quotation as a tool by which literature can be seen to engage with larger cultural energies. The formal heterogeneity of these plays, critically accessible through their patchwork quotation, provides an ideal medium for new historicist analysis. By examining how New Historicism has interpreted cultural quotations in early modern plays, we can better fathom its strengths as well as its weaknesses and why it increasingly seems such a limited way of reading.

Focus on New Historicism here requires a definition, for although few terms have figured so centrally in current debates about early modern drama, none has produced more ambiguity. Difficult as definition has proved, so frequently do critics attempt to define New Historicism and so varied are their results, that it is sometimes hard to tell whether it is, on the one hand, a large critical school unified by a common set of beliefs or, on the other, merely a handful of influential essays by a relatively few critics. Most definitions fall somewhere between these extremes and often involve divergent issues.[40] One can define New Historicism, for example, as a rhetorical form, a generational project, an interdisciplinary phenomenon, and a sign of analytical and ethical decay or progress. The partiality of these definitions is heightened by the understandable reluctance of "New Historicists" to wear that badge and by the fact that academic presses continue to introduce under this label new and diverse work that compels us to expand our already capacious definitions of New Historicism. How, then, to define it?

Characterized as a procedure, new historicist analysis tends to fasten onto part of a text contiguous with something outside that text, reading contemporaneous events, documents, and phenomena beside and into literary works: a novel and a scientific lecture, a play and a riot, a poem and a battle. Such readings see various objects as interinanimated by proximity: comparing them tells us more about a culture than would reading either of the objects in isolation. New Historicism thus relies on the quotations of literary texts, and it has made remarkable achievements with these quotations. Yet for all the insight this critical genre has given us into the cultural and the historical, its penchant for the synchronic, for the "next-to-in-time," has occluded the process and implications of literary composition. Ironically, the recent "return" to History in literary studies embodied by New Historicism has repressed the diachronic, the sequence of before and after, which has traditionally defined the historical. New Historicism has also changed the objects that criticism examines. Where still invoked, sources have become democratized; rarely now does criticism privilege books as either originary or teleological objects. If in stressing the particularities of Lyly's worldly "hodgepodge," New Historicism is less bookish than older forms of historicist criticism (which had long read "sideways"), another salient difference between it and its precursors lies in the vocabulary and concepts used to convey the relations it describes. With its interest in the synchronic, and following the critical shift away from "source," New Historicism refers to "intertextuality" rather than to "source" and to "circulation" instead of to "borrowing."

Unfortunately, this change in nomenclature has obscured the history of criticism itself, especially the connections between New Historicism and the traditions of source study. For instance, while Stephen Greenblatt begins an early version of his influential essay "Shakespeare and the Exorcists" by saying his "concern is with the relation between" Samuel Harsnett's *A Declaration of Egregious Popish Impostures* (1603) and Shakespeare's *King Lear* (1605), he almost immediately claims that "Source study is, as we all know, the elephants' graveyard of literary history."[41] Greenblatt offers instead an approach called "cultural poetics," one that sees texts, events, and institutions as actively *exchanging* ideas, arguments, and energy. Source study, in his model, is entirely philological:

[P]ossible borrowings [by *King Lear* from Harsnett's *Declaration*] have been carefully catalogued, but the question of their significance has been not only unanswered but unasked. Until recently, the prevailing model for the study of literary sources, a model in effect parceled out between the old historicism and the new criticism, blocked such a question. As a freestanding, self-sufficient, disinterested art-work produced by a solitary genius, *King Lear* has only an accidental relation to its sources: they provide a glimpse of the "raw material" that the artist fashioned. In so far as this "material" is taken seriously at all, it is as part of the work's "historical background," a phrase that reduces history to a decorative setting or a convenient, well-lighted pigeonhole. But once the differentiations upon which this model is based begin to crumble, then source study is compelled to change its character: history cannot simply be set against literary texts as either stable antithesis or stable background, and the protective isolation of those texts gives way to a sense of their interaction with other texts and hence to the permeability of their boundaries.[42]

This paragraph indicates how older forms of criticism interested in quotation are commonly represented. Greenblatt's genealogy connects source study with "old historicism" and "new criticism" to explain how source study views literature and literary relations. But here the logic behind these statements asks us to pause and consider his claims. Can any source study ever believe, as Greenblatt holds, that any work is "a freestanding, self-sufficient, disinterested art-work produced by a solitary genius"? By definition, does not source study reveal a composite, dependent, "interested" artwork produced by an artist immersed in a material complex of texts, persons, and often events?

Concerned with various literary, historical, and social quotations that make up Renaissance drama, older studies such as Henry Green's *Shakespeare and the Emblem Writers* (1870), Gunnar Boklund's *The Duchess of Malfi: Sources, Themes, Characters* (1962), and Geoffrey Bullough's generally nondiscursive *Narrative and Dramatic Sources of Shakespeare* (1957–75) contradict the preceding characterization of source study. And even studies that use the rhetoric Greenblatt alludes to do not always do so to the effect he claims. For instance, the first sentence of an old historicist study, T. W. Baldwin's *On the Compositional Genetics of "The Comedy of Errors"* (1965), calls into question Greenblatt's sense of "decorative setting" and "stable background" by offering a more fluid relation: "*The Comedy of Errors* was written within the political and intellectual background of London in the late 'eighties, and *the political background has entered basically into the composition of the play.*"[43] With only slight rewording (the substitution, for example, of "milieu" for "background"), this statement could pass as the beginning of a typical new historicist essay. For, although phrased in terms of background, Baldwin's statement describes a permeability between the cultural and the literary that is integral to New Historicism.

Dependent on inadequate generalizations about previous scholarship, Greenblatt's remarks nevertheless indicate a relation between New Historicism and one vision of source study. Source study is itself an important source of Greenblatt's own essay and, further, an important source of New Historicism, the name that "cultural poetics" would come to be known by. Frequently depending on source study, the New Historicism is a version of this methodology, changed (as Greenblatt concedes) in character. Although these changes are significant—"Shakespeare and the Exorcists" is what source study looks like after Michel Foucault, Clifford Geertz, Raymond Williams, and Pierre Bourdieu—the similarities are crucial for many reasons, not the least of which that they are so often and so forcefully repressed. Greenblatt rightly indicates that previous critics had not done enough with Harsnett and *Lear*: an essay by Kenneth Muir, which Greenblatt cites in a note, is admittedly little more than a long list of borrowings by Shakespeare from *A Declaration of Egregious Popish Impostures*.[44] But this essay is also no *less* than a long list of Shakespeare's borrowings from Harsnett (many unrecognized prior to the publication of the essay), and, along with Muir's edition of *King Lear* in the Arden series (1952), it adds to our collective knowledge of the play and its culture. We need Muir's work even as we need philology and historical scholarship in general. We know what we know about early modern drama in part from such works as H. R. D. Anders's *Shakespeare's Books* (1904) and R. W. Dent's *John Webster's Borrowing* (1960)—both "long-list" works without a narrative structure or a conscious concern with politics, but works that nonetheless add to our knowledge and our potential knowledge of the period's plays. We should not undervalue the scholars and critics whose labor has brought the material relations of the past to our attention.

However much it underestimates source study, Greenblatt's essay depends on the fact that Harsnett is Shakespeare's source. Greenblatt's source, in turn, is Muir. Yet as "Shakespeare and the Exorcists" went through its many stages, Greenblatt's dependence on Muir and his source study became less apparent. In its first, four-page incarnation, Greenblatt's essay primarily notes the interesting involvement of Harsnett's text in *Lear,* saying, "We happen to know one of the books that Shakespeare had been reading and seems indeed to have had open before him as he revised the old play of *King Leir.*"[45] The tone of this remark is like that of a lecturer presenting commonplace details to an audience unconcerned with academic endeavor. It implies, with its "We happen to know," that there is little effort involved in the acquisition of knowledge and fact, and little real or symbolic capital associated with producing new information. This early version of the essay formed something like the first step away from, and beyond, what Greenblatt saw as conventional source study. A later version added the preceding critique of source study. Still later, another version deleted this critique, testifying, perhaps, that New Historicism had transcended source study, obviating the need to address its influence and making a rhetorical break with it. In contemporary debates about New Historicism, in fact, the latter's connections with source study seldom receive notice—one reason we need to explore source study's implications for New Historicism and, by extension, for how we read texts and what we consider them to be.

Lest it seem that too much is made of one essay here, we should turn to other examples of New Historicism and their relation to source study. Other new historicist essays bring to bear texts and phenomena occurring *after* the canonical texts in question; it could be argued that, in doing away with priority, these essays abolish the positivistic assumptions of traditional source study, rendering the concept of "source" obsolete. Here Simon Forman's dream (1597) in Louis Montrose's now classic essay on *A Midsummer Night's Dream* (1596) remains a prime example. Montrose calls his essay an "intertextual study of Shakespeare's *Midsummer Night's Dream* and symbolic forms shaped by other Elizabethan lunatics, lovers, and poets."[46] Adopting the rhetoric of intertextuality, Montrose moves from the chronological (Old Historicism and literary history) to the intertextual "field" of the cultural (New Historicism). Can this self-consciously innovative essay be considered source study? And if so, to what end?

Like "Shakespeare and the Exorcists," Montrose's essay participates in, even as it alters, the critical genre of source study. Montrose pays homage to traditional modes of source study by discussing prior studies of the sources of *A Midsummer Night's Dream* at some length in his notes. The body of his essay, however, clusters a variety of cultural "sources" from around the time *A Midsummer Night's Dream* was written: these sources include, in addition to Forman's dream, extracts from contemporaneous diaries, letters, and travel writings. His emphasis on contemporaneous texts can be misleading, however. It seems telling that, when Montrose cites the *Problems* of Aristotle, he does so in an English translation published in 1597, the year of Forman's dream, and just one year after we believe *A Midsummer Night's Dream* was written. Citing this edition of Aristotle serves to point out that the opinions articulated therein were indeed available as Shakespeare composed the play. But because this text and its positions had long been available to readers—Aristotle's *Problems* had been a staple text of medical thought for hundreds of years—Montrose's citation of this synchronically adjacent edition implies a confirming, even urgent authority that the edition itself did not necessarily possess.

Like other new historicists, Montrose retains the importance of exterior texts, turning source study sideways—even backwards—and stressing the synecdochic and the synchronic. "Sources" no longer add or cause or need to precede literary texts; they are instead part of a single cultural organism or system—sources primarily for *us,* aiding our insight into texts. We now think about sources in relation to cultures, to critics, and to other belated readers, instead of to authors (themselves, of course, readers), in relation not to the writing of a text, but to the critical *re*production of texts. We have moved from a "writerly" intertextuality to a "readerly" intertextuality. As representative anecdotes, sources form the intertextual building blocks not of literary works but of the cultural "text" that the new historicist essay works to produce—or, in its words, to identify.[47]

We need to remember that the word "intertextuality" was coined (almost serendipitously) by Julia Kristeva to describe the necessary dependence of literary texts upon those that came before. That is, it was initially chronological, not synchronic; successive, not sideways. According to Kristeva, and in the translation by Jonathan Culler, a literary text is "constructed from a mosaic of quotations; any text is the absorption and transformation of another."[48] Kristeva's original formulation was merely a sophisticated way of talking about how writers make texts. But Culler's subsequent gloss points to a certain looseness of definition surrounding "intertextuality" over the following decades: "A work can only be read in connection with or against other texts, which provide a grid through which it is read and structured by establishing expectations which enable one to pick out salient features and give them a structure."[49] Culler's interest in structuralism leads him to omit mention of priority or even of textual production; he concerns himself more with how readers reproduce the work in relation to other works. This flattening of intertextuality—stressing the "sideways," synchronic textures of literature—underwrites much of the New Historicism and limits its ability to talk about historical change.

Traditional source study posits an active author who produces texts by quoting material from other "texts"—literary, historical, and social. A kind of *bricoleur,* this author fashions works by quoting. In this schema, if we take Shakespeare as author, source texts (which might number in the hundreds, if not thousands) could include Harsnett's *Declaration* (1603), Sidney's *Arcadia* (pub. 1593), and *The True Chronicle History of King Leir* (1590). The "final" text in this instance is *King Lear.* I put "final" in quotation marks here because I have deliberately chosen a vexed example: the various texts of *King Lear* remind us that any model of composition for this period and this literary business has to be flexible enough to account for revision, multiple texts (themselves potential sources for later versions of the "same" play), and collaboration, authorial and otherwise. Contrary to Greenblatt's characterization, the category of author here need not be conceived as solitary or static (or even in terms of genius); the author instead remains part of history and actively *makes* texts, over time, out of other materials.

In contrast, New Historicism changes this traditional model. Among the compositional sources of its new cultural texts stand more generalized quotations—stories, incidents, utterances, slices of time, symbolic forms—and canonical literary texts. Both *King Lear* and Harsnett's *Declaration* go into the cultural text in "Shakespeare and the Exorcists," as *A Midsummer Night's Dream* combines with Simon Forman's bawdy dream about Queen Elizabeth to establish the field of the cultural in Montrose's "Shaping Fantasies" essay. This cultural text is often portrayed as dynamic but seems, in the long view, static and unchanging. Montrose's turn to *Pericles* (1608, 5.1.195) to close his essay—"*A Midsummer Night's Dream* . . . shapes the fantasies by which it is shaped, begets that by which it is begotten"—calls on the chiasmic, even circulatory formulation so common to New Historicism that one could describe it as New Historicism's hallmark trope.[50] We hear this in Richard Helgerson's statement: "Texts, nations, individual authors, particular discursive communities—all are both produced and productive, productive of that by which they are produced."[51] And we will also recall Greenblatt's vision of continuing exchange between Harsnett and "Shakespeare's theater": "Who knows if Harsnett has not already, in a deep sense, borrowed from Shakespeare's theater what Shakespeare borrows back?"[52] One problem with this circulatory model is that things change and change other things: the theater Harsnett may have borrowed from, writing in 1603, was not the same theater (nor was Shakespeare the same playwright) that may have borrowed "back" from Harsnett. Actors, plays, playwrights, even the location of the playhouse itself had changed in the decade before 1603, and some of these would change again between Harsnett's *Declaration* and the first version of *King Lear* circa 1605–6.

While Greenblatt rightly questions an easy differentiation between texts and history-as-background, we also need to sense the differences that time brings. To insist on exchange without difference is to repress change and to forget that exchange itself is a powerful instrument of transformation. Reading sideways, reading "circulation," can bring us new insights, but it can also lull us into believing we can step into the same river twice. A study of dramatic quotation that asks questions about change and difference can help us put the comparatively static field of the cultural into motion. If moving to a circulatory model of society, and seeing the cultural as a text to be read, transforms "source" from building material to something resembling a tissue sample, we still have a criticism that aligns canonical works with lesser-known "texts." This hierarchy is often disguised in leveling metaphors like circulation and exchange and through the seemingly neutral rhetoric of intertextuality, but there remains a basic dedication to the canonical texts on which traditional source study had expended its energies. While New Historicism often takes up "sources" chronologically close to (even after) a literary work and expands traditional definitions of source to include ideas, forces, and other phenomena outside books, it repeats source study's commitment to well-known texts.

New Historicism's understanding of this repetition, and of its relation to its critical sources, is often impaired by a repression of its own history, even of the history of scholarship itself. *King Lear* appears to bring Harsnett's *Declaration* to our attention by quoting it; between the two works, and between Greenblatt and *Lear*, however, lie dozens of scholars and editors who helped identify and preserve the quotation as quotation. That the development of New Historicism came only at the price of a tension with this tradition is evident in the Greenblatt paragraph quoted above. Witness "elephants' graveyard" in the sentence "Source study is, as we all know, the elephants' graveyard of literary history." Why, we might ask, this figure? That is, why use a patently fictional metaphor—the elephants' graveyard—to talk about a real practice? If there seems an unconscious revelation in this move, Greenblatt's recourse to an accepted fiction also indicates a larger mythology of origins, a story of "how we got here" that New Historicism has come to accept. Much of this mythology is evident in Greenblatt's generalizations about New Criticism, Old Historicism, and the ostensibly ahistorical beliefs of philology and formalism. Reading Greenblatt's story of origins as a fiction, one can say that source study is what must be censured to validate the foundational narrative of New Historicism.

What difference does it make where New Historicism came from? At this point, it may be clear that I believe the answer to this question has relevance for literature's relation to its compositional materials. Quotations tell us what a work is materially *tethered* to: what lines of relation tie it to texts, people, events, ideas, and discourses. By following these tethers and by scrutinizing the differences that occur in every remaking, we can come to a deeper understanding of the works we study. I have dwelled on New Historicism's representations of source study out of a belief in the affinities between critical and literary indebtedness, and out of a conviction that a "flow" between these categories is inevitable. Criticism, like literature, is a material practice. To understand provenance and relation in literature, we must make every effort to get it right where it concerns us. We should not repress the diachronic—our history as well as the history of texts and authors we are studying—in our move toward the synchronic. And we cannot afford to forget that things, including arguments and ideas, are constructed out of, and with, other things.

Positioning Quotation

Increasingly fewer interpreters believe in "whole" texts, that such a play as *The Winter's Tale* (1611) or *The Duchess of Malfi* (1614), for example, forms an independent, highly integrated microcosm of words, themes, and meaning.[53] Concentrating instead on the significance of parts of plays and on the relation of these parts to elements in the surrounding culture, readers today often concede (however implicitly) the fragmentary nature of early modern drama. Surely they are not wrong to do so. The contemporary metaphors for playwriting we have seen—tailoring, bricklaying, cart building—offered good analogies because dramatists of early modern England constructed their plays in ways that do not hold, necessarily, for later periods. To begin with, most plays were collaborations.[54] A manuscript like *[The Book of] Sir Thomas More* (1595), with its diverse hands indicating multiple contributors (Shakespeare most likely writing this speech and scene, Dekker, Munday, Chettle, and Heywood others) formed the rule, not the exception. To this collaboration on new works, one could add the revision, even rewriting of extant plays—the belatedness of *Hamlet* has already been invoked—and the practice of adding scenes and speeches to established dramas for revivals. Here Henslowe's notation that he paid Jonson for "adicians in geronymo the some of xxxxˢ" (i.e., additions to Kyd's *The Spanish Tragedy* [1587]) remains only one instance of a common practice.[55] Companies also fragmented plays for the purposes of performance. After playwrights turned their manuscripts over to acting companies, scribes would typically write out fair copies; one of these copies might be cut apart, speech by speech, and pasted together according to part—a "side," as it was then called, for each actor. Looking at the surviving side of Edward Alleyn for the title role of Greene's *Orlando Furioso* (1591) is to confront the manner in which texts were physically dispersed after composition.[56] Censors also could isolate a passage for excision, especially if it too forwardly "quoted" a person or issue. And we have already seen Nashe as only one of countless auditors who cribbed attractive pieces of these plays, a practice formalized in this era by printed collections. All these practices argue against seeing plays as organic wholes, as undifferentiated creations of a single author. To stress parts of plays, then, seems merely to follow their inherently fragmentary nature.

Yet if we read parts of plays, including their quotation of the world, we rarely discuss these *as* parts. Nor do we usually see the drawbacks of analyzing these particulars in increasingly conventional ways or of using formal relations to read social energy. My reading of New Historicism and its relation to traditional forms of criticism has tried to show that New Historicism's penchant for synchrony limits our field of inquiry, diminishing our perception of the history in and behind early modern drama. Joined to its reliance on such familiar, potentially chiasmic metaphors as circulation, exchange, and negotiation, the synchronic window of New Historicism makes it difficult to see that these plays quote a variety of ideas, practices, persons, and events, from a variety of times. Because these plays are in turn quoted by later writers, their lines of appropriation stretch both backward and forward in time. Texts are too historical, in every sense of the word, to read sideways. We need, therefore, to rethink precisely how they are historical and how our criticism will describe their historicity.

Stressing the diachronic forms something like a first step, for restoring motion to the history connected with early modern plays will help us see them as richer documents even as it gives us a vocabulary for describing historical change. Critics have already begun to do so in significant ways. Recent developments in criticism concerning texts and occasion in early modern England, for example, call into question the utility of New Historicism's attraction to the synchronic. Joined to a new interest in multiple versions of play texts, an expanded idea of events and their afterlife asks that we consider early modern drama "historical" in multiple ways.[57] While New Historicism has given us richer historical contexts than did much previous criticism, the contexts that New Historicism commonly reads are expanding to degrees its synchronic window cannot encompass.

Neither contexts nor texts explain themselves, of course, and although I have argued that we need to consider quotation and history in more supple ways, to this point I have shown primarily that certain tendencies of current historicist criticism lessen its analytical and explanatory abilities. While what I have called "quotation" clearly involves more than purely literary issues, precisely how it sheds light on anything outside texts themselves has yet to be accounted for here. We might begin to fill this gap by noticing that, by definition, quotation links unlike things. For representation means partiality, and even the verbatim re-presentation of words from an earlier text can never reproduce their initial context. Every instance of borrowing can be said to foreground difference, and differences no less than similarities can offer valuable information about the cultural, historical, and political positions of literary texts.

Perhaps the most familiar instances of these meaningful positions come when authors explicitly disagree with the texts they quote. We immediately recall such polemics because they are often joined as companion

pieces in classrooms, anthologies, and histories, neatly answering our need
to see the past as a struggle with identifiable sides. Among these many
texts are "The Nymph's Reply" talking back to "The Passionate Shepherd"
toward the end of Elizabeth's reign; *The Woman's Prize, or The Tamer
Tamed* (1611) responding, after two decades, to *The Taming of the Shrew*
(1592); and *Eikonoklastes* countering *Eikon Basilike* "point by point" in
1649.[58] Whether the issue involves the status of time and pleasure, the arrangements of power between women and men, or the legality of regicide,
the debates of these texts show how quotation speaks to charged issues
outside the work in question. Many critics have seen the conflict represented in these debates as a metaphor for literary relations generally:
texts, that is, fight through quotation.

Parallel to this belief, a stress on a hierarchy of Renaissance *imitatio* often prejudices our thoughts about the significance of various kinds of borrowing. We might take as example of both tendencies Thomas Greene's
influential study, *The Light in Troy* (1982). Greene most admires the no-
ticeable, "civilized violence" of what he calls "dialectical" *imitatio*. He describes this type of imitation as fierce struggle: "[T]he diachronic structure
of the humanist text . . . had to expose the vulnerability of the subtext
while exposing itself to the subtext's potential aggression. . . . By exposing
itself in this way to the destructive criticism of its acknowledged or alleged
predecessors, by entering into a conflict whose solution is withheld, the
humanist text assumes its full historicity and works to protect itself against
its own pathos."[59] Here literary relations are red in tooth and claw: "expose
the vulnerability," "aggression," "destructive," "conflict," "protect itself."
Where the best kind of *imitatio* is self-conscious and erudite, it is also
wholly violent. Great texts and authors survive, this rhetoric implies, because they are the strongest and smartest of their kind. But while a conflictive model that stresses literary antagonism might hold for some early
modern plays and playwrights (and, perhaps apropos here, even some contemporary English departments), it cannot begin to account for the range
of dramatic texts in the era.[60]

Similarly, attempting to explain plays through a select tradition of
books and authors runs contrary to the fact that early modern playwrights
commonly borrowed from decidedly noncanonical texts and authors.
Greene's interest in erudite and creative imitation works well, for example,
for such authors as Petrarch and Jonson, authors who seem exceptionally

aware of themselves as authors and conscious of their place in a long tradition of literary creation.[61] But if we think of a writer like Thomas Heywood, who claimed to have had a hand (or at least a "main finger") in making two hundred and twenty plays, a graded scale of *imitatio* that values intensively self-conscious, careful wrestling with select literary models and forbears seems not merely unfair but unhelpful. Common quotation finds little place in this criticism because it draws no attention to itself. Yet it is precisely through such quotation that texts are most deeply inscribed in the world.

So although the debates of the companion texts mentioned previously may make the best case for literature as extremely *positioned,* texts quote in ways that exceed argumentative dialogue. Even as unattributed quotation was the norm in early modern plays, so were their positions toward other texts less direct and vehement than these polemics would imply. In contrast to Harold Bloom's theory of agonistic literary associations, for instance, the quotations of early modern drama show us that conflict is only one of many possible relations among texts and authors.[62] Playwrights patched together their works, making many decisions that can reveal their relations to the materials they used. Here Michael Baxandall's remarks about "influence" in art history apply equally to literary relations:

> If one says that X influenced Y it does seem that one is saying that X did something to Y rather than that Y did something to X. . . . If we think of Y rather than X as the agent, the vocabulary is much richer and more attractively diversified: draw on, resort to, avail oneself of, appropriate from, have recourse to, adapt, misunderstand, refer to, pick up, take on, engage with, react to, quote, differentiate oneself from, assimilate oneself to, assimilate, align oneself with, copy, address, paraphrase, absorb, make a variation on, revive, continue, remodel, ape, emulate, travesty, parody, extract from, distort, attend to, resist, reduce, promote, respond to, transform, tackle . . .[63]

We can take from Baxandall's commonsensical observation both a language for describing the heterogeneous activity of literary quotation and a map for charting the variety of literary relations. Relations among texts and authors are too varied to be accounted for in narrow, programmatic ways. The range we see in Baxandall's list of possibilities gives us a channel between the Scylla of "conflict" tropes and the Charybdis of neutral "circulation," for the way in which his purposeful agents position themselves toward earlier texts is limited less by the critic than by the agents themselves.

With this word "position" I hope to convey the orienting potential of quotations and, correspondingly, how an analysis of borrowings can bring texts into sharper, sometimes startling relief. Position, then, can mean both the situation of a text—that is, its larger position *toward*—and the internal postures or attitudes of a text—its various positions *on* things. Where quotation implies relation, positions beg for a more specific definition of relations and offer us a way of describing differences among texts and authors. For instance, by following the tethers of quotations and studying the differences they reveal, we can gain information that countless close readings might never produce. As I will show in my next chapter, when dramatists quoted Marlowe's "The Passionate Shepherd" in their plays, this "golden" anthology piece often appears as a poem of latent sexual violence. Tracing it into these plays, we can see how early modern writers positioned the lyric and what they must have felt the poem's own positions were. And while it might be alleged that a comparison of any texts, regardless of quotation, could prove informative (surely it could), it is my contention here that material truths can lead us to more certain knowledge. Realizing, for instance, that authors had particular texts before them, or even in mind, can shed light on a template from which they diverged. It can show us a possibility—not only what was borrowed for the later work but also what was not: a set of possessions left in place, a road not traveled.

Whatever promise this way of reading may hold, even in the outline sketched so far, we might anticipate at least two immediate objections. Each of these objections alleges a falsification of early modern plays, and each could apply to new historicist practice as well as to the modified way of reading I am suggesting here. The first of these objections is general and holds that to search for the positions of plays—whether cultural, political, or historical—goes against their grain. Why treat these pleasurable stories as informative documents? Why read *plays,* that is, if we are interested in history, politics, and culture? Why look for the worldly when these plays concern *other* worlds and the worlds of the imagination? One could argue convincingly, in fact, that "position" itself is a word entirely alien to the poetry of this period.[64] It would appear much more at home, for example, in a work like *Dangerous Positions and Proceedings, Published and Practised Within This Island of Britain, Under Pretence of Reformation,* brought out in 1593 by Richard Bancroft (then Canon of Westminster and soon to be Bishop of London).[65] This fascinating sally against reformist writings, the author declares in a preface, was written to "set down by way of an historical narration, what he had observed touching certain positions holden." Bancroft's method is to provide, "through . . . manifold quotations," nothing "which is not to be found either in Books and writings published to the view of the world . . . or in public records."[66] There follow pages and pages of "positions"—quotations, that is, from both sources and authorities Bancroft approves of (Tertullian, Augustine, Chrysostom, certain parts of the Bible) and from contemporaries whose positions he finds dangerous: Knox, Goodman, Buchanan, and Martin Marprelate, among others. The "paper-sea" Florio would soon describe was, in part, both cause and content of Bancroft's text; as Bancroft concedes in the preface, much of his book consists of the words of others, from others' books. The utterly controversialist character of his work, apparent on every page, speaks to how, through print, Reformation energies had multiplied the dangerous positions Bancroft found it necessary to address.

Watchful authorities like Bancroft helped ensure that positions were dangerous almost by definition, that the word "position" itself might strike authors as overly controversial. For example, Shakespeare himself uses the word four times in his plays, and the characters who deploy it—Malvolio, Ulysses, and Iago—offer a reason to distrust its controversial implications, a reason "positions" themselves could seem dangerous.[67] We share with the early modern era, of course, this sense of position as an "assertion" or "advanced opinion."[68] And on the face of it, nothing could seem more formally alike yet substantively different than Bancroft's text, with its catalog of dangerous positions, and poetic quotations in such catalogs as *Politeuphuia; Wit's Commonwealth* (1597) and *Belvedere; Or, The Garden of the Muses* (1600). Bancroft gives us polemical utterances; the latter catalogs, mellifluous ones. It might be argued, however, that Bancroft's choice of words defines a useful analytical category for us. A decade before *Dangerous Positions,* he had written against Robert Browne and against what he would call *The opinions and dealings of the Precisians.* Although, like *Dangerous Positions,* this manuscript "relies on authorities and piles up quotations," it consistently inveighs against "platforms," not "positions."[69] What might such a change indicate?

This shift in nomenclature appears to signal Bancroft's awareness that what he objects to is something smaller and more concise than a platform. Granting such awareness, the similarities between works like *Dangerous Positions* and *Politeuphuia* become more significant. Seen historically, both testify to a late-sixteenth-century emphasis on small units of writing. Although it had many causes, this emphasis testified both to the success of humanist pedagogical formations earlier in the sixteenth century and to the educational revolution of its second half. It appears not merely in the various collections of resonant quotations and in the notebook method of composition but also in such increasingly popular, shorter forms as the sonnet, the ayre, the satire, the libel, and the epigram, in essays, aphorisms, maxims, apothegms, and sententiae, and in innovations in the theory and practice of translation such as those of Joseph Webbe, who pioneered a phrase-by-phrase method of translating Latin texts around the beginning of the seventeenth century.[70] One of the legacies of humanism is that writers in the sixteenth century became increasingly interested in, and sophisticated at, manipulating smaller verbal units—including quotations. We might note an awareness of this concentration of scale in a number of familiar conceits: Donne's "little rooms," Shakespeare's "posy of a ring," Marlowe's "infinite riches in a little room," Jonson's "lily of a day." The process of patching together early modern plays unfolded, then, in an atmosphere congenial to small groupings of words. But although we may tentatively accept that *Dangerous Positions* and quotation collections such as *Politeuphuia* and *Belvedere* speak to changes in discursive practice, the differences among them remain too obvious to dismiss. Whereas holding the positions that Bancroft collects could lead to one's execution (perhaps on, as well as for, a platform), the positions in these collections of literary quotations seem decidedly safe. Why, then, should we look for positions in dramas of the period when doing so might make plays seem more polemical than they are?

Were one to have answered this objection a decade ago, a response might have begun with a bald statement about the inherently political nature of the early modern playhouse. As marginal institutions located in the limbo of London's liberties, so the prevalent interpretation held, theaters were the sites and the instruments of the culture's most radical self-critiques.[71] Analyzing the various positions of the dramas performed there would mean uncovering only what was most crucial to the theaters' agency. To pass over these positions would be, according to this way of

reading, something like accepting the existence of a machine while denying its working parts.[72] But recently it has become clear that critics have
exaggerated the political force of sixteenth- and seventeenth-century playhouses. Paul Yachnin, for instance, has argued that the early modern
theater in London was a "powerless theater" made possible by its very inefficacy. For although these stages "persistently represented the issues of the
moment . . . these representations were seen to subsist in a field of discourse isolated from the real world, and . . . such representations were seen
normally as incapable of intervening in the political arena."[73] Other commentators have contributed to this vision by stressing the commercial
goals of playing, leaving us with playhouses devoted more to entertainment than to polemic.[74] Compared with the intensively polemical dramas
of the Henrician era and the midcentury, for instance, plays of the commercial theaters of the later sixteenth and early seventeenth century indeed
seem less directed, less hortatory, and even wholly unlikely tools for political commentary and change. It is undoubtedly this earlier, more pointed
form of drama that *Hamlet* remembers in its augmented play-within-the-
play, *The Murder of Gonzago*. That Hamlet's otherwise unsubtle mousetrap
produces notoriously ambiguous results might even be seen as a metaphor
for the political inefficacy of drama in the late Elizabethan era. Of course,
theatrical representations occasionally made powerful figures unhappy. We
have many records to this effect, from those about Elizabeth herself to the
well-documented affair of Count Gondomar in the 1620s. But even in a
society controlled by powerful aristocrats, irking individuals does not in itself spur significant cultural or political change. Staging a play to alter a
political scene, as Essex's followers discovered, was to ask a venue and a
medium to do more than they could.

Plenty and Patterns

There is little reason to see early modern playhouses as radical places. At
the same time, we have to acknowledge that, far from lacking political positions, early modern drama had them in abundance. The worldly "hodgepodge" that Lyly saw in early modern plays meant a *copia* of views, claims,
and postures on a variety of topics. A typical play might feature an overplot, plot, and subplot and, in these, a heterogeneous assortment of characters and speeches that, however closely woven or individually pointed,
take audience members and readers in a bewildering number of directions.

We might see the proclivity of the commercial theaters *for* this *copia* as one cause of its powerlessness; early modern drama, in this reading, offered too many positions to make anything happen, too many directions to prompt or expect a significant response. Perhaps because this *copia* remains so central to what early modern drama is, critics have seldom stopped to discuss its implications: it is the enabling condition of discussion itself.

Criticism has usually dealt with these plays' *copia* by seeing it as dichotomous in nature. Traditionally, for instance, Shakespeare criticism has responded to the abundance of his plays by channeling it through what we might call the two-party system: Norman Rabkin's rabbit/duck, Joel Altman's *argumentum ab utramque partem,* even the two-faced Janus produced in the rival readings of Tillyard and Dollimore.[75] This criticism shows us, finally, that Shakespeare has things *both ways.* Characters are one thing and its opposite, contradictory ideas are asserted and affirmed, and both sides of any issue appear equally plausible. This model implies that just as Hal immobilizes Francis the drawer in his tavern psychomachia, so does Shakespeare "freeze" readers interested in finding univocal positions in his plays. On this account, the political messages of any of his plays remain too bifurcated to compel action; "How long halt ye between two opinions?"

However persuasively this mode of criticism seems to account for divergent ideas in the drama, it seems overly wedded to binaries. For instance, even when it does not see these plays taking one side of a debate, criticism's tendency to understand them *as* debates limits what these plays are heard to say in a manner that the plays themselves rarely do. Categories like subversion/containment and radical/conservative falsify the heterogeneity of these plays. So while we can take from this criticism reason to reject a monological Shakespeare, replacing one voice with two equally constricts our interpretation of these acutely copious dramas. To be sure, Shakespeare differs in significant ways from many of his contemporaries, and the interpretive bind that his *copia* places readers in is not always produced by the works of contemporary playwrights, works sometimes less obviously full of copious matter. But if we consider such plays as *The Spanish Tragedy* (1587), *Friar Bacon and Friar Bungay* (1589), *The Jew of Malta* (1589), *Every Man in His Humour* (1598), *The Malcontent* (1604), *The Knight of the Burning Pestle* (1607), *The White Devil* (1612), *Bartholomew Fair* (1614), and *Women Beware Women* (1621)—some of them influencing Shakespeare's practice, some of them influenced by it—we find that they share with the plays of their better-scrutinized contemporary many of the heterogeneous features discussed above. Their *copia* likewise raises the problems of overdetermination posed by Shakespearean drama: How can we satisfy ourselves that these plays mean anything when they often appear to mean everything? How can we identify a direction in them when they seem to contain the whole world?

By raising this second objection we have almost inadvertently answered the first; in conceding the exceptional worldliness of early modern plays we have found good reason for scrutinizing their positions: cultural, political, and historical. These positions often differ greatly, of course, from the polemical, "dangerous positions" Bancroft quoted from his religious opponents. But surely we have expanded our definitions of what counts as significant in the arrangements of power and authority in early modern England. Defining the political more generously (as concerning, for instance, bodies, events, and ideas outside court and parliament), we have begun to see that the worldliness of their positions formed an important part of what these plays were. Therefore, if our first objection questioned the reading of positions, this second reservation involves which positions we choose to read. We might call this the problem of *pars pro toto,* or "part for the whole." Whether stressing an incident, anecdote, or archival passage, the current habit of reading slices of time and texts asks us to ask *which* passage, anecdote, incident, or other cultural fact has a claim to representativeness, and why.[76] We have seen that New Historicism typically opens its readings with single quotations. Because new historicist critics present these quotations in evocative prose at the outset of an argument, it is easy to see the quotations as "given," to accept without question their claim to representative status even as they seem to offer a natural purchase on the play at hand. Once we have accepted the representative quotation, however, the terms of our response have already been dictated. It sometimes seems that we are persuaded by the logic of new historicist essays, when it is actually as often their arrangement of texts, coupled with a seductive writing style, that compels our attention and assent. What would it mean, we might ask, to resist such provocative alignments? To imagine others? To see plays as entities composed of manifold quotations, some of them provocative and intrinsically "dramatic," some of them by comparison unexciting, but all of them potentially significant?

We have to understand the risks that accompany selectively reading these plays, even when such selectivity comes in the service of searching for *patterns* in early modern works—a possible solution to the problem of selective quotation. If one finds a pattern of sentiments, arguments, or ideas in a particular text or group of texts, for instance, it might imply that a larger tradition, orientation, or belief system was behind them. But an inherent danger in reading for patterns is that we will find only those patterns with which we are comfortable or that we have been conditioned to recognize by individual or institutional habits. Such a concern might be seen in relation to Richard Strier's *Resistant Structures* (1995), a study that argues against the potentially misleading influence of preconceived templates and paradigms in the reading process. In the following sentences, Strier articulates a rationale for reading the patterns of Shakespeare's works:

> [H]ow would one go about showing that Shakespeare had views, let alone radical ones? We have no pamphlets or tracts by him, and, of course, it would not necessarily settle the issue if we did (though it would certainly establish presumptions). The following procedures seem reasonable. We must see whether certain views are expressed by characters of whom, it seems clear, we are meant to approve or with whom we are meant to sympathize; we must see if there is a *pattern* of such views being expressed, so that they seem to be something that the playwright was truly interested in; and, finally, we must see whether such views are expressed in a number of plays, whenever contexts arise where they might be appropriate. If all these conditions are met, it seems reasonable to think that we have found something that Shakespeare believed.[77]

Strier attempts to fashion an objective procedure for the determination of "views," a procedure that leads carefully from hypothesis to conclusion. By his account, one is merely stating what others could confirm by following the same steps.

But this procedure has a number of shortcomings. We might notice first that, as Strier frames the procedure, he folds in an ancillary term, "radical," to the primary aim, the determination of views. Although this move is telling, and symptomatic of a larger tendency in criticism today, it is not in itself the main problem. Nor, even, is the questionable assumption that one could generate a list of "characters of whom . . . we are meant to approve or with whom we are meant to sympathize." Characters in most plays of the period are too complex to be placed in groups stamped "approved" and "unapproved," and the plays themselves offer a variety of events and actions that can make such things as approval and sympathy only intermittently true. For example, is Lear a character of whom we "approve" or with whom we "sympathize"? In act one? Act five? What about Portia, Hal, or Falstaff? This brief list of characters—characters who have traditionally prompted great ambivalence in readers and audience members—could be extended indefinitely, of course, and would include hundreds of characters in plays by Shakespeare's contemporaries. Clearly, then, Strier's use of "sympathy" or "approval" as a foundation to his way of reading is more hopeful than he indicates.

But however much the preceding issues call into question Strier's proposed way of reading, its main problem is that it tells him what he wants to hear. Strier begins with the hypothesis that Shakespeare held a certain type of belief, looks for and finds confirmation of that hypothesis in plays, and thus comes to believe that he has found Shakespeare's belief. Notice how the object in the passage quoted above slides from the plural "views" to the apparently singular "something that Shakespeare believed." We might ask, indeed, if the procedure is actually as objective as is implied, given a potential plurality of "views" in Shakespeare. That is, in looking for and finding one thing, a critic may neglect to notice other things; that oversight can call the truth of one's findings into question. As David Kastan reminds us, "Too often . . . a revealing word or phrase is used to prove an intentional commitment of the author to a political or philosophical position with too little sense of how the language functions in its particular context."[78] When dealing with copious works, what is not noticed can directly contradict what is (even as it can qualify or otherwise add to the topic at hand).

We might ask: What if one were to look for material that might falsify a hypothetical link between a pattern and an author's belief? What if, for instance, one were to look for an opposite pattern? How would Strier's search for patterns look, that is, were one to replace "radical" with "conservative" in the preceding passage? It might look a great deal like Allan Bloom's study, *Shakespeare's Politics* (1964), which itself sought patterns in Shakespeare's works, confirming them in the way Strier suggests, and which went on to present not a radical but a conservative Shakespeare. Bloom, for instance, felt that Shakespeare "tried to develop a sensible view of what the English regime is and how it should be accepted and revered by succeeding generations of Englishmen."[79] It should give us pause to note that, throughout their efforts, Bloom and Strier both seem confident in their accounts of a political Shakespeare. Those politics differ so profoundly, however, that we should be unwilling to embrace either account as true.

The reason these critics find a Shakespeare whose political orientation is so comfortable to them is that each focuses on what he is looking to find in a body of work with many patterns. Each of these critics can be seen as both enabled and misled by fundamental errors of approach: where Bloom treats Shakespeare's works like political philosophy, Strier reads the plays as though they were metaphysical poems. In the end, neither critic succeeds in avoiding the seductive call of his own desire because neither recognizes the *copia* that defines Shakespeare's plays. As Hamlet seems to realize, if we look for a whale, or a camel, in a sky full of clouds, chances are that we can find one. Shakespeare is not a Rorschach test, of course, but the *copia* of his plays should prompt us to enforce a skepticism about what we believe we have discovered in his works. The procedure described by Strier avoids a necessary step before we satisfy ourselves with the interpretation of patterns: we need, in short, to try to disprove our conclusions, to lend them validity by considering under what circumstances they would not be true. That is, if one wishes to establish a radical Shakespeare, one needs to acknowledge that such a portrait would be false (at the very least, in need of serious qualification) were one able to find compelling evidence for a conservative or otherwise oriented Shakespeare.

I invoke Strier's example here not for its exceptionality but because it articulates how most of us go about reading the plays of Shakespeare and his contemporaries. We tend to find what we look for; we grab parts and convince ourselves that we have retrieved wholes. To address the *pars pro toto* problem, we need to admit that reading quotations means reading partially, and we need to negotiate with care the dangers of that partiality. While it might be argued that we can do nothing other *than* read parts, that writing history and writing literary criticism entails such partiality, we nevertheless need to remind ourselves of the implications of reading this way and to work against the foreseeable errors it can lead us into. As we have seen, in reading quotations without considering what it means to do so, recent criticism risks obscuring the formal and cultural heterogeneity of early modern plays. Although following plays' lines of appropriation can put texts into striking, even startling relations, we need to be diligent about both how we do so and how we analyze what we find. Acknowledging that we read parts of these dramatic texts will force us to be more responsible to them as texts—not as integral wholes, perhaps, but as composite entities. This approach will also compel us to account more rigorously for our claims about the status of quotations. We can begin to do so by looking for patterns and habits behind quotation and by evaluating the significance of any quotation in relation to tendencies it may represent.[80]

As authors are to their cultures, so are their works to them, and quotations to their works. Our analysis of any of these elements should seek to admit the full range of each, even if doing so points out the exceptionality of the object, individual, or issue examined. To see Shakespeare or any of his contemporary dramatists as (alternately) radical, conservative, Catholic, Anglican, or Puritan because a few scenes, characters, speeches, or sentences from a play overlap with something outside that play is to read irresponsibly. Early modern plays have too many quotations, and these quotations are too varied in nature, to read selected ones as representative of the text's or the author's positions.

I began this introduction by describing early modern plays as mosaic-like works, thick with history, culture, and the political. It is through their *bricolage,* I argued, that dramatic texts quoted the world around them. These quotations tether early modern plays to a variety of works, institutions, events, practices, and individuals, from a variety of times. The historical sweep of quotation in any work makes a narrow analytical window incompatible with the materials that both contributed to and were borrowed from these plays. By analyzing the differences that result from every instance of quotation, we can better see the positions of early modern plays. It has been the burden of the paragraphs immediately preceding this one to show that the overdetermination of positions is both a characteristic of these dramas and a hurdle to critics interested in reading them *for* their positions. In the wealth of their *copia,* many plays appear to say everything, and this feature (sometimes beneficial, sometimes a liability) often goes unrecognized by critics interested in hearing only certain things. I have claimed that looking for patterns, habits, and other instances of meaningful repetition can help us gain a more accurate understanding of what these plays are about.

In this sense, the preceding remarks offer less a groundbreaking methodology than a qualification of current ways of reading. I have argued for this qualification based on a formal and historical description of early modern plays because reading objects with a concern for their production can lend richness to our interpretations. I do not mean to imply that I have described the only way to read plays of this period, or even the only way to read for the kinds of content that a culturally oriented criticism often looks for. The dense *copia* in early modern plays makes any critical approach only one of many that can seek to interpret them. Yet as long as we see a close identification of context and content in these plays, as long as we remain interested in how they quote, we need to read their quotations with more care and deliberation. For where early modern dramatists and actors regularly performed the Herculean feat of bringing the world into the commercial playhouses, our task—a very different labor—involves explaining the nature and import of their plays' worldliness.

CHAPTER 2

Quoting Marlowe's Shepherd

You must lay lime to tangle her desires
By wailful sonnets, whose composed rhymes
Should be full-fraught with serviceable vows.
    PROTEUS, in *The Two Gentlemen of Verona* (1593)

With adjectives we bait our lines
When we do fish for gentlewomen's loves,
And with their sweetness catch the nibbling ear
Of amorous ladies.
    CAPTAIN, in Shirley's *Love in a Maze* (1632)

Like all literary works, the plays that the Globe's actors carried in their heads were products, made things. Because every work of literature is not only made but made in part out of other works (something especially apparent in revisions, sequels, and parodies), and then itself may be borrowed from by others, literature should also be seen as an unending process. The epigraph to this book, from Emerson's "Quotation and Originality," argues for the truth of process in its denial of anything new under the sun, and in its analogy of time to an ever-moving loom: "Old and new make the warp and woof of every moment. There is no thread that is not a twist of these two strands." Seen in terms of Emerson's loom, literature indeed seems made up of strands of other works and of elements from the world itself. These strands are so numerous, of course, that what they produce perhaps more closely resembles a thick rope than a slender thread. To extend the analogy, we might say that this rope is continually unraveled by later writers, who pull at particular fibers and wind them into their own constructions. The result is a massive, ungainly web, a web that the perspective of history and the literary canon sometimes persuade us is a neat and decorous tapestry.

Yet there are patterns in this web. Cultures as well as authors have tendencies that motivate them to read, borrow, and refashion in particular ways. This chapter takes up just such a cultural pattern by examining both the "winding" and "unwinding" of one of the most celebrated lyrics from the Elizabethan era: Christopher Marlowe's "The Passionate Shepherd." Published in *England's Helicon* in 1600, one version of the poem reads as follows:

Come live with me and be my love,
And we will all the pleasures prove
That valleys, groves, hills, and fields,
Woods or steepy mountain yields.

And we will sit upon the rocks,
Seeing the shepherds feed their flocks
By shallow rivers, to whose falls
Melodious birds sing madrigals.

And I will make thee beds of roses
And a thousand fragrant posies,
A cap of flowers and a kirtle
Embroid'red all with leaves of myrtle;

A gown made of the finest wool
Which from our pretty lambs we pull,
Fair-lined slippers for the cold
With buckles of the purest gold;

A belt of straw and ivy buds
With coral clasps and amber studs.
And if these pleasures may thee move,
Come live with me and be my love.

The shepherds' swains shall dance and sing
For thy delight each May-morning.
If these delights thy mind may move,
Then live with me and be my love.

The durability of this short poem was recently brought home to audiences of Richard Loncraine's film version of *Richard III* (MGM 1995), which stars Ian McKellen. This film sets Shakespeare's play in what appears to be a fascistic, late-1930s era England. The calm-before-the-storm of Shakespeare's play is conveyed in the film by a nightclub setting, where a chanteuse performs an upbeat, period-sounding song that we gradually, and with a surprised delight, realize is a swing version of "The Passionate Shepherd." Marlowe's lyric, of course, was written some four centuries before this version of *Richard III* was filmed and in a poetic dialect almost as distant from the "era" in which the film locates its story. So while it is a love lyric, the poem's inclusion in the film perhaps seems a gratuitous in-joke on the part of the director, a coy reward to audience members for having studied English literature. To be sure, other readings could take the poem's presence more seriously. One approach, for instance, might argue that the lyric's function is to contrast with the horrors that follow. Certainly the rapid onset of violence in the film puts the poem in counterpoint. Love poems, after all, are about love, not war—a point driven home when the tranquilizing cadences of the lyric give way to the story's more brutal realities.

But as surprising as the film's quotation of this lyric seems, Loncraine's juxtaposition of "The Passionate Shepherd" with violence is anything but novel. It would have been far from startling, for instance, to those who saw and read plays of the early modern era. Marlowe's popular lyric during and after his lifetime was often placed in the context of violence, in situations where an apparently harmless invitation is followed by threats and aggression. Why might this have been? What, we might ask, does a love poem have to do with violence? Although we can begin to answer these questions by scrutinizing how "The Passionate Shepherd" was received in its day, we will also be aided by examining the resources it drew upon. As this chapter seeks to demonstrate, one way of understanding this poem and its reception—one way of not being surprised by its situation in later texts— is to read its own quotations before examining how it was quoted by others. Obviously, the kind of formalism described in such a process is not wedded to close reading, to concentrating primarily on the poem's words, phrases, imagery, structure, or logic. However valuable reading in "slow motion" may be (surely it is an indispensable tool), in this instance such close reading tells us less about "The Passionate Shepherd" than we need to know. Accordingly, the mode of reading employed in this chapter understands form as both internal and external to literary works. It is important to note that the external is here conceived as more than the synchronic slice that New Historicism typically takes up. Even as a word-by-word close reading of "The Passionate Shepherd" leaves us with an extremely incomplete understanding of this lyric, a new historicist account of Marlowe's poem circa 1588–89 can tell but a small part of the complex story relating to the poem. Only by looking at works written before Marlowe's poem, and at works written after it, may we be in a position to grasp its significance.

Background and Resources

Like Sidney, Marlowe was eulogized as a shepherd.[1] When Phebe quotes the "Dead Shepherd" in *As You Like It* (1599, 3.5.81–82), she not only extends Shakespeare's practice of anonymous quotation but describes with this epithet one of the most resonant aspects of Marlowe's contemporary reputation. Mighty line and Scythian Tamburlaine notwithstanding, it was with his erotic poetry generally, and with the words of another compelling shepherd in particular—those of "The Passionate Shepherd to His Love"—that Marlowe most clearly affected the literature of his immediate posterity.[2] Adapted for six ballad tunes and mentioned in the title sheets of at least nine separate ballads, the lyric generated an impressive literary legacy.[3] That "The Passionate Shepherd" attained popular currency is well attested by Parson Evans's use of it in *The Merry Wives of Windsor* (1597, 3.1.17–29), a quotation to which this chapter will return. Shakespeare, however, was far from the first or only writer to quote this poem. Indeed, "The Nymph's reply to the Shepherd," the methodical counter-argument usually attributed to Ralegh, which follows Marlowe's lyric in *England's Helicon,* remains only the most famous in a series of visions and revisions of the poem during the Tudor and Stuart periods. This lyric clearly fascinated its contemporaries: Greene, Drayton, Lodge, Deloney, and Walton are only a few of the many authors who quote "The Passionate Shepherd" in their works. In addition to the extent of such interest, the specific reception that the lyric earned hints that it was not only popular but also somewhat scandalous in its time. Why might this seemingly innocuous lyric have seemed scandalous? One way of answering this question is to look at how and where it was quoted.

Although, like a number of the poem's rebuttals and parodies, "The Nymph's Reply" takes lyric form, many responses to "The Passionate Shepherd" came in a dramatic context. Throughout the early modern era, playwrights avidly incorporated the Marlovian lyric into their plays; their reworkings of the invitation allowed for extended treatment of character, motivation, and situation. Quoting Marlowe's poem within their heterogeneous dramatic narratives, playwrights set these two "representational modes" in juxtaposition.[4] Such quotation spoke to key differences of form and outlook: it was in such borrowings and reformulations that dialogue arose within and between modes, the tension between Shepherd and Nymph manifested not only in a passion/reason debate but in the differences between lyric and dramatic as well. By appropriating and reforming the lyric, dramatists highlighted a variety of received differences between these two modes. Their reworkings of the invitation in dramatic context also revealed an aggression unstated in the form and process of the proposal as written by Marlowe. This "invitation not an invitation" figured importantly in the way playwrights adapted Marlowe's lyric, suggesting that its single-voiced rhetorical world was inherently dangerous to the objects of its desire.

A traditional approach to this lyric might stress its literary context by examining the social poetics of the pastoral. I choose here to place more emphasis on the poem as an individualized object—not, that is, as self-sufficient or freestanding but as something more than a version of the pastoral. My remarks explore the power dynamics of the Marlovian invitation as illustrated both in the works that it quoted and in works that quoted it. By doing so, I hope to keep focus on received properties of this lyric that go beyond the pastoral, however influential the traditions of the pastoral were to early modern literature.[5] After tracing the classical and biblical precursors quoted by Marlowe's poem, and after situating the lyric in a tradition of piscatorial poetry, I turn to the modal tension between lyric and dramatic evoked by "The Passionate Shepherd." To explore the differences of these modes is to take our understanding of Marlowe's poem beyond the confines not only of the pastoral but also of "answer poetry" in the early modern era.[6] The last section of this chapter examines how early modern dramatists quoted Marlowe's poem in their works and what their patterns of quotations mean. As positioned by its contemporaries in their works, "The Passionate Shepherd" was, in large part, a poem about power and authority. What seemed monological rigor in it invited alternate accounts of what had been left out, the repressed ultimately finding expression in revisionary, often violent versions of Marlowe's haunting lyric.

An examination of Marlowe's poem might begin with the resources available to him. Many readers in his time, for example, would have recognized that "The Passionate Shepherd" evolved out of a long tradition of amatory invitations. Among its literary forerunners, the Song of Songs and Catullus's *vivamus, mea Lesbia, atque amemus* would have been seen as providing familiar models. Important in this series was Theocritus's eleventh idyll, the lament of the Cyclops to Galatea, a sea nymph who has not requited his love. Offered as consolation by the poet to his friend Nicias of Miletus, a poet-physician, the idyll is prefaced with a description of the lament's scene, characters, and circumstances. In an anonymous translation published at Oxford in 1588—just prior to the likely date of composition for "The Passionate Shepherd"[7]—Theocritus's eleventh idyll is one poem in a small collection fully described by its title page: *Sixe idillia: That is, Sixe Small, or Petty poems, or Æglogues, Chosen out of the right famous Sicilian Poet Theocritus, and translated into English Verse.*[8] Because it has rarely been published elsewhere, because Marlowe and his readers may have known it, and because it can help us understand the role of power in Marlowe's poem, I give the idyll in full here as found in the *Sixe idillia*.

THE XI IDILLION

Argument

Theocritus wrote this Idillion to Nicias a learned Physician, wherein he sheweth by the example of Polyphemus, a Giant in Sicilie, of the race of the Cyclops, who loved the water Nymph Galatea, that there is no medicine so sovereign against love, as is Poetry. Of whose love-song, as this Idillion is termed Cyclops, so he was called Cyclops, because he had but one eye, that stood like a circle in the middle of his forehead.

Cyclops

O Nicias, there is no other remedy for love,
With ointing, or with sprinkling on, that ever I could prove,
Beside the Muses nine. This pleasant med'cine of the mind
Grows among men, and seems but light, yet very hard to find.
As well I wot you know, who are in Physic such a leech,   5
And of the Muses so belov'd, the cause of this my speech,
A Cyclops is, who lived here with us right wealthily,
That ancient Polyphem, when first he loved Galate;
When with a bristled beard, his chin and cheeks first clothed were.
He loved her not, with roses, apples, or with curled hair,   10

But with the Furies' rage, all other things he little plied.
For often to their fold, from pastures green, without a guide
His sheep returned home, when all the while he singing lay
In honor of his love, and on the shore consumed away
From morning until night, sick of the wound, fast by the heart   15
Which might Venus gave, and in his liver stuck the dart.
For which, this remedy he found, that sitting oftentimes
Upon a rock, and looking on the Sea, he sung these rhymes.
"O Galatea fair, why dost thou shun thy lover true?
More tender than a Lamb, more white than cheese when it is new,   20
More wanton than a calf, more sharp than grapes unripe I find.
You use to come, when pleasant sleep my senses all do blind.
But you are gone again, when pleasant sleep doth leave mine eye,
And as a sheep you run, that on the plain a Wolf doth spy.
I then began to love thee, Galate, when first of all   25
You with my mother came, to gather leaves of Crowtoe small
Upon our hill, when I as usher, squired you all the way.
Nor when I saw thee first, nor afterward, nor at this day,
Since then could I refrain; but you, by Jove, nought set thereby.
But well I know, fair Nymph, the very cause why you thus fly.   30
Because upon my front, one only brow, with bristles strong
From one ear to the other ear, is stretched all along.
'Neath which, one eye, and on my lips a hugie nose there stands.
Yet I, this such a one, a thousand sheep feed on these lands.
And pleasant milk I drink, which from the strouting bags is pressed.   35
Nor want I cheese in summer, nor in Autumn of the best,
Nor yet in winter time; my cheese-racks ever laden are,
And better can I pipe, than any Cyclops may compare.
O, Apple Sweet, of thee, and of my self, I use to sing,
And that at midnight oft. For thee, eleven fawns up I bring,   40
All great with young, & four bears' whelps, I nourish up for thee.
And let the bluish-colored Sea beat on the shore so nie,
The night with me in cave, thou shalt consume more pleasantly.
There are the shady Bays, and there tall Cyprus-trees doe sprout,
And there is Ivy black, and fertile vines are all about.   45
Cool water there I have, distilled of the whitest snow,

A drink divine, which out of woody Ætna mount doth flow.
In these respects, who in the Sea & waves would rather be?
But if I seem as yet, too rough and savage unto thee,
Great store of Oaken wood I have, and never quenched fire;   50
And I can well endure my soul to burn with thy desire,
With this my only eye, then which I nothing think more trim.
Now woe is me, my mother bore me not with fins to swim,
That I might dive to thee, that I thy dainty hand might kiss,
If lips thou wouldst not let; then would I Lilies bring Iwis,   55
And tender Poppy too, that bears a top like rattles red.
And these in summer time, but other are in winter bred,
So that I cannot bring them all at once. Now certainly,
I'll learn to swim of some or other stranger passing by,
That I may know what pleasure 'tis in waters deep to dwell.   60
Come forth, fair Galate, and once got out, forget thee well
(As I do sitting on this rock) home to return again.
But feed my sheep with me, & for to milk them take the pain,
And cheese to press, and in the milk, the rennet sharp to strain.
My mother only wrongeth me, and her I blame, for she   65
Spake never yet to thee, one good or lovely word of me,
And that, although she daily sees, how I away do pine.
But I will say my head and feet do ache, that she may whine
And sorrow at the heart, because my heart with grief is swollen.
O Cyclops, Cyclops, whither is thy wit and reason flown?   70
If thou wouldst baskets make, and cut down browsing from the tree,
And bring it to thy Lambs, a great deal wiser thou shouldst be.
Go coy some present Nymph, why dost thou follow flying wind?
Perhaps an other Galate, and fairer thou shalt find.
For many maidens in the evening tide with me will play,   75
And all do sweetly laugh, when I stand hark'ning what they say,
And I some body seem, and in the earth do bear a sway."
    Thus Polyphemus singing, fed his raging love of old,
    Wherein he sweeter did, than had he sent her sums of gold.

Following this poem in the *Sixe idillia* is a Latin tag identified as "Polyphem's Emblem": *Ubi Dictamum inveniam?* This could be translated as "Where shall I find something to say?" perhaps a fitting motto for an unrequited lover. After finishing the poem, though, we may feel that this emblem flies in the face of the lyric itself, for Polyphemus *has* found something to say—something called here both a "remedy" (lines 1, 17) and a "pleasant med'cine of the mind" (line 3). In each instance of its use, the English "remedy" translates *pharmakon,* a word encompassing "any artificial means, especially for producing physical effects." Medicine, drug, remedy, philter, antidote, poison: all are possible meanings for *pharmakon.*[9] As a closer examination of Theocritus's idyll suggests, however, the *pharmakon* of invitational poetry acts most specifically as a kind of stimulant.

Some invitations of the early modern era invite even as another of their roles—sometimes, apparently, the primary one—is to empower the self. In Theocritus's poem, we see that this invigorating effect forms a kind of "working through." By the end of his lament, and perhaps as early as line 58, Polyphemus has ceased to address Galatea and turns his speech toward himself. We see this in the simple fact of address here: "you" and "thou" in the first part of his speech refer to Galatea; after line 70, "thou" refers to Polyphemus. Clearly by this point in the poem, Polyphemus has begun not only to address himself but also to "cheer himself up," as T. S. Eliot describes the way Shakespeare's tragic heroes talk to themselves at the end of their plays with therapeutic speech. Discussing this "attitude of self-dramatization," Eliot quotes Othello's final speech—"Soft you; a word or two before you go. | I have done the state some service . . ." (5.2.33–39)—and observes: "What Othello seems to me to be doing in making this speech is *cheering himself up.* He is endeavouring to escape reality, he has ceased to think about Desdemona, and is thinking about himself."[10] In a similar vein, Helen Vendler has argued that carpe diem poems, one of the more popular of the classical forms revived in the early modern era, always have a twofold purpose and subject, and are as much self-address as address to another: "The profound object of commiseration is always really the poet himself."[11] We might take Eliot's description of Othello's speech and Vendler's observation about carpe diem poems as jointly pointing out a general truth about "The Passionate Shepherd" when quoted in later works: early modern writers consistently see this lyric as filling the empty spaces in the characters who speak it, providing words for them to exist by—the invitation, that is, as equipment for being.

Poetry at Work

In observing that this form of utterance can *do* things—cheer oneself up, allow for commiseration—Vendler and Eliot are pointing out something that would have been second nature to readers and writers in Marlowe's time. Marlowe's contemporaries expected poetry to do something. A work of literature, according to models current in the early modern era, is not primarily self-expression, as is often one's assumption when dealing with more recent poems and poets. More than a reservoir into which poets pour their feelings and experiences, a literary text was seen, in contrast, as a functioning object, a thing that works. Certainly, writers of the early modern era did not discount that literature teaches and delights, that it improves readers, or that poets are physicians of the soul. One often encounters these general descriptions of literature and of those who write it in poetic treatises of the period. But even in such works as Sidney's *Defence of Poesy* and Puttenham's *Arte of English Poesie,* where versions of these general descriptions appear, there is clear evidence that literature was also thought to work specifically and through genre.

As Rosalie Colie and Stephen Cohen have reminded us, in the early modern era various genres were believed to possess particular functions; these poetic kinds made certain things happen.[12] We might take as an initial example here Sidney's analysis of the "parts, kinds, or species" of poetry in *The Defence of Poesy* (c. 1581–83). The long *confirmatio* of the *Defence* uses as its instances various kinds of poetry—kinds that, Sidney argues, produce beneficial effects when employed in "right use." The pastoral poem, for example, shows the plight of the people under bad rulers; satire makes us laugh at folly; tragedy makes kings "fear to be tyrants."[13] At one point, Sidney jokes that Plato cannot have banished poetry out of his commonwealth because of its corrupting influence, for Plato allows "community of women." Sidney unpacks his logic for us as follows: "poetical sonnets [could not] be hurtful when a man might have what woman he listed."[14] Sonnets, according to the reasoning here, are for seducing women; when women are freely had, whatever might have been objectionable about sonnets would no longer be objectionable. The conviction behind this train of thought is, again, that specific forms do specific things. Because this belief runs throughout the *Defence,* readers are not surprised by Sidney's concluding "curse" on those who resist or ridicule poetry: "that while you live, you live in love, and never get favor for lacking skill of a sonnet, and, when you die, your memory die from the earth for want of an epitaph."[15] Sonnets win love; epitaphs win memory.

Put bluntly in this manner, neither of these assertions is likely to startle. Whether choosing a greeting card or an inscription for a tombstone, we are familiar in our own lives with literary forms as diverse as love poems and epitaphs and with what such forms are supposed to do. But often we do not apply our own experience of poetic forms to works of other periods, especially with regard to the functions of literary kinds. Compounding the problem, we sometimes ignore other periods' pragmatic utterances in favor of grander statements. For instance, so frequently do we choose to hear the major chords of Sidney's treatise ("the poets only deliver a golden [world]," etc.) that we typically miss the notes of its melody. While the *Defence* does present a larger argument about the benefits of poetry, it is noteworthy that Sidney points to specific forms and to what they can do when he needs to press home to us poetry's actual virtues.

We find an even greater emphasis on the specific efficacy of individual literary kinds in Puttenham's handbook. Puttenham's *The Arte of English Poesie* (pub. 1589) exceeds Sidney's treatise in its pragmatism and likewise stresses the working parts of literature. Throughout his work, Puttenham is at pains to tell the fledgling poet how verse, forms, and figures function; how, when, and why one should employ them; and what one can anticipate their effects will be. Puttenham's understanding of poetry relates strongly to his understanding of life. He begins with the assumption that all lives have within them certain occasions, and that for many of these occasions, a correspondent literary form has evolved. To Puttenham, the various forms and genres of poetry respond to situations provoked by our bodies and conform to the rituals that society constructs around those bodies.[16] For instance, love (what Puttenham calls "the amorous affections and allurements") leads to "odes, songs, elegies, ballads, sonnets and other ditties, moving one way and another to great compassion."[17] The need for rejoicing, in turn, produces such "triumphall" forms as the encomia ("carols of honour"); lamentation, obsequies and elegies; childbirth, "*genethliaca*," that is, "natal or birth songs"; and marriages and weddings, epithalamia, or "ballads at the bedding of the bride."[18]

Only after providing these instances of undeniably *social* occasions— what the *Arte* refers to as "civil" matters—does Puttenham give us an example of poetry's more personal use. Describing the origin of epigrams, Puttenham confesses that no social arrangement can prevent a certain kind of aggression in verse:

> all the world could not keep, nor any civil ordinance to the contrary so prevail, but that men would and must needs utter their spleens in all ordinary matters also: or else it seemed their bowels would burst, therefore the poet devised a pretty fashioned poem short and sweet (as we are wont to say) and called it *Epigramma* in which every merry conceited man might without any long study or tedious ambage, make his friend sport, and anger his foe, and give a pretty nip, or show a sharp conceit in few verses.[19]

This passage comes closest to the therapeutic role that the lyric takes in Theocritus's idyll. Whereas Puttenham describes the *effects* of epigrams socially—they amuse one's friends, anger one's enemies, nip, and display one's talent in a short form—the initial *cause* of the epigram is personal and physical: "must needs utter their spleens . . . or else it seemed their bowels would burst." The epigram, then, acts first in a medicinal fashion, as a kind of purgative that helps the poet; only after it is finished and distributed can it function as the more social form it remains by reputation.

These selections from Sidney and Puttenham help to remind us not only that there were complex theories of the poetic forms and their functions during the early modern era but also (and this is especially apparent in the Puttenham material above) that some commentators understood poetry to have a particularly therapeutic role that did not depend on persuading the poem's reader or listener. A contrasting instance might help clarify the point at hand. In Sidney's *Astrophil and Stella,* Astrophil famously chains together a series of causes and effects in the first four lines of the initial sonnet: loving, wanting to show his love in verse, hoping that Stella might take some pleasure in his pain(s), that this pleasure might cause her to read these poems, that reading might lead her to know of his love, that knowledge might win pity, and that, through this pity, Astrophil might obtain "grace." His success depends upon a sympathetic and responsive reader and a predictable sequence of events. (That these events do not unfold as Astrophil hopes is, of course, the basis for Sidney's poetic sequence.) Astrophil's plan is classically rhetorical. It is perhaps tempting to think of the invitational form in relation to such a pattern: an invitation is carefully framed; enticements for the listener are offered in seductive language, with the speaker hoping to obtain physical or spiritual "grace" from the desired party in much the way that Astrophil describes his quest. But to think of the invitation primarily as a social form—even when the society is a party of two and even when the goal is primarily selfish—is potentially to misunderstand its role in early modern literature, where the invitation often functions as a *pharmakon* that aids the self. Perhaps more than any other poem of its time, "The Passionate Shepherd" shows how powerful invitational speech could be for its speaker, regardless of who else is listening.

We can begin to test the truth of this assertion by looking at Shakespeare's quotation of "The Passionate Shepherd" in one of his plays. Shakespeare quotes this poem, again, in *The Merry Wives of Windsor,* through a nervous and frightened Hugh Evans. Evans is a Welsh parson who has been challenged to a duel. Few characters in the play seem less likely fighters, and Shakespeare uses Evans's fear of the impending duel, as well as the parson's accent, for a comic soliloquy. Alone at what he believes to be the site of the duel (he and his rival have been sent to separate locations), Evans launches into a passage of consoling speech:

How melancholies I am! I will knog his urinals about his knave's costard when I have good opportunities for the ork. Pless my soul!   [*Sings*]

> "To shallow rivers, to whose falls
> Melodious birds sings madrigals;
> There will we make our peds of roses,
> And a thousand fragran posies.
> To shallow—"

Mercy on me! I have a great dispositions to cry.   [*Sings*]
> "Melodious birds sing madrigals—
> When as I sat in Pabylon—
> And a thousand vagram posies.
> To shallow, etc."
>   (3.1.13–26)

Evans's words unfold the comedy of the situation. "Jeshu pless my soul!" he says after Peter Simple leaves him, "how full of chollors I am and trempling of mind!" (11–12). Thinking he faces death, Evans calls upon a popular song, Marlowe's "Passionate Shepherd," to bless his soul. Alone he latches upon the invitational lyric even though there is no one to invite. This seeming paradox appears less so, however, in light of what the invitational form does in Theocritus's idyll, where the lyric is less about others than about the self. Here, in fact, the invitation seems to draw a kind of mandala, or charmed circle, around its speaker.

Much of the sequence's humor comes from Evans's mingling of things. Even as his soliloquy blends English words with a Welsh pronunciation, for instance, so does he blend Marlowe's lyric with words from a less secular—though equally popular—source. For, in singing "When as I sat in Pabylon," Evans combines Marlowe's lines with those of a metrical version of Psalm 137. The first two stanzas of this psalm in the collection of Sternhold and Hopkins run as follows:

> When as we sat in Babylon
> the rivers round about
> And in remembrance of Sion
> the tears for grief burst out.
>
> We hang'd our harps and instruments
> the willow trees upon:
> For in that place men for their use
> had planted many one.[20]

The reasons for Evans's confusion of the two songs seem clear. We notice that, in speaking of "harps and instruments" and "willow trees," the psalm itself appears to invoke the apparatus of the pastoral mode, which infuses Marlowe's secular lyric. Shepherds play harps, and willow trees hint of a setting hospitable to the pastoral. Verbal similarities also play a part. For instance, the second stanza of "The Passionate Shepherd" unfolds as follows: "And we will sit upon the rocks, | Seeing the shepherds feed their flocks, | By shallow rivers, to whose falls | Melodious birds sing madrigals." Evans, we soon realize, confuses Marlowe's shepherd and that shepherd's beloved, who will "sit" by "shallow rivers," with the Israelites who once "sat in Babylon." Evans seems to do so in part because of generic similarities and in part because of verbal parallels ("sit"/"sat"; "rivers"/"rivers") between the two poems.

That Evans, a parson, turns first to a popular song (rather than to a psalm) to console himself provides further humor to the sequence. Yet if the poems are not interchangeable, they have enough in common for us to understand why Evans confuses the "celestial" and the "terrestrial" (a distinction that the Host of the Garter will make shortly after this passage in *The Merry Wives*) and why Marlowe's poem struck Shakespeare as a likely secular double for the consoling biblical poem. One thing we might learn about "The Passionate Shepherd" from this instance of quotation, in fact, springs from the association of Marlowe's poem with the psalms. For nowhere in early modern poetic theory was the insistence upon poetry's function, an insistence that we have seen in Sidney and Puttenham, carried to such an extreme as in relation to these holy songs.

Useful Psalms

Publishing records indicate that the psalms were the most popular poems in early modern England.[21] These overwhelmingly popular lyrics were often accompanied in print form by a "treatise . . . concerning the use and virtue of the Psalms" ascribed to Athanasius the Great (293?–373), an early saint to whom was also ascribed the better-known Athanasian Creed. What makes this treatise so important for our reading of "The Passionate Shepherd," and what makes it worth discussing as a third instance of poetic theory here, is its detailed assertions concerning the individual functions of the psalms. The prose paragraphs that begin the treatise make the psalms sound like elements of a Renaissance handbook of conduct: "For as he which intendeth to present himself to a King will first compound himself to set in good order both his gesture and his speech, lest else he might be reputed rude and ignorant; even so doth this godly book inform all such as be desirous to lead their life in virtue."[22] Such information is by definition multifaceted, and the psalms accordingly "inform" us in various ways: "Moreover, the psalms inform and teach every man with divers instructions." These instructions see the psalms as idiosyncratic. That is, where Puttenham's *Arte* correlated specific literary *forms* to certain situations in life (e.g., marriage, births, death), the Athanasian treatise recommends individual *psalms*. Of the seven pages of this treatise, six and a half are taken up by ninety-nine individual "If" instructions, a brief sampling of which is offered here:

> [*1*] If therefore thou wouldest at any time describe a blessed man who he is, and what thing maketh him to be so, thou hast the 1, 32, 41, 112, 128 Psalms. . . .

19 If thou dost wonder at the order of things created by God, considering the grace of the divine providence, sing the 19, 24 psalms. . . .

35 If thou seest many poor men to beg, & wilt shew pity to them, thou mayst both thyself receive them to mercy, and also exhort other to do the same, saying the 41 psalm.

So particularized are such instructions that the treatise recommends some psalms for certain days of the week. Other situations the treatise describes are so specific that one might never have recourse to the psalms it recommends. The twenty-third instruction, for instance, is for when "thine enemies cluster against thee & go about with their bloody hands to destroy thee," and the forty-third, for one who "hast suffered false accusation before the King." The treatise recommends Psalm 137, the psalm that Hugh Evans happens to confuse with "The Passionate Shepherd," for the following situation: "If thou beest holden in thralldom under straying and wandering thoughts, & feelest thyself drawn by them, whereof thou art sorry, then stay thyself from henceforth, and tary where thou hast found thyself in fault, set thee down, and mourn thou also as the Hebrew people did, and say with them the 137 Psalm." This description appropriately conveys Evans's situation in *The Merry Wives of Windsor* as he awaits the duel with Dr. Caius. His thoughts are "straying and wandering" and hold him in their thrall; he feels himself "drawn by them" and is "sorry" (i.e., distressed, sorrowful).

Like Theocritus's idyll, Shakespeare's quotation of "The Passionate Shepherd" underscores the relevance of Sidney and Puttenham to our reading of the lyric at hand. The latters' emphasis on the function of various forms is put into practice through lyrics in Theocritus and in *The Merry Wives of Windsor*. In each instance, a lyric appears to have been called upon to make something happen. Evans's recourse to "The Passionate Shepherd" in *The Merry Wives* also asks us to consider the lyric in relation to the psalms. By examining the treatise ascribed to Athanasius, we have seen that not only poetic forms but even individual poems could be thought to have a highly particularized function. The treatise's description of Psalm 137 and of its putative function seems to square with what Evans calls upon the two poems to do—to offer consolation against the "thralldom" of heavy thoughts, to comfort him. But if such explains their function within a work, it may also explain something about how texts themselves were seen as working; the correlation of Evans's two poems with this claim concerning the psalm's function gives us reason to see patterns of response to specific poems as more than coincidental. That is, if we find that a particular poem was quoted and responded to in a highly patterned way, the Athanasian treatise's insistence on the distinctiveness of individual poems could indicate why. Like the treatise itself, certain early modern readers may have been accustomed to seeing individual poems as distinct in their functions.

For instance, although Izaak Walton's *The Compleat Angler* (1653) sets "The Passionate Shepherd" firmly in a context of fishermen and fishing, he is careful to indicate that, depending on one's position in life, it is possible to have distinct uses for, and responses to, poetic bait. When Piscator meets a milkmaid and her mother in Walton's text, he begs them to perform again a pair of songs he had heard them sing "about eight or nine days since." The pair of songs consists of Marlowe's invitation and Ralegh's response. What remains interesting for this argument is how the milkmaid's mother describes these songs:

> O, I know it now, I learned the first part in my golden age, when I was about the age of my poor daughter; and the latter part, which indeed fits me best now, but two or three years ago, when the cares of the World began to take hold of me . . .[23]

The milkmaid's mother learned Marlowe's lyric when she was young; after the "cares of the World" began to press her, however, she realizes that it is Ralegh's rejoinder that best embodies her situation. As her life changes, so must the poem that "fits" her. Far from embracing a poem for any transcendental truth, she casually acknowledges that various poems are appropriate for various times and situations. It is perhaps only a small step from this offhand acknowledgment to the catalog of functions in Athanasius's treatise on the psalms.

So far, the patterns that the invitation follows in Theocritus, Shakespeare, and Walton are comedic. Hapless speakers turn to the invitation for comfort. In none of these instances do we see any violence or aggression; even though Evans fears a conflict, audience members and readers of *The Merry Wives* know that this fear is unjustified, that the parson will be safe. Once again, then, we should ask: What can a lyric have to do with violence? This question might seem less than rhetorical were we to read the whole of Psalm 137. For what begins in an almost pastoral mode, as a song of mourning and memory, ends with a fierce wish related to the people of Babylon. Here are the final two stanzas of the psalm:

Even so shalt thou (O Babylon)
at length to dust be brought,
And happy shall that man be called,
that our revenge hath wrought.

Yea blessed shall that man be
that takes thy children young,
To dash their bones against hard stones
which lie the streets among.

To be sure, nowhere in Evans's confusion of the two popular songs does the violence of these stanzas surface. And given the quick pace of a dramatic performance, even the most devout audience member would scarcely have the time to dwell long enough on the quoted line from Psalm 137 to ponder the relevance of lines that are not quoted. But what remains clear from the last two stanzas of Psalm 137 is that apparently tranquil poems can have aggressive aspects to them and that readers and audience members in the early modern era would have realized this possibility.

As *pharmakon,* Theocritus's lament restores Polyphemus to himself: "For many maidens in the evening tide with me will play, | And all do sweetly laugh, when I stand hark'ning what they say, | And I some body seem, and in the earth do bear a sway" (75–77). Seeming "some body": while in Theocritus this restoration is harmless, even comic, with later authors the poem as *pharmakon* often precedes—even makes possible—acts of violence against others. We can see the beginnings of such a tradition in Vergil's second Eclogue, itself an imitation of Theocritus's idyll. In Vergil's poem, Corydon, a lovesick shepherd, laments his unrequited love for the fair boy Alexis. Speaking to his love in apostrophe, Corydon lists enticing natural objects that Alexis could have if he joins Corydon. These include fine cattle and lambs, flowers in overflowing baskets, fruits, nuts, laurels, and myrtle. Corydon ultimately calls his unrequited passion madness; he resolves that the woods are the best place for his passions, since there "The grim lioness follows the wolf, the wolf himself the goat, the wanton goat the flowering clover, and Corydon follows you, Alexis."[24] In these woods,

Corydon says, *trahit sua quemque voluptas*: "Each is led by his liking" (line 65). Even as the lion seeks to eat the wolf; the wolf, the goat; and the goat, clover, so Corydon wishes to devour Alexis. Love is a violent desire that consumes its object.

A more pointed example of such aggression comes in the story of Polyphemus and Galatea in the thirteenth book of Ovid's *Metamorphoses*.[25] Like Vergil's second Eclogue, Ovid's story clearly imitates Theocritus's rustic monster and song. Ovid's Cyclops and his famous appeal—*iam, Galatea, veni, nec munera despice nostra!* ("now come my *Galat*, come away, | And of my present take no scorn" [lines 985–86])[26]—laid the foundation for many subsequent pastoral invitations. The difference between Ovid's version and those of Theocritus and Vergil is that Ovid dramatizes the invitation; where the speakers in these earlier poems apostrophized their loves, Ovid has his Polyphemus speak directly to the object of his desire. In Ovid's version, Polyphemus offers the Nymph all his possessions and is careful to enumerate and describe them in sensuous detail. Arthur Golding's translation underscores the delight taken by Tudor authors in this luxurious mode of description:

> Gay Apples weighing down the boughs have I, and Grapes like gold,
> And purple Grapes on spreaded Vines as many as can hold,
> Both which I do reserve for thee. Thyself shalt with thy hand
> The soft sweet strawberries gather, which in woody shadow stand.
>
>   (956–59)

Galatea loves Acis, however, and she refuses Polyphemus's offer. Angry at her denial and jealous at seeing the happy pair, Polyphemus then throws a massive rock at Acis and crushes him. Illustrations from early modern editions of the *Metamorphoses* sometimes "freeze" the pair of lovers beneath the rock upraised in Polyphemus's hands, making it impossible to identify the object of the Cyclops's anger.[27] Whom, exactly, does the Cyclops want to kill? Acis? Galatea? Both? This ambiguity is important. Indeed, in early modern treatments of the invitation/denial scenario, this violence toward the unfortunate lover frequently becomes aggression toward the denying beloved.

Marlowe and his literary heirs fused the material provided by Theocritus, Vergil, and Ovid into a basic arrangement that, on the surface, is anything but aggressive. It begins with a direct address, stating the action that the speaker desires the listener to take: "Come live with me, and be my love." Following this invitation (usually put so forcefully that it verges on the imperative mood, as an obligation), the speaker typically recites an ordered list of sensuous commodities and experiences—a "catalogue of delights"—to be given the listener if the first condition of the lyric "contract" is fulfilled.[28] Typically, these come from the distillation of natural objects, the refinement of the many into the select through the hyperbolic production of the pastoral world: "A gown made of the finest wool" and "buckles of the purest gold." Often a relaxing retreat is promised, with the speaker and addressed party casually viewing a rural court and kingdom. Just as the identity of the bridegroom in the Song of Songs vacillates between king and shepherd, so is it unclear whether the speaker in Marlowe's lyric is actually a passionate shepherd or merely one who intends to *watch* passionate shepherds: the title of the poem, which is of questionable authority, remains the only evidence for the former. In the end, the lyric voice belongs to one who will remain separate from the shepherds, watching them work and having them dance for his love. Birds sing madrigals for their enjoyment; more important, a form of theatrical servitude is promised: "The shepherds' swains shall dance and sing, | For thy delight each May-morning."

Perhaps of greater consequence than the invitation's elements are its general mood and effects. With each element building on the richness of the previous enticement, seducing both speaker and listener with its cadence, the invitation of the Passionate Shepherd is a kind of sexual foreplay; the process of enumeration is intended to excite. If the speaker can draw the listener into shared delight at the many luxuries he or she catalogs, physical contact may become moot. Sometimes this secondary goal is indeed anticlimactic, for at times in the drama the successful suitor quickly ignores or gives away the "possession."[29] A good illustration of how the mechanism worked in plays of the period comes with Thomas Nabbes's *Hannibal and Scipio* (1637), where the conquering general, Scipio, seduces a captive Spanish lady with soft and winning words only to give her away quickly thereafter.[30] What remains of primary importance is the erotic force of the invitation itself, not its aftermath. The creation of this exotic world (however short-lived) springs from the power of the lyric genre to fashion an intensely charged, highly enclosed world of the personal. Because little dialogue is customary in this genre of poem, the lyric speaker has the ability to overwhelm opposition with powerful language—language so rich and entrancing that the possibility of denial decreases in the face of the lyric speaker's determination and poetic ability. This vocal discrepancy comprises the monological power underlying the Shepherd's sensuous "invitation."

Responding to the Shepherd

Response to "The Passionate Shepherd" came in various modes, and even lyric rejoinders assumed a number of forms. "The Nymph's Reply" in *England's Helicon,* for example, erects a point-by-point rebuttal of the Shepherd's promises: passion, though once hot, inevitably cools; time passes; "the flowers do fade"; and all the luxurious items are "soon forgotten." This reply stresses rationality and the "plain" over sensuality.[31] One critic sees it as "confronting the world as it is, directly and without apology."[32] True to the form of "answer" poems, it carefully replicates Marlowe's phrasing. The lyric concludes:

> But could youth last, and love still breed,
> Had joys no date, nor age no need,
> Then these delights my mind might move,
> To live with thee, and be thy love.[33]

Stoically conceiving the transitory nature of things, "The Nymph's Reply" argues against an eternizing conceit never made fully explicit by Marlowe's Shepherd. In this way the answer poem bases its argument on an ideology presumed to be behind "The Passionate Shepherd" itself, responding to a poem Marlowe seems not to have written. But perhaps the author of the reply read a subtext of Marlowe's lyric correctly, for in the lyric immediately following "The Nymph's Reply" in *England's Helicon*—an expansive imitation of Marlowe's poem—the Shepherd speaks of "Eternal ditties" and of reveling "all the year." From this quotation of Marlowe's poem, we might begin to see that Ralegh understood the Shepherd's invitation—an invitation to come to his *locus amoenus*—to imply an invitation to a *locus amoenus et aeternus*. This understanding persists even though the Shepherd's gesture may be undercut by the ephemeral nature of the entice-ments—"roses," "posies"—that he offers the Nymph.

Another strategy of counterargument comes through rewriting the in-vitation; by so doing, lyric poets present their position both parodically and metaphorically. Donne's "The Bait," beginning "Come live with me, and be my love, | And we will some new pleasures prove," is probably an early example of such an attempt at disclosing the hidden agenda of the invitational lyric.[34] Donne repeats the commonplace scenario of fish (courtiers) caught by the charms of the beautiful woman, but, in using Marlowe's "Passionate Shepherd" as core of his lyric (and quoting the first line without alteration), he points up another part of the Marlowe poem that has gone unstated. That is, the Shepherd uses his description of the luxurious as bait to catch his own fish. The list of rich substantives is dangled before the listener like a lure on a sharp hook. Early modern drama was especially aware of, and sensitive to, this formulation. Cleopatra, frequent reverser of gender roles, imagines a scenario for catching her fish/lover:

> My bended hook shall pierce
> Their slimy jaws; and as I draw them up,
> I'll think them every one an Antony,
> And say, "Ah, ha! y' are caught!"
>   (2.5.12–15)

Likewise, James Shirley underscores this aspect of the invitational lyric when one of the Shepherds in *Love Tricks* (1625) promises:

> Walk unto the silver brook,
> You shall need no other hook,
> To catch the dancing fish withal,
> But a song or madrigal.
>   (5.2)[35]

This passage points out the nature of the Shepherd's activity: the "song or madrigal" is the bait and "hook | To catch the dancing fish withal." It is no coincidence, of course, that (as was pointed out above) "The Passionate Shepherd," "The Nymph's Reply," and "The Bait" all appeared in Izaak Walton's *The Compleat Angler*. Not only do the three lyrics reflect the pastoral setting of Walton's angling world, but also all three contain a poetic enticement that seems much like fishing. "The Bait," and perhaps "The Nymph's Reply" as well, implies that "The Passionate Shepherd" entices its listeners the way a fisherman lures a fish. In "The Bait," catching fish becomes the patently innocuous double of seduction or rape. As a metaphor for what the lyric can accomplish, the notion of bait underscored what many early modern playwrights saw in "The Passionate Shepherd": the predatory nature of the monological.

Voice and Response

Because early modern drama in England embraced divergent voices and modes and because such variety became thematically as well as structurally important to drama as a mode, it often questioned—sometimes even ridiculed—the written lyric's perceived emphasis on the monological.[36] It is important to note that, as used here, "monological" means something more than self-addressed speech. Early modern plays are full of soliloquies, for instance, which cannot be described as truly monological in that they feature sustained "dialogue": Faustus and Hamlet are only two of many characters who engage in animated, and memorable, conversations with themselves. Though spoken alone, their speeches are far from monological. By "monological," then, we might understand discourse that is not only self-addressed but also self-absorbed in a manner that denies or ignores the difference the outside world offers. Clearly, Faustus and Hamlet are guilty of self-absorption. But when playwrights wish to convey this quality in an obviously critical way, they frequently have characters overheard as they speak to themselves, generating humor, irony, or other distance at such characters' expense. We might consider Malvolio in *Twelfth Night* (1601, 2.5.23–185), Macbeth (1606, 1.3.128–50), or Beatrice-Joanna in *The Changeling* (1622, 2.2.40–50), each of whom is overheard by other characters in a moment of self-absorbed discourse. These characters seem so preoccupied with personal concerns that they do not realize that their "soliloquies" are not private at all. When characters speak to themselves this way in the company of others, their self-isolation is often presented negatively by their respective plays.

Malvolio, Macbeth, and Beatrice-Joanna give us practical instances of monological speech in the midst of drama. Literary theory also provides a way of thinking about the conflict between individual voice and social dialogue. We might turn here to relevant remarks on the monological in Marxist literary theory—which, perhaps more than any other theoretical mode, has pondered the social shape of language. To Mikhail Bakhtin, the monological is empty speech. Bakhtin's definition of the monological fits closely with what I have called "self-absorbed" discourse. "A single voice,"

Bakhtin maintained in *Problems of Dostoevsky's Poetics,* "ends nothing and resolves nothing. Two voices is the minimum for existence."[37] To Bakhtin, social language precedes being. Georg Lukács would echo this in claiming that "The language of the absolutely lonely man is lyrical, i.e. monological."[38] The "lonely man," that is, speaks a lyrical speech that falls short of dialogue. Like Bakhtin, Lukács valorizes the many over the singular. Even as speech determines social existence, communication depends on difference and exchange. Both critics exhibit an underlying mistrust of the individual voice. And while their viewpoints offer us a modern resistance to impulses that might be considered part of the post-Romantic lyric, it is a resistance, I would argue, that early modern drama often anticipated in its responses to the monological tendencies of some lyric forms.

Shakespeare's plays, for example, frequently portray the love sonnet as the immature effusion of youth, something that we can see in part as satire on the lyric excesses of the day. Often, however, the satirized excess appears to be that of the love lyric itself. Hamlet's lyric "To the celestial, and my soul's idol, the most beautified Ophelia" (2.2.109–24) follows the sonnets of *Love's Labour's Lost* (1595) in its bathetic extravagance. Almost speaking for the drama itself, Polonius—an unreliable messenger who often carries valid messages—interrupts his recitation to say: "That's an ill phrase, a vile phrase; 'beautified' is a vile phrase." (The "in-joke" here—Shakespeare responding to Robert Greene's "upstart crow, beautified with our feathers"—only strengthens the point by making the word stranger than it would otherwise seem.) The lyrics of *As You Like It* are similarly the object of ridicule. Orlando's gushing creations, hung on trees throughout the forest of Arden, provide easy targets for Rosalind's biting wit; they neatly illustrate the type of passionate impulse she undercuts in replying "Say 'a day' without the 'ever'" to Orlando's vow to love "For ever and a day" (4.1.145–46). Monologue like Orlando's ignores or attempts to deny the external. Responding to this solipsism, early modern drama sought to socialize the formal lyric's emphasis on what Lukács would call the "absolutely lonely man," the isolated and narcissistic subject. Where the lyric, aspiring toward the eternal, often promises stasis, the drama, incorporating and acknowledging process, insists on recognizing change.[39]

Typically a single-voiced utterance, the lyric as a mode tends to eschew dialogue. This tendency should not be taken to imply that no lyrics, and no lyric sequences, were dialogical; like soliloquies, many were. From

Wyatt's "They Flee from Me" through Herbert's "The Collar," a number of short poems with multiple speakers and subject positions spring immediately to mind. Likewise *Astrophil and Stella* captures Stella's voice responding to Astrophil. Yet in this period dialogue most often remained outside what the lyric could easily (and convincingly) integrate into its vision.[40] The textual dialogue that "The Passionate Shepherd" developed in *England's Helicon,* for instance, remained a social one, extrinsic to the individual poems and ideologically self-contained. It happened not in the poems but *between* them, as one poem quoted another. That "The Passionate Shepherd" invitation begs a reply is shown by the number of imitations and responses that arose during the early modern era. Such quotation indicated a perceived incompleteness about the original poem. The vehemence of response betrays a larger, perhaps even cultural, anxiety over the power of the invitational lyric.

Plays of the period often staged this anxiety, revealing—in their treatment of the invitation scenario—latent aspects of the seduction impulse. The first playwright to quote "The Passionate Shepherd" was apparently Marlowe himself. Over a dozen instances of this form of invitation occur in Marlowe's own plays.[41] In the Second Part of *Tamburlaine* (1588), for example, Marlowe uses invitational language like that of "The Passionate Shepherd" in a scene of imprecation. Theridamas, king of Argier, attempts to seduce the recently widowed Olympia with honeyed words:

> Leave this, my love, and listen more to me.
> Thou shalt be stately queen of fair Argier,
> And, cloth'd in costly cloth of massy gold,
> Upon the marble turrets of my court
> Sit like to Venus in her chair of state,
> Commanding all thy princely eye desires;
> And I will cast off arms to sit with thee,
> Spending my life in sweet discourse of love.
> (4.2.38–45)[42]

The exotic enticements of his "sweet discourse of love" fall on closed ears, however, as Olympia asserts loyalty to the memory of her dead husband. Her denial focuses eerily on death:

> No such discourse is pleasant in mine ears,
> But that where every period ends with death,

And every line begins with death again.

I cannot love, to be an emperess.

   (4.2.46–49)

Like "The Nymph's Reply," Olympia's argument points toward the inevitable end of passion, drawing on a *memento mori* trope to undercut the immediacy of the Shepherd's plea. Theridamas, angered by this rebuttal, quickly makes his reply:

Nay, lady, then, if nothing will prevail,

I'll use some other means to make you yield.

Such is the sudden fury of my love,

I must and will be pleas'd, and you shall yield.

Come to the tent again.

   (4.2.50–54)

The soothing poetry here resolves itself, upon the woman's rejection, into a pointed closing: "Come to the tent again." These five sharp words make it appear that the invitation was less than sincere. The resort to "some other means" is, I would argue, exactly what the contemporaries of "The Passionate Shepherd" took it to conceal.

Satisfying the will is all important in Marlowe's drama.[43] As Tamburlaine himself congratulates Theridamas in *1 Tamburlaine* (1587): "Well said, Theridamas! Speak in that mood, | For 'will' and 'shall' best fitteth Tamburlaine" (3.3.40–41). Here Tamburlaine refers to "martial triumph"; yet, as with other Marlovian supermen, the will establishes his existence and imbues every part of his life. Will is both the reason for and method of triumph, whether military or amatory. Theridamas, then, only repeats a scenario established by Tamburlaine early in the first play, when the Scythian conqueror began to woo Zenocrate:

A hundred Tartars shall attend on thee,

Mounted on steeds swifter than Pegasus.

Thy garments shall be made of Median silk,

Enchas'd with precious jewels of mine own,

More rich and valurous than Zenocrate's.

With milk-white harts upon an ivory sled

Thou shalt be drawn amidst the frozen pools,

And scale the icy mountains' lofty tops,

Which with thy beauty will be soon resolv'd.

(1.2.93–101)

Like "The Passionate Shepherd," Tamburlaine's lyrical exposition is not designed to elicit a measured or independent response; it impresses its immediate, on-stage audience the same way it impresses those in the theater, as a seductive aria.

That such lyric exposition can prove nakedly functional in Marlowe's plays becomes apparent in 2 *Tamburlaine* (1.3). In this play, Callapine uses a similar catalog of exotic possessions to bribe Almeda, his keeper, to release him from bondage. It is important to note that the role of Shepherd should not be exclusively identified with the male, nor should the role of the Beloved be exclusively identified with the female. For instance, in Marlowe and Nashe's *Dido, Queen of Carthage* (1586), Dido attempts to seduce Aeneas with the following:

> Aeneas, I'll repair thy Trojan ships,
> Conditionally that thou wilt stay with me,
> And let Achates sail to Italy:
> I'll give thee tackling made of rivell'd gold,
> Wound on the barks of odoriferous trees;
> Oars of massy ivory, full of holes,
> Through which the water shall delight to play;
> Thy anchors shall be hew'd from crystal rocks,
> Which, if thou lose, shall shine above the waves;
>
> . . . .
>
> So that Aeneas may but stay with me.
>
> (3.1.113–33)[44]

The pattern replicates that of "The Passionate Shepherd": imperative address, followed by enumeration of luxurious, natural objects fashioned into useful items, and finally a repetition of the first, invitational imperative. Later in this play, Dido's Nurse persuades Cupid—disguised as Ascanius—to accompany her home:

> thou shalt go with me unto my house.
> I have an orchard that hath store of plums,
> Brown almonds, services, ripe figs, and dates,

Dewberries, apples, yellow oranges;
A garden where are bee-hives full of honey,
Musk roses, and a thousand sort of flowers;
And in the midst doth run a silver stream,
Where thou shalt see the red-gill'd fishes leap,
White swans, and many lovely water-fowls.

. . . .

Ay, so you'll dwell with me, and call me mother.
   (4.5.3–16)

Changing the speaker and the person addressed, Marlowe alters as well the objects used as bait and the desired end. The luxurious objects become sweets, the position of lover that of son, and we move from the sphere of mature sexuality to that of the familial fantasy. Even the *l* alliteration of "The Passionate Shepherd"'s "live . . . love" is changed to *m* in "me . . . mother" (although the *l* sound appears to survive in the ultimate position, in "you'll dwell . . . call"). What this somewhat homely transformation of "The Passionate Shepherd" does not disguise, however, is that the method of lyrical persuasion remains the same.

The sequence from *Dido* is fairly innocuous, much like the invitations in *The Merry Wives* and in Theocritus. In fact, just once in Marlowe's dramatic works—in the Theridamas/Olympia episode discussed above—does one encounter a violent end connected directly with the sequence: force (and the threat of force) used to overcome denial. Likewise, with the exception of the eerie close of Barnabe Barnes's *Parthenophil and Parthenophe* (perhaps the strangest of the English Renaissance lyric collections), rape is not an option for plot among the Petrarchan lyricists.[45] While most often lacking the ability to respond directly, the addressed woman is forced neither to choose nor to defend herself.[46] Instead, the seduction sequence is thoroughly explored primarily through the freedom offered by dramatic presentation and the responsibility arising from characters' sustained interactions.

Quoting Marlowe

A group of dramatists contemporary with Marlowe quoted the Passionate Shepherd sequence in their works. These dramatists wrote in the 1589–90 period, just following the likely composition date of "The Passionate Shepherd." They sometimes mocked the invitational sequence but more often appear to have been commenting seriously on the psychology behind it. After Marlowe's own plays, the dramatic works of Robert Greene are perhaps the earliest to take up the Marlovian invitation. His plays and those of George Peele see the invitation related to a growing Elizabethan mythology of other worlds. Fueled by a nationalist spirit that reached its zenith shortly after the defeat of the Spanish Armada, England turned outward with increasing curiosity and ambition in the late 1580s and 1590s. The year 1588 witnessed the publication of Bigges's *Summary and True Discourse of Sir Francis Drake's West Indian Voyage* and Harriot's *Brief and True Report of the New Found Land of Virginia*; in 1589 Hakluyt issued the first version of his *Principal Navigations, Voyages, and Discoveries of the English Nation*. These titles give some indication of the rising interest in the outside world. Plays also reveal this interest. Like Marlowe, such playwrights as Greene and Peele engaged the cultural voyeurism of their audiences with rich dramatic tableaux. Their theatrical documents included fantasies of exploration and expansion. As the dream screens of nascent capitalism, playhouses sold England its own fantasies. We have seen that these fantasies were so numerous that they sometimes contradicted one another. Indeed, the heterogeneous nature of plays (shaped in part by the heterogeneity of many theater audiences) tended to ensure a dialogic response to the singular claims of colonialism. Their *copia* meant that no aggressiveness went entirely unchallenged, even when it coincided with nationalistic impulses.

We can see this complexity of response in Greene's *Friar Bacon and Friar Bungay* (1589). In Greene's play, Prince Edward becomes infatuated with Margaret, the "Fair Maid of Fressingfield," and sends his friend Lacy, Earl of Lincoln, to woo her in his place. Yet, after Lacy and Margaret fall in love, Edward still makes a desperate attempt to seduce her:

> I tell thee, Peggy, I will have thy loves.
> Edward or none shall conquer Margaret.
> In frigates bottomed with rich Sethin planks,
> Topped with the lofty firs of Lebanon,
> Stemmed and incased with burnished ivory,
> And overlaid with plates of Persian wealth,

Like Thetis shalt thou wanton on the waves,
And draw the dolphins to thy lovely eyes
To dance lavoltas in the purple streams.
Sirens, with harps and silver psalteries
Shall wait with music at thy frigate's stem
And entertain fair Margaret with their lays.
England and England's wealth shall wait on thee;
Britain shall bend unto her prince's love
And do due homage to thine excellence
If thou wilt be but Edward's Margaret.
    (8.51–66)[47]

This speech is sensuous. We find an initial address (here a statement rather than an invitation), enumeration of exotic enticements—natural objects worked into useful shapes—and the promise of servants: "Sirens . . . | Shall wait with music . . . | Britain shall bend . . . | And do homage." Edward makes explicit the sine qua non of the contract: "If thou wilt be but Edward's Margaret." The parallel between the seduction and colonization is strengthened through the word "conquer" and through references to "Persian wealth" and frigates loaded with plunder. Dominion will not cease, however, at foreign trade or plunder (that the latter is suggested may follow upon the resonances of the word "conquer" in the second line above). England and Britain themselves will become the source of wealth and homage.

Ironically, Edward foregrounds for Margaret the very process of objectification to which she is submitted when he stresses the servitude she is to enjoy. Greene's play advances this servitude in a much blunter fashion than does Marlowe's poem. Margaret rejects his offer, however, holding that "Not all the wealth heaven's treasury affords, | Should make me leave Lord Lacy or his love" (72–73). With this last line, Greene intensifies Marlowe's *l* alliteration, and we may still hear echoes of the famous "live | love" figure. The violent end of the cycle emerges in Edward's animosity toward Lacy as the Prince vows to "bathe | My poniard in the bosom of an earl" (79–80). Yet in an aside Edward reasons through the situation and, deciding that reconciliation and generosity should prevail, agrees to the romantic match.

In *Alphonsus, King of Arragon* (1587), Greene's title character has no such conscience. Delaying a clash of arms with the warrior-maiden Iphigena, he lapses into invitational rhetoric of the Marlovian mode:

> An if thou wilt vouchsafe
> To entertain Alphonsus' simple suit,
> Thou shalt ere long be monarch of the world:
> All christen'd kings, with all your pagan dogs,
> Shall bend their knees unto Iphigena;
> The Indian soil shall be thine at command,
> Where every step thou settest on the ground
> Shall be received on the golden mines;
> Rich Pactolus, that river of account,
> Which doth descend from top of Tmolus Mount,
> Shall be thine own, and all the world beside,
> If you will grant to be Alphonsus' bride.[48]

Here Alphonsus rehearses a catalog of orientalism. With servants and wealth dangled before her, however, Iphigena responds quickly and negatively: she prefers death. Alphonsus, angered by her pride, changes the terms of the contract; she is to be his concubine instead. Iphigena replies that she would "rather die than ever that shall hap." His ire—and desire—increased even further, Alphonsus assures her: "And thou shalt die unless it come to pass." The stage directions tell us that the two fight, and Iphigena flees, pursued by Alphonsus. But we should note that this scene began with the *reverse*: a strong Iphigena chases a fleeing Alphonsus (reluctant to fight) onto the stage, taunting him and his amatory disposition. His actions, she says at that point,

> were fitter to be writ
> Within the tables of dame Venus' son
> Than in god Mars his warlike registers.

His mind, she continues, "is busied in fond Cupid's toys." In the context of the play, she seems correct in these observations, for Alphonsus's effusive, amatory invitation follows almost directly on this last line. Iphigena fails to understand, however, that this language is not weakness but the source of his strength. The power Alphonsus can tap is the power of the invitation itself, the power of the lyric voice. He gains in strength whether she accepts or denies his suit.

This invitation, again, is not always spoken by a man to a woman. We can see this in the anonymous *Lust's Dominion* (1600), a play attributed to Marlowe on the title page of the 1657 quarto (perhaps *because* it contains a Marlovian invitation). This play reverses the typical gender roles of the invitation. Just as Dido wooed Aeneas in the works of both Marlowe and Nashe, so does the Queen Mother of Spain, King Philip's wife, use the invitational form in her efforts to seduce Eleazar, a Moor. While Philip lies on his deathbed, the Queen Mother importunes an unwilling Eleazar to "Look smoothly on me," "Come, let's kiss," "speak to me, and chide me not" before settling on her penultimate wish:

> Smile on me, and these two wanton boys,
> These pretty lads that do attend on me,
> Shall call thee Jove, shall wait upon thy cup,
> And fill thee nectar: their enticing eyes
> Shall serve as crystal, wherein thou may'st see
> To dress thyself, if thou wilt smile on me.
> Smile on me, and with coronets of pearl,
> And bells of gold, circling their pretty arms,
> In a round ivory fount these two shall swim,
> And dive to make thee sport:
> Bestow one smile, one little little smile,
> And in a net of twisted silk and gold
> In my all-naked arms thyself shalt lie.
>   (1.1.73–85)[49]

The Queen Mother's final image is significant. Following her aquatic picture—two servant boys diving like creatures of the water—she promises the Moor that he shall lie first "in a net," then in her arms, conflating the separate entities. We might think here of the net that in mythology Vulcan uses to catch Mars and Venus having sex.[50] But choosing this image (subsequently a metaphor with Donne and Walton) to cap her invitation also points to a coy awareness of the relation between rhetorical bait and fishing. When Eleazar refuses her offer, the Queen Mother threatens violence: she orders her servant boys to shout to the court that she is being murdered. Quick to sense his fate unless he relents, Eleazar immediately gives in, calling her "dear love," and promises that "Come, | Now I'll kiss thee; now I'll smile upon thee." The threat to his life following upon, and perhaps lurking behind, the sensuous invitation compels his submission. His repetition of her conditions shows his understanding of the contract form. Like Edward in *Friar Bacon* and the title character in *Alphonsus,* the Queen Mother of *Lust's Dominion* first couches her invitation in a fantasy of dominion, then, after the invitation is refused, turns the fantasized power against the invitation's object.

Jonson and After

If the last decade of the sixteenth century saw the invitation framed by colonialist rhetoric, the first decade of the seventeenth saw it set in the language and imagery of the court. In a famous scene from Jonson's *Volpone* (1606), for instance, the foxlike title character pretends he is near death to lure Celia close. Once she is sealed in his chamber, he delivers a lengthy and sensuous description of the delights he will provide if she consents to be his lover. The first lines of his song—"Come, my Celia, let us prove, | While we can, the sports of love" (3.7.166–67)—and its carpe diem tone generally are most likely adopted from Catullus's *vivamus, mea Lesbia, atque amemus,* with Jonson borrowing the Marlovian words at initial and ultimate positions. (It was Jonson's poetry, we will remember, that led Eliot to call him "the legitimate heir of Marlowe."[51]) Volpone promises her voluptuous banquets:

> The heads of parrots, tongues of nightingales,
> The brains of peacocks, and of ostriches,
> Shall be our food: and, could we get the phoenix,
> (Though nature lost her kind) she were our dish.
>   (202–5)

Celia refuses all these enticements, saying that she "Cannot be taken with these sensual baits" (209). However, neither her perception of this offer as seduction (compare "baits") nor her refusal can dissuade Volpone, and once more he presses his case. If the picture he paints is somehow familiar, perhaps it is because Volpone's ideal world sounds much like the fantasy world of the Jacobean court.[52] Her baths will be all flowers and milk, their drink of gold and amber, and, importantly, Volpone's dwarf, eunuch, and fool will live for their entertainment—the servitude conceit never far away. They will dress in exotic costumes, and he will have Celia

Attired like some sprightly dame of France,

Brave Tuscan lady, or proud Spanish beauty;

Sometimes, unto the Persian Sophy's wife;

Or the grand-Signior's mistress; and, for change,

To one of our most artful courtesans,

Or some quick Negro, or cold Russian.

(227–32)

Many of Jonson's characters are obsessed with erotic game-playing and costuming. Here this theme is yoked with the typical enumeration of sensuous objects, giving voice to the role-playing and costume motifs present in "The Passionate Shepherd" in the description of the "cap of flowers and a kirtle | Embroid'red all with leaves of myrtle," the "belt of straw and ivy buds | With coral clasps and amber studs," the "gown made of the finest wool" and "Fair-lined slippers for the cold." To be the Shepherd's love is not only to indulge in the fantasy of the pastoral but to dress for the according role as well. Jonson appears to realize this implication and its logical extension: when one costume becomes boring, the role-playing must continue in other forms. Celia's refusal elicits a violence that Volpone had concealed: "Yield, or I'll force thee" (266). The change from wooing suitor to desperate rapist becomes more remarkable when we remember that (as noted above) only minutes before Volpone had pretended to be on his deathbed. Like Alphonsus, Volpone uses the invitational lyric to invigorate himself, as a kind of Theocritean *pharmakon*. And like Alphonsus, he turns ultimately to rape.

Why should playwrights so frequently have connected "The Passionate Shepherd" with violence? It is a poem, after all, that seems on the surface tranquil and pleasant, encompassing a pastoral setting, love, and enjoyment. What, then, might explain the pattern of quotation we have seen in the preceding pages? One answer might be that Marlowe's own reputation, no less than the "literary" reputation of the invitational form as grounded in Ovid's Polyphemus, came to be associated with what he wrote. Marlowe's grisly death in 1593, for instance, appeared to follow a life full of radical and threatening activities. Such alleged activities as freethinking, espionage, counterfeiting, and sexual libertinism, among others, contributed to a dangerous reputation. Like his dramatic supermen, Marlowe was seen by some of his contemporaries as a scourge of all that was proper.[53] In this way, then, the mythology of Marlowe's life and death may have joined with various literary models for "The Passionate Shepherd" to shape readers' understanding of his famous lyric invitation.

To such an explanation, however, we might add another answer—one that by no means excludes or diminishes the first. I have shown in this chapter how plays put Marlowe's lyric into motion. Dramatic form provides the freedom for a reply to the invitation (often negative) and allows the Shepherd figure to make a counter offer, often through a violent *raptus*. Prose treatments, I should point out, had a similar formal latitude. Moral use of the Passionate Shepherd scenario can be seen, for instance, in the prose tract *Barley-break* (1607), in which the reveler Streton, via a stock Marlovian lyric, seduces, impregnates, and ultimately abandons a young woman. We can hear strong echoes of Marlowe's poem throughout Streton's invitation, which includes the following stanzas:

> When thou shalt feed on Olives, Nuts, and plums,
> Delicious Figs and Almonds finely peel'd,
> The Muses' food, such as of Violets comes,
> With drink forth of the purest grape distill'd:
>
> .   .   .   .
>
> If these delights, with many thousand more,
> May in thy breast move matter of regard,
> Let me no longer thus distressed implore:
> But with a smile my loyal love reward.[54]

Evident in the moral use to which this sequence is put in *Barley-break,* and in the dramatic scenes treated above, is that the timeless and golden world of the lyric invitation is almost always challenged when it meets another representational mode. Criticism of this kind of invitation takes on many forms in the drama, among them ethical, political, and religious. Often as telling as the responding voice, however, is the subsequent action of the Shepherd. Where most lyric voices—from Sidney's Astrophil to the poetic speaker of Shakespeare's Sonnets—remain largely locked in Petrarchan inaction, the Passionate Shepherd of the drama responds in a way reminiscent of the brutal urges of Polyphemus in Ovid's *Metamorphoses.* As lyric and drama become interwoven, they argue over the power of poetry and the nature of time. Also contested, of course, is dominion itself. The luxurious enticements offered the desired party in the Renaissance invitation and the violence with which this party is threatened upon denial make explicit a relation to an expansionist project: such is apparent in the lists of exotic commodities and human servitude promised and in the geographic place names detailed in such catalogs.

The scenario also has important implications for our understanding of the dynamics of gender and subjectivity in early modern literature. As we have seen, the invitation scenario builds authority in terms of a powerful rhetoric and with special frequency in male characters. Many invitations examined here actively suppress the voices of female characters, anticipate them, or channel the conditions of their speech into narrow categories of response. As has been noted, however, the dramatic quotations of Marlowe's lyric sometimes feature a woman in the role of dominant invitor: Dido and the Queen of *Lust's Dominion*. The intricacies of the invitational process thus refuse to be reduced to the polarization of male/female. "The Passionate Shepherd" asserts the primacy of persuasion (physical and linguistic alike) over sexual identity, and reminds us that the self is the first, and sometimes the most important, audience for this persuasion. The primacy of power over identity might also have come as no surprise to early modern subjects: with Elizabeth's status and political agency providing one model for a rhetorical grammar that acknowledged gender's subordination to power, "The Passionate Shepherd" functioned as a particularly Elizabethan script of ambition. It was a script of which not every reader disapproved. In the next chapter, for instance, we will see that the power of Marlowe's Shepherd struck one of his contemporaries as far from malign. In Shakespeare's plays, that is, the controlling authority of "The Passionate Shepherd" invitor becomes, for Marlowe's exact contemporary, something like a paradigm for political agency.

CHAPTER 3

The Agency of Quotation
in Shakespearean Comedy

Our remedies oft in ourselves do lie,
Which we ascribe to heaven.
      HELENA, in *All's Well That Ends Well* (1602)

So let the poetic ideal be sloganized as *Iago-plus-Ariel.*
      KENNETH BURKE, "Semantic and Poetic Meaning"

Marlowe's Shepherd survives in Shakespeare, though not through the verbal quotation we have seen in *The Merry Wives of Windsor* (1597) and *As You Like It* (1599). Instead, the assertive speaker of "The Passionate Shepherd" finds parallels in the eloquent, controlling characters who appear to resolve several of Shakespeare's plays. Portia in *The Merchant of Venice* (1596), Vincentio in *Measure for Measure* (1604), Prospero in *The Tempest* (1611), and the dopplegängers Theseus and Oberon in *A Midsummer Night's Dream* (1596), for instance, all seem to wield considerable influence over the outcome of their plays. These figures often come from the aristocracy and bring about the drama's denouement by discovering and controlling information about the social world they attempt to govern. The information they discover usually involves familial or romantic relations and is commonly obtained through disguise and deception with the assistance of subordinate characters—"Acting by others' action," in the words of Walter Ralegh.[1] Versions of these controlling figures can be found in Shakespeare's histories in characters like Richard III and Hal, as both Prince and King. They appear as well in the tragedies, in characters like Iago and Hamlet, where, however intended, their machinations bring unfortunate and unhappy results.[2] It is primarily in the comedies and the romances, however, that such figures enjoy seemingly limitless dramatic control.

In light of this control, these figures are frequently seen as symbolic dramatists. With his "great globe itself" speech, for example, Prospero traditionally, even notoriously, has been described as embodying Shakespeare's own position as playwright—something examined more fully in the next chapter. This assertive "playwright" figure is so powerful in, and so present to, Shakespeare's plays that it has been seen as central to his dramatic vision.[3] In an essay on "The Personal Shakespeare," for instance, William Kerrigan observes that "The impressive characters in Shakespeare, beginning with Richard, Duke of Gloucester, are often plotters, schemers, disguisers, stage managers, role players—actors, in a word, acting having been, of course, the author's first profession. Illeism, self-reference in the third person, is a recurrent feature of their rhetoric. The traditional doctrine of the king's two bodies seems almost to have been made for Shakespeare."[4] Kerrigan's remarks indicate the extent to which the histrionic governs character—and, especially, governing characters—in Shakespeare's plays.[5]

The offhand comment to the effect that "acting" was "of course, the author's first profession" is reassuring, though it is, of course, a fantasy. We do not know that acting was Shakespeare's first profession: he may well have been a teacher or butcher or something else before he came to London. The implicit suggestion that the theater itself formed a deep source of the theatrical, controlling characters in Shakespeare's work should give us pause for several other reasons as well. First, there were other actor/playwrights of the era whose dramas do not make such characters central to their playworlds' social order. Playwright/actors like Jonson, Heywood, Field, and Rowley, for example, diverge from Shakespeare in their relations to theatrical manipulation. Where disguise and deception have a role in such plays as *The Alchemist* (1610), *The Golden Age* (1610), *Amends for Ladies* (1611), and *The Changeling* (1622), sometimes as the temporary means by which social excess is corrected, these works do not, as do Shakespeare's plays, endorse theatrical manipulation as a sufficient form of governance. We might take Lovewit's return at the end of *The Alchemist* as a statement by Jonson regarding the limits of actor-characters as they relate to government. A second, and related, reason to question "the" theater as a source of Shakespeare's dramatic tendencies is that there were many theaters and many playing spaces in early modern England, with diverse audiences and repertories. Even acting as a category begs the question, for the roles within plays written for various repertories differed significantly. Also Richard Burbage, rather than William Shakespeare, likely performed many of the controlling roles that Shakespeare wrote.[6] So while we might see Shakespeare's acting career as a powerful resource for his controlling characters, it was perhaps not first, or even foremost, among such resources.

Where, then, might we look for a source of these theatrical controllers in Shakespeare's plays? His books seem a likely place to begin, for before he was an actor, Shakespeare was a student and a reader. His reading and education obviously shaped his dramatic worlds. Part of that reading surely formed an important resource for his theatrical controllers. The playwright figure in Shakespeare's plays, I believe, was quoted from Plautus, the Roman dramatist whose works were a staple in the Elizabethan grammar school. Plautus's dramatic works are typically associated with a superficial, comparatively artless dramaturgy, with identical twins and jealous fathers. But this stereotype fails to account for both the complexity of Plautus's craft and for a character type important to his plays: the resourceful, directing *servus* or slave. Shakespeare appears to have depended heavily on this character for his controlling figures. Such dependence, however, came with revisions, chief among them Shakespeare's tendency to displace the agency of the resourceful slave upward on the social scale. In contrast to Plautus, Shakespeare most often gives this agency to aristocrats and others in positions of established authority. While these revisions embody common prejudices in early modern England concerning rank and hierarchy, such prejudices were not the only alternatives for imagining power, agency, and control in that time and place. The tendency to push agency upward, I believe, speaks to a Shakespearean (if not *Shakespeare's*) orientation regarding agency, regarding where power should and does lie. In contrast to Marlowe, whose Passionate Shepherd invites his listener to a world that appears to be outside typical societies and governments, Shakespeare takes a figure from the lower orders and translates this figure's somewhat subversive power into a more traditional form of authority.

Shaping Agencies

Plays are shaped by many things, of course, and if characters can be seen as standing in for their drama's author(s)—thus speaking to the authority of writers themselves—one can also ascribe a kind of mediating authorship to the specific influences of various individuals (e.g., actors, managers) associated with theaters, to conventions of form and genre, to the general horizon of expectations that playwrights work within, and even to the larger arrangement of cultural forces that "writes" through authors. This last element alludes to Stephen Greenblatt's conception of the "circulation of social energy" and the general new historicist project dealing with early modern England.[7] For Greenblatt, "The 'life' that literary works seem to possess long after both the death of the author and the death of the culture for which the author wrote is the historical consequence, however transformed and refashioned, of the social energy initially encoded in those works."[8] As this claim suggests, and as we have seen in the introduction to this study, new historicist criticism derives some of its paradigmatic features and direction from a shift toward "intertextuality" (itself shaped by the "death of the author" thesis advanced by Barthes and revised by Foucault). Here the author of a work is only one component in a network of forces that mold a text; theater audiences and the desire encoded in titles like *What You Will* (1601) and *As You Like It* are also part of this network. New Historicism thus stresses the external, "authorizing" forces that produce and shape what we call literature.

Yet New Historicism is far from the first mode of criticism to see a complexity of cause and power in the Shakespearean universe. For example, an early and still provocative discussion of dramatic mediation was offered by Denton J. Snider in his *System of Shakespeare's Dramas* (1877). Operating on the Hegelian premise that drama is itself a mediating form—a middle term between epic objectivity and lyric subjectivity—Snider stressed what he saw as the fundamentally *ethical* nature of drama. It is precisely because "ethical principles are both numerous and of very different kinds," however, that dramatic conflict arises.[9] To Snider, "the Shakespearian Drama unfolds the order of ethical principles as realized in the Individual, and in him moving through conflict to final reconciliation. It, therefore, portrays a movement—a movement through struggle to repose."[10] Although Snider identified various sources of this "final reconciliation" and "repose," genre remains the ultimate determinant in his schema: where "Tragedy portrays the collision of opposing ethical ends, which cannot be mediated except through the death of the person or persons who are carrying out these ends . . . [c]omedy, on the other hand, portrays the collision of opposing ethical ends, which can be mediated, and thus the participants do not perish."[11] This argument seems circular because it offers as evidence something (the generic category) that is sometimes fixed almost arbitrarily in the final scenes of a play rather than through qualities inherent in certain "opposing ethical ends." If the genre of a play can be changed by altering its ending, can genre really be related so strongly to the ethical issues that the play addresses? With its replaceable ending, for instance, the Lear story—whose stage history stretches from *The True Chronicle History of King Leir* (1590) through Shakespeare's *The Tragedy of King Lear* (1605; title from 1623 [Folio]), Nahum Tate's *The History of King Lear* (1681), and beyond—suggests the forced relation of genre and idea in Snider's master plot.

Snider's argument is worth considering, however, because it poses a question central to understanding the politics of Shakespeare's drama: who or what is responsible for bringing plays to their conclusion? In plays that end "well," how do we get from "*O Dolentis*" to "ha, ha, he"—the frame of comedy as described by D'Amville in *The Atheist's Tragedy* (1611)?[12] Or, as A. R. Braunmuller asks in less playful language: "[H]ow do the playwrights persuade their audiences that the plot issues from individually-differentiated motives through individually-selected actions towards specific and various goals? How do they persuade us that the plot, the change of fortune in time, arises from the interaction of the dramatis personae rather than from a chronologically prior aesthetic, moral, philosophical or political design?"[13] Significantly, Snider's emphasis on systems leads him to underestimate not only the contingency of dramatic genre but also (and this aspect is closely related) the extent and importance of individual agency in the plays—what Braunmuller describes as a combination of "motives" and "actions." For example, while in such plays as *The Merchant of Venice* and *All's Well That Ends Well* (1602), Snider saw Portia ("the Friend's Wife") and Helena ("the Wife") as the primary agents responsible for comedic endings, in other "groups" of plays, he identified mediation with modes of "Life" and with "Worlds." Snider thus understood *Measure for Measure* as resolved not by Vincentio but by "Monastic Life"; similarly, *The Tempest* is brought to resolution not by Prospero but by the "Spirit World."[14]

Articulated over a century ago, these modes and "worlds" come strangely close to the amorphous nature of "social energy" in the New Historicism. As though ascribing, as Helena puts it, "remedies . . . to heaven," both critical positions take power from individuals and vest it in vaguely defined systems (however frequently these systems are bound up in the New Historicism with monarchical regimes of power). Nothing, perhaps, could seem more distant from the experience of many of Shakespeare's plays, where *characters* seem to make things happen and to do so directly. No matter how skeptical one wants to be of these plays' fictions, clearly such fictions are important to the plays—important enough that we need to take them seriously. Shakespeare recurrently emphasizes a corollary of the character that Manfred Pfister, in his transhistorical analysis of dramatic form, calls a "producer figure."[15] To Pfister, "this figure serves as a mediator between the internal dramatic level and the audience. Transcending the merely explanatory and reflective function of the chorus, he appears as the fictional authorial subject presenting the internal dramatic system."[16] The examples Pfister offers of this figure (Brecht's "Singer" in *The Caucasian Chalk Circle,* the "Stage Manager" of Wilder's *Our Town*) speak to a narrational style of dramatic mediation somewhat atypical of the dramaturgy of Shakespeare's theater—with the Chorus of *Henry V* (1599) and Gower in *Pericles* (1608) as partial exceptions to the rule. Nonetheless, we find an anticipation of this privileged figure in such characters as Portia, Prospero, and Vincentio. While many individuals, structures, and energies shape the plot of specific plays, Shakespeare's drama makes repeated recourse to figures that channel these disparate influences, to a focal character or close group of characters that consciously mediates dramatic action.[17]

As a mediating character, the Shakespearean producer figure stands between the play's action and its audience as well as among competing groups of characters within the play. This mediation depends on what is loosely called "agency," a term and concept central to literary theory during the past several decades. The etymology of "agency" can help give content to what may otherwise seem a vague term. From the Latin *agēns* [*agere*], "acting, driving, doing," agency has come to refer not only to the sense of "active working or operation; action, activity" (OED) but also to the capability and/or power to act, often in a self-directed, instrumental capacity. We can also take a provisional definition here from Anthony Giddens, who uses agency (and "action") to refer "not . . . to a series of discrete acts combined together, but to a continuous flow of *conduct*."[18] As this definition might suggest, how we think about agency in relation to literature can have strong ramifications for how we address issues outside texts. Things happen: do we credit a Who or a What? Both? To what extent is something or someone responsible for events? How we answer such questions can affect our answers to questions about the world. Our answer to How free are characters? for instance, can shape our response to How free are *we*? "Novels both have and are agents," Bruce Robbins points out: "Indeed, one way in which they are agents is by producing and propagating fictions of agency and agent-characters which have worldly consequences in encouraging or discouraging various forms of action."[19] Robbins's observation has equal relevance, of course, for our understanding of agency in drama: plays "both have and are agents," and produce and propagate "fictions of agency and agent-characters" that implicitly, and, at times, explicitly, shape readers' and audience members' thoughts on political questions.

To understand the fictions of agency in plays from the early modern era, it can be helpful to examine the language that authors used to describe it. While Shakespeare nowhere employs the word "agency" itself, ideas and actions associated with it are frequently phrased through some form of the word in his plays. For instance, when, at the end of *Troilus and Cressida* (1602), Pandarus laments "thus is the poor agent despis'd!" (5.10.36–37), he plays off an earlier moment when he had "predicted" that his name would become slang for an agent of prostitution: "If ever you prove false one to another, since I have taken such pain to bring you together, let all pitiful goers-between be call'd to the world's end after my name; call them all Pandars" (3.2.199–202). But where Pandarus claims to see his own agency (that of a goer-between) as unrewarding and unsatisfactory, other Shakespearean characters see their actions as contributing to the drama's plot and as consonant with its successful resolution. We might turn to the Queen in *Cymbeline* (1609) and to her disparagement of Pisanio for an example of how such agency (here, ironically, a misunderstanding of it) can be understood by characters within the plays:

> A sly and constant knave,
> Not to be shak'd; the agent for his master,
> And the remembrancer of her to hold
> The hand-fast to her lord.
>   (1.5.75–78)

In the Queen's mind, Pisanio has special control, ability, and tenacity. A "remembrancer" who goes between characters as an "agent," Pisanio seems both a stand-in for Posthumus and also a kind of living link to him. One might witness this linkage in the vocabulary of the above: "constant . . . Not to be shak'd . . . agent . . . master . . . remembrancer . . . her . . . hold . . . hand-fast . . . her lord." Chained through the Queen's speech is the language of relation and duty. The Queen feels that, through Pisanio's service, Posthumus remains close to Imogen. This dynamic is indeed Ralegh's "Acting by others' action."

The range of vocabulary in this *Cymbeline* passage suggests the rich variety of terms used in early modern drama to describe agency and its surrounding phenomena. Such terms include, among others, "direct" and "direction," "trick," "motion," "business"—as well as "practice," "project," and "plot" (the latter three terms as both nouns and verbs). Words for instrumental subordinate characters include, among many others, "actor," "agent," "aider," "assistant," "doer," "drudge," "factor," "factotum," "fairy," "familiar," "go-between," "instrument," "intelligencer," "mediator," "moderator," "motive," "servant," "undertaker," and "vassal."[20] With "mediate" and "agency," such words formed a cluster of the possible from which Shakespeare and other playwrights would construct their controlling figures and the characters who worked with these figures.

These controlling figures have garnered almost as many descriptive labels in criticism as in the plays themselves, in part because these figures appear in many, and many types of, plays. The controlling figures also find homes in a wide range of nondramatic texts. In his study of the Renaissance "confidence man" in Machiavelli's works, Wayne Rebhorn speaks of the proliferation of such characters in literature of the era:

> Machiavelli's world is saturated with confidence men. He detects them at every level of the social hierarchy, just as other Renaissance writers did. Of course, Machiavelli, like those other writers, also knew that not all confidence men are alike, and he did discriminate between the slightly clownish Callimaco and the consistently serious Cesare Borgia, just as Shakespeare did between the comic Falstaff and the sinister Iago. . . . if one takes Machiavelli's vision of society as seriously as one takes the comparable views of Boccaccio and Shakespeare, Jonson and Molière, then what we are dealing with looks more like a continuum of characters, an immense family of confidence men and women, ranging from tricky peasants to brutal princes, than a series of discrete and unrelated types. Before we begin to discriminate among them, we must recognize, as so many Renaissance writers did, their profound similarity.[21]

Rebhorn's observation reminds us how great a role such controlling figures assumed in the literature of Shakespeare's time. The notion of "a continuum of characters" as well as the need to discriminate among these characters will be useful to the following analysis of Shakespeare's dramatic controllers. For we must see, first, those things that Shakespeare shared with others in the early modern era and, second, that writers can respond to larger cultural influences in quite idiosyncratic ways—borrowing from various materials to construct characters that may share a "family resemblance" to those of other authors but remain in many ways distinct.

As Rebhorn's study suggests, many modern commentators—having before them the early examples of Marlowe's Machiavel and Barabas in *The Jew of Malta* (1589) and Shakespeare's Aaron in *Titus Andronicus* (1594)—have followed Bernard Spivack's *Shakespeare and the Allegory of Evil* (1958) in tracing this assertive controlling figure back to the medieval Vice, the grotesque, and the Renaissance Machiavel.[22] As we have seen, critics have also been drawn to the playwright as explanatory metaphor. Hazlitt early on described Iago as an "amateur of tragedy in real life," who "instead of employing his invention on imaginary characters, or long-forgotten incidents, . . . takes the bolder and more desperate course of getting up his plot at home, casts the principal parts among his nearest friends and connections, and rehearses it in downright earnest, with steady nerves and unabated resolution."[23] A. C. Bradley took up this observation in calling Iago an "artist" whose "action is a plot, the intricate plot of a drama, and in the conception and execution of it he experiences the tension and the joy of artistic creation."[24] Along these lines, Sidney Homan refers to Iago as "Shakespeare's own sinister portrait of the artist," while Sigurd Burckhardt calls him a "built-in playwright, who, presented with a donnee and glorying in his subtlety and skill, sets about shaping a play from it."[25] And in an essay on Prospero as manipulative dramatist, Richard Abrams combines these metaphors in arguing that Prospero's roots lie in the villain-playwright of the Machiavellian tradition, adding that "of various character-types on the Shakespearean stage, it is the Machiavel who most faithfully gives back to the playwright the image of his own powers and aspirations, his privilege to do nearly whatever he pleases within his artistic creation."[26]

To playwright, however, must be joined still other models of dramatic agency. Bertrand Evans read across genres to find the "practicer"—rep-

resented by such characters as Hamlet, Iago, Tamora, and Aaron; by phenomena in certain plays (e.g., "Fate" in *Romeo and Juliet* [1596]); and even,
in *Macbeth* (1606), by the dramatist himself.[27] If intrigue and the "discrep-
ant awareness" produced by deception are critical to his definition of
"practice," Evans's plurality here recalls Snider in assigning responsibility
to extracharacterological forms (witness "Fate"). In his study of Shakespeare's history plays, John Blanpied draws a distinction between the controlling impulses of the Machiavel and the anarchic energy of what he calls
the "antic." Where the "machiavel" is "a plotter, a manager of appearances
toward a future revelation, a manipulator of others' perceptions and expectations, a weaver of designs," the "antic" is "Jester to the machiavel's so-
briety . . . in his purest form . . . the fool, materialized from a blurred background of anarchic energy."[28] Building on these critical positions, Richard
Hillman has more recently delineated the role of the subversive "trickster"
across the Shakespeare canon. Saying that "The trickster's essence is his
shape-changing, and he can only be known indirectly, through his entan-
glements," Hillman proposes that "a wide variety of subversive practices in
Shakespearean drama . . . a principle of subversiveness can be distilled
that, in cutting across context and consequence, cuts deeper than particular 'subversive voices.'"[29] By stressing a category of "troublemaker" over the
received models of Clown/Vice/Machiavel, Hillman is able to connect
characters from ostensibly unrelated political and social spheres—such
characters, for example, as Katherina, Cloten, Puck, and Richard III.
These characters engage in politically charged and potentially subversive
activity; their disruptions are invariably social and challenge the status
quo.

My differences with Hillman lie partly in focus and partly in the conclusions we draw. We both see a "making" in the plays, but, in contrast to
Hillman, I stress not destructive troublemaking but constructive will-to-
government. Where Hillman emphasizes subversion and disruption, I
sense affirmation of politics by design. And if Blanpied's machiavel "culti-
vates disorder . . . in the interests of a broader order," my interest lies in
how this "broader order" is often achieved through the Shakespearean
maker's exercise of power over and through subordinates. It should be
pointed out that this relation is sometimes based on a contract. As Spivack, Rebhorn, and Abrams make clear, the Vice/Machiavel tradition undoubtedly influenced Shakespeare's controlling characters. Yet in depend-

ing on active subordinates like Puck and Ariel to bring about the drama's resolution, the maker or producer figure enacts a social dynamic into which the more independent, self-marginalizing Vice/Machiavel enters only with reluctance. Because the contract between controller and agent tends to work against the isolation of tragedy as a form, this dynamic—important to Shakespeare's drama—is ultimately comedic rather than tragedic.

While the traditions of machiavel and trickster undoubtedly shaped early modern plays, Shakespeare appears to have based his controlling figure on a powerful prototype from Roman New Comedy, the Plautine *poeta,* roughly translatable as "maker" or "producer." A *servus* or slave, the Plautine *poeta* can accomplish things for his master (usually an *adulescens amans,* or young lover) precisely because his low status in the social world of the comedy affords him a substantial latitude of agency and activity.[30] He most often brings about the comedic resolution through an *inventio,* an inspired construction of an object or device by which he can manipulate characters and events in the drama. He often writes and directs (even critiques) plays within his play. An intelligent character, the Plautine *poeta* typically talks to himself in the kind of soliloquies we hear from Shakespearean characters, meditating out loud in speeches that indicate psychological depth and self-consciousness. This Plautine figure is represented by, among others, Pseudolus and Epidicus in plays of the same name, by Toxilus in *Persa,* Libanus and Leonida in *Asinaria,* and by Chrysalus in *Bacchides.* I propose that Shakespeare's controlling figures draw on the tradition of this slave/*poeta* character and were based on Shakespeare's early familiarity with Plautus's works. I will examine the basic structure of the master-servant relation in Plautus, tracing the role of the *servus* as *poeta* and the relation of Shakespeare's aristocratic producers or "playwrights" to the Plautine figure and his dramaturgical powers. When Shakespeare adapts the master-slave dyad, wit and intelligence (the source of the servant/*poeta*'s power) are generally taken from the servant figure and ascribed to the aristocratic master.[31] What remains of the Plautine complex after this alteration, however, figures importantly in the comedic praxis of Shakespearean drama. Inverting the comedic pattern of authority and agency, Shakespeare suggests a political bias that has profound implications for the entire body of his work.

Makers

Plautus's comedy embraces the *poeta* as "maker" in a classical tradition frequently alluded to by early modern poetic theory. The tendency of early modern commentators to see this maker as a sagacious and respectable lawgiver, politician—even god—formed a pattern that Shakespeare would extend in lending his makers established authority. Let us examine a central statement regarding the powers of poetry in Julius Caesar Scaliger's *Poetices libri septem* (1561). Scaliger contrasts poetry with history and oratory on the basis of its almost limitless possibilities. While the orator deals with the politics of the present and the historian with the details of the past, the poet is bound by nothing save imagination:

Sola poesis haec omnia complexa est, tanto quam artes illae excellentius, quod caeterae (ut dicebamus) res ipsas, uti sunt, representant, veluti aurium pictura quadam. At poeta & naturam alteram, & fortunas plures etiam; ac demum sese isthoc ipso perinde ac Deum alterum efficit. Nam quae omnium opifex condidit, eorum reliquae scientiae tamquam actores sunt. Poetica vero quum & speciosius quae sunt, & quae non sunt, eorum speciem ponit; videtur sane res ipsas, non ut aliae, quasi Histrio, narrare, sed velut alter deus condere.

[Poetry alone has included all these things, more outstandingly than the former arts inasmuch as the others (as we were saying) represent events themselves as they are, just like some aural portrait. The poet, on the contrary, represents an alternate world, and, for that matter, a larger set of circumstances. And, ultimately, by that very deed, he makes himself just like a second God. For the remaining disciplines are like actors for the creations that the Maker of all things has brought forth. But when the poetic discipline produces an image of what is not or, in a more beautiful image, what is, it appears not to retell events—as if a mime—as other disciplines do but to create the events themselves, just like a second God.][32]

Scaliger sees the poet as a *Deus alter,* or "another God." Connecting the poet and this God is their ability to *make,* to fashion, to produce. Scaliger grounds this connection in the etymology of "poet," ultimately from the Greek for "maker." English writers often elaborated this sense of making in their explanations of poetry and poets.

Following Scaliger, and Phillipe de Mornay's reiteration of the *Deus alter* conceit, for instance, Sidney famously gave voice to the idea of poet as maker in his *Defense of Poesy,* in which he cites the etymology of "poet" before lending poets the "high and incomparable" title of "maker."[33] His example would be taken up by a chorus of writers. In *Timber, or Discoveries,* for example, Ben Jonson provides a definition typical of poetic treatises in early modern England by answering the question *"What is a Poet?"*

> *A Poet* is that, which by the *Greeks* is call'd κατ᾽ ἐξοχὴν, ὁ Ποιητὴς, a Maker, or a fainer: His Art, an Art of imitation, or faining; expressing the life of man in fit measure, numbers, and harmony, according to *Aristotle*: From the word ποιεῖν, which signifies to make, or fayne. (vol. 8: 635, lines 2346–51)

Puttenham had begun *The Arte of English Poesie* with *"What a Poet and Poesie is,"* stating that

> A Poet is as much to say as a maker. And our English name well conforms with the Greek word: for of ποιεῖν to make, they call a maker *Poeta.* Such as (by way of resemblance and reverently) we may say of God: who without any travail to his divine imagination, made all the world of nought, nor also by any pattern or mould as the Platonics with their Ideas do phantastically suppose. Even so the very Poet makes and contrives out of his own brain, both the verse and matter of his poem, and not by any foreign copy or example.[34]

Puttenham suggests ("reverently") that a poet/*poeta* is similar to God in the way he "makes and contrives." Like Sidney and Jonson, he follows Scaliger's lead in exploring poetry's basis in making, or production, through the etymology of the Greek ποιεῖν, to "make" or "produce." This borrowing literalizes its etymology in early modern drama by becoming one of the standard metaphors for defining how the *poeta* brings about a comedic resolution.

The connection between production of poetic texts and production within them came about partly because, for Puttenham and others, the poet is more than just a general "maker." The heading for the third chapter of *The Arte of English Poesie,* for example, gives an indication of the poet's extensive professional history: "How Poets were the first priests, the first prophets, the first Legislators and politicians in the world."[35] Because poets were curious about nature, Puttenham argues, they became "the first Priests and ministers of the holy mysteries." And because, as priests and ministers, they lived chastely and they meditated, they were "made apt to receive visions, both waking and sleeping, which made them utter prophesies, and foretell things to come." As "the first Prophets or seers," they were to be "the first lawmakers to the people, and the first politicians, devising all expedient means for th'establishment of Common wealth, to hold and contain the people in order and duty by force and virtue of good and wholesome laws, made for the preservation of the public peace and tranquility."[36] Puttenham's fourth chapter expands this praiseful genealogy of poets by stating that it will describe "How the Poets were the first Philosophers, the first Astronomers and Historiographers and Orators and Musicians of the world." For Puttenham, then, the poet had always been a maker and always *more* than a maker. As a fundamental trope, "making" described the visionary, imaginative, and legislative roles necessary to civilization.

Such "making," sometimes including a kind of "devising" of "expedient means" and a "hold[ing] and contain[ing]" of "people in order," had long been an ability of many poet figures in literature itself, including those in the Roman New Comedy that Shakespeare would draw on for plot material. Pseudolus, wily *servus* in Plautus's play of the same name, succinctly deploys this metaphor for production and does so in a way that reminds us of his origins in the lower orders (hence his difference from Puttenham's governing poet, whom he resembles, nonetheless, in his ability to see and control). Stranded without the means to resolve his young master's difficulties, he seizes upon an idea:

> sed quasi poeta, tabulas quom cepit sibi,
> quaerit quod nusquam gentiumst, reperit tamen,
> facit illud ueri simile quod mendacium est,
> nunc ego poeta fiam: uiginti minas,
> quae nunc nusquam sunt gentium, inueniam tamen.
>
> (lines 401–5)

> [But just like a poet, taking up his tablets, searches for what is nowhere on earth, but finds it anyway, and makes the false seem true, I'll be a poet myself: the twenty minae, that are nowhere on earth now, I'll find them anyway.][37]

Pseudolus is the slave of Calidorus (a typical *adulescens amans,* or young lover), who has lost his beloved through a pimp's breach of contract. Pseudolus takes it on himself to rectify the situation by stealing the girl out from under the pimp's nose. The predicament is typical to Plautus, running throughout his plays. With the onus of plot resolution placed on him, Plautus's *servus* triumphs through inspired discovery, becoming "quasi poeta," that is, "like a poet."

What Pseudolus needs to discover is "nusquam gentiumst"—"nowhere on earth" (literally, "which sort is nowhere"). In the conceptual map of Plautus's dramatic world there are usually two avenues for such a discovery: above and below. Pseudolus declares later in the same passage that "ex hoc sepulcro uetere uiginti minas | ecfodiam ego hodie quas dem erili filio" ("From this old tomb today I'll dig up the twenty minae to give my young master" [lines 412–13]). Succor from a similar location is obtained in *Rudens,* in which a chest holding the means of dramatic resolution is fished out of the sea (lines 906ff.). And in *Asinaria,* when the *servus* Libanus is faced with a seemingly irresolvable problem, he responds: "iubeas una opera me piscari in aere, | uenari autem rete iaculo in medio mari" ("You might as well order me to go fishing in the air, or even go hunting in the middle of the ocean" [lines 99–100]). Here humorous juxtaposition fixes the two places of resolution. When Libanus does find a solution, the inspiration comes from above:

> unde sumam? quem interuortam? quo hanc celocem conferam?
> impetritum, inauguratumst: quouis admittunt aues,
> picus et cornix ab laeua, coruos, parra ab dextera
> consuadent; certum herclest uostram consequi sententiam.
>   (lines 258–61)

> [Where to find it? Whom to cheat? Where to steer this little boat? (pause) I've got the omens, the auguries: the birds let me go wherever I want, woodpecker and crow on the left of me, raven and owl on the right—they all agree; by god I'll certainly follow your advice.]

Aerial augury leads Libanus to success, giving him from above what in *Rudens* appears from below. This trope could be said to characterize the Plautine: the *servus* schemes toward resolution, achieving it, finally, through (super)naturally bestowed or aided inspiration. Invention is accomplished with assistance, and intrigue hinges on something outside the intriguer.

"Playwright" might be an accurate gloss here for *poeta,* because to bring about the resolution, the tricky *servus* often writes and directs a play within the play. For example, Plautus has Pseudolus select his own actor (rejecting one applicant as unsuitable), dress him in a carefully chosen costume, and rehearse him in his part (lines 694–766; 905–55). Toxilus in *Persa* (lines 159, 465ff.) and Milphio in *Poenulus* (lines 579ff.) discuss what they do in explicitly theatrical terms as well. Frequently in Plautus, as George Duckworth noted, "the characters frankly refer to themselves as actors and joke about stage conventions and stage machinery."[38] Niall Slater expands on this observation in describing a recurrent role in Plautus's plays, from *Pseudolus* to *Bacchides* to *Epidicus*, as that of "poet," "playwright," and dramatic "writer with first-night jitters."[39] In this way these Roman dramas foreground the artifice of the *poeta* figure even as they make public the mystery of comedy.

Shakespeare and Plautus

Most critics recognize the enormous influence Plautus had on Shakespeare's development as a playwright, especially as both *Menaechmii* and *Rudens* were important to what may have been his first comedy, *The Comedy of Errors* (1592). Yet many are generally unwilling to see Plautus as much more than a schoolboy resource whose influence Shakespeare soon outgrew, this despite Plautine themes and topoi throughout the canon. Why such an erroneous portrait? The commonplace early modern grouping of Plautus with Terence is potentially misleading here. For instance, that even the highly traditionalistic Polonius chooses Plautus rather than Terence in his windy praise—"Seneca cannot be too heavy, nor Plautus too light" (2.2.400–401)—gives us some sense that, for Shakespeare, Plautus and Terence were not dramatic equals. But critics have continued to consider the two playwrights together, often seeing their influence as intertwined.[40] To distinguish the two is, I would argue, to begin to sense Plautus's distinctiveness as resource no less than as a playwright.

For a long time, scholars tried to make Terence important to Shakespeare. And although T. W. Baldwin has argued that Terence's *Andria* provided the structural basis of such comedies as *The Comedy of Errors* and *Twelfth Night* (1601), neither Kenneth Muir nor Geoffrey Bullough has been able to cite *any* quotation of Terence in Shakespeare's plays.[41] In his recent study of Plautus's influence on Shakespeare, Wolfgang Riehle argues that Terence was most popular among the humanists and Plautus among playwrights, pointing out that "Nicholas Udall turned to Terence when looking for examples of first-rate Latin [in his *Flowers for Latin-Speaking, Selected and Gathered out of Terence and the same translated to*

Englysshe (1533/34)], and to Plautus when he set himself the task of writing a specifically English 'Roman' comedy."[42] Shakespeare almost certainly would have read Plautus in grammar school, and it is likely that Plautus's plays—better acted than cribbed for wisdom—were performed there as well. Baldwin examines a list of grammar school texts "published in London in 1581," which includes *Pseudolus*; in *De Discenda Graeca Lingua Oratio Secunda,* one G. H. (Gabriel Harvey?) related: *Legunt pueri . . . Plauti Amphytrionem; Epidicum: Menaechmos: Pseudolum* ("The boys read . . . Plautus's *Amphtiruo; Epidicus; Menaechmii; Pseudolus*").[43] Plautus's influence may not be confined to comedy. *Pseudolus,* as a comedy, shares certain features with the tragedy of *Hamlet* (1601). Timothy Moore's recent reading of *Pseudolus* emphasizes the play's metatheatricality, which involves in large part the title character's consciousness that he is organizing and executing a play for the audience.[44] Moore notes the irony of the characters' concern with "time in general, and with the place of performance in particular" in a play "where so many extra characters, scenes, and monologues have been added with such self-consciousness" and where the main character, Pseudolus, teasingly delays the implementation of his comedic plans.[45] Exploring the comedic matrix of *Hamlet,* Susan Snyder describes Hamlet as "role player, manipulator, crafty madman, wit, and eiron," terms that closely fit Pseudolus and his New Comedy character type.[46] George Duckworth has noticed in *Hamlet* another possible quotation ("Assume a virtue, if you have it not" [3.4.160]) from Plautus's comedy, *Amphitruo* ("Even if you have no modesty, you might at least assume a little" [*Amphitruo* 819]).[47] However, one needs look no further than *Hamlet* 2.2, where Hamlet mentions the Roman comedian Roscius (2.2.390–91), and remember Polonius's reference to Plautus, to understand how present Roman New Comedy is to Shakespeare's tragedy.[48] What remains most important, though, is how Shakespeare changes Plautus.

Shakespeare's reversal of the model of smart slave/straight-man master in *Hamlet* happens over and over in his plays. As is apparent in the exchange between Hamlet and Horatio, Shakespeare transformed the dynamic between characters: his comedies, like his tragedies, are most often controlled by aristocrats rather than by characters below them. Horatio is relatively powerless here; Hamlet and Shakespeare choose to have Hamlet do everything by himself—writing plays within the play, directing them, commenting on them. Where Jonson in plays like *Every Man in His Humour* and *The Alchemist* would give temporarily free rein to *servus* figures, respectively, Brainworm ("Musco"), and Face ("Jeremy"), Shakespeare tends to locate his "practicer" in the upper registers of society. Instead of a servant manipulating the action, an aristocratic figure is frequently accorded the imagination and control necessary for resolution. As if borrowing a page from Puttenham and other authors of poetic treatises, who theorized poetic governance, Shakespeare connects political and dramatic power in practice.

When we encounter abstract theorizing about poetry in Shakespeare's plays, it is often by characters who have the power to translate thought into action. Witness, for instance, Duke Theseus's famous exposition in *A Midsummer Night's Dream,* which offers a strong parallel with the type of inspiration guiding Pseudolus:

> The lunatic, the lover, and the poet
> Are of imagination all compact.
> One sees more devils than vast hell can hold;
> That is the madman. The lover, all as frantic,
> Sees Helen's beauty in a brow of Egypt.
> The poet's eye, in a fine frenzy rolling,
> Doth glance from heaven to earth, from earth to heaven;
> And as imagination bodies forth
> The forms of things unknown, the poet's pen
> Turns them to shapes, and gives to aery nothing
> A local habitation and a name.
>
> (5.1.7–17)

Some scholars gloss this passage by pointing to the trope of *furor poeticus* and the idea of the inspired poet, which traces its origins ultimately to Plato.[49] But Theseus's model also remains aligned in many ways with the imaginative faculty of the Plautine *poeta,* the maker who snatches from a height or depth (witness "from heaven to earth, from earth to heaven") that "habitation and a name" that has been, until now, "aery nothing."

Shortly after this speech, Theseus embodies his definition of poet, becoming a *poeta* by grounding the conceit in dramatic application. Philostrate, master of revels, brings to Theseus a list of the plays to be considered for the nuptial ceremony. Significantly, the three plays correspond closely to the categories of Theseus's discourse on imagination. The "riot of the tipsy Bacchanals, | Tearing the Thracian singer in their rage" (5.1.48–49) recalls the frenzied Dionysian revelers who dismembered Orpheus and coincides with the concept of madness in Theseus's speech. Ovid's "sed enim temeraria crescunt | bella, modusque abiit, insanaque regnat Erinys" is rendered in Arthur Golding's 1567 translation: "But rash | And heady ryot out of frame all reason did clash, | And frantik outrage ranged."[50] The "battle with the Centaurs" (5.1.44) alludes to the centaurs' attempted rape of Hippodamia, Pirithous's bride, agreeing with Theseus's "lover" even as it brings to mind the Duke's own abduction of Hippolyta (witness 1.1.16–17). Ovid's "tam virgine visa | ardet, et ebrietas geminata libidine regnat" becomes with Golding "so | Assoone as thou behilldst the bryde, thy hart began too frayne, | And doubled with thy droonkennesse thy raging lust did reigne."[51] One might remember that Antipholus of Syracuse, who enjoys at least the attention of—if not intimate contact with—Adriana, his brother's wife, resides at the Centaur Inn in *The Comedy of Errors* (1.1.19), the image of the centaur literalizing the notion of (bestial) lust in man.[52] Finally, the "thrice three Muses mourning for the death | Of learning," the third play in Philostrate's list, invokes Theseus's poet in its allusion to the inspiring Muses. Lunatic, lover, poet: the thematic parallels between the dramas and the categories of his discourse on imagination are complete. Yet Theseus rejects all three plays. What remains, then, for their nuptials?

In setting up three categories of received inspiration and distancing himself from them, Theseus creates a space for his own powers of poetry. This space reveals itself when Philostrate mentions one play that he neglected to suggest previously because it is "nothing, nothing in the world" (5.1.78). The phrasing here resonates with Plautus's "quod nusquam gentiumst," that which is "nowhere on earth." To Philostrate, the nothingness of the Mechanicals' play disqualifies it from serious consideration. But both dramas require that the impossible become real—indeed, that a *poeta* figure accomplish it *through* this very nothingness. So Theseus, over all objections, chooses the play that is "nothing in the world," the play we know as *The most lamentable comedy and most cruel death of Pyramus and Thisby*. He does so with a short exposition on perceiving something where there appears to be nothing:

> Trust me, sweet,
> Out of this silence yet I pick'd a welcome;
> And in the modesty of fearful duty
> I read as much as from the rattling tongue
> Of saucy and audacious eloquence . . .
>
> (5.1.99–103)

Theseus defends Quince's play as the poetry that seems more real: where the drama of "The thrice three Muses" is "some satire, keen and critical" (5.1.54), the play of Pyramus and Thisby is tendered by "simpleness and duty" (5.1.83). That it is "nothing, nothing in the world" seems to remain its chief attraction to Theseus. In contrast to Lear, who fails to perceive the something behind Cordelia's "nothing" (1.1.87ff.)—an unimaginative act that contributes to their tragedy—Theseus displays a poetic insight that leads to a comedic ending. During the Mechanicals' presentation, he serves not as the worldly, literary poet of "The thrice three Muses" but as the active, comedic *poeta* who stands side-stage during the dramatic production, sometimes supporting, sometimes criticizing the play. In his careful deliberation of plays to be performed and in his metadramatic commentary on Bottom's special performance, Theseus shows an aesthetic side to the governmental role he assumes in bringing about the resolution of *A Midsummer Night's Dream.*

Theseus's actions and decisions appear to resolve the "mortal" plot of *A Midsummer Night's Dream.* He is paralleled in this agency, of course, by Oberon and Puck in the play's green world. As Peter Brook's famous 1970 production helped to demonstrate, Oberon and Theseus (and Titania and Hippolyta) possess many similarities in terms of character and dramatic function. Theseus's use of Bottom and the Mechanicals in the pageant of aristocratic condescension, in fact, is anticipated by Oberon and Puck's use of Bottom in the erotic subordination of Titania. Oberon's dramatic role, like Theseus's, is that of comedic *poeta.* His plan for furthering the action of the fairy drama revolves around an inspired making. Having met "proud Titania" in a wood near Athens and having been rebuffed in his attempt to acquire the "changeling boy," Oberon summons Puck to his side and recalls a time when he (Oberon)

> saw (but thou couldst not),
> Flying between the cold moon and the earth,

Cupid all arm'd. A certain aim he took
At a fair vestal throned by the west,
And loos'd his love-shaft smartly from his bow,
As it should pierce a hundred thousand hearts . . .
   (2.1.155–60)

This arrow, Oberon recalls,

> fell upon a little western flower,
> Before milk-white, now purple with love's wound,
> And maidens call it love-in-idleness.
> Fetch me that flow'r; the herb I showed thee once.
>   (2.1.166–69)

Several things about Oberon's speech stand out. First is the coy allusion to Elizabeth in the reference to "a fair vestal throned by the west." What remains important about this allusion in relation to the present argument is its role as a metaphor for the politics of the larger drama. That is, in acknowledging their sovereign (and every acting company's ultimate patron), the playwright and actors acknowledge the master/servant dynamic. Just as Shakespeare makes obeisance to Elizabeth in this passage, Puck listens to his master's instructions and replies, "Fear not, my lord! Your servant shall do so" (2.1.268).[53] But "high" depends on "low." Oberon may retrieve the "love-in-idleness," it seems, only with the assistance of Puck, who can "put a girdle round the earth | In forty minutes" (2.1.175–76). The emphasis on the physical separation of *poeta* and object or symbol of dramatic resolution is, as we have seen, typical of comedic praxis, and in employing Puck as a "wanderer" (2.1.247), Oberon testifies to the utter dependence of upper-class characters in Roman New Comedy on their servants. In contrast to New Comedy, however, *servus* figures in Shakespeare are important not for their wit or intelligence but rather for their geographical and social mobility.

By social mobility, I mean the ability temporarily to move through and among various social classes. This social freedom is a version of what we most frequently associate with servants' geographical ubiquity. Ariel and Puck, for instance, are portrayed as covering a great deal of terrain in their plays. Like Puck, Ariel's practical role in his play is mainly that of tool. Although given an evocative moment in *The Tempest* that bears witness to emotional depth—that is, when he teaches Prospero mercy—Ariel is normally employed by Prospero as a tremendously mobile spy. "Thou . . . think'st it much," Prospero scolds him,

> to tread the ooze
> Of the salt deep,
> To run upon the sharp wind of the north,
> To do me business in the veins o' th' earth
> When it is bak'd with frost.
> (1.2.252–56)

The importance placed on geographical mobility—both vertical and horizontal—and on Puck's ability to "put a girdle round the earth | In forty minutes" might be seen in part as embodying New Comedy's emphasis on the (super)natural source of invention that resolves comedic plots and in part as making physical the hyperbolic scope of imagination in such descriptions as Theseus's "from heaven to earth, from earth to heaven."

The relation between the centralized and centralizing controllers of Oberon/Theseus and Prospero and their *servus* accomplices surfaces in what Robert Weimann explores as the *platea* and *locus* areas of the medieval and early modern theater.[54] In Weimann's explication, the *platea* is an "extension of the acting area" by a nonrepresentational, "unlocalized 'place,'" while the *locus* is a more restricted acting area, corresponding (in terms of the medieval theater) to "a scaffold, be it a *domus, sedes,* or throne," which can "delimit a more or less fixed and focused scenic unit." The *platea/locus* division is especially helpful for understanding the comedic praxis of Shakespearean drama because it highlights the discrepancy in mobility between the *poeta* and the controller's subordinate. Shakespeare's controller is most often associated with a central "place" from which he or she manipulates elements of action in the play. We might think of Theseus's court and Prospero's island cell as representative of this *locus* space. The controller's subordinate, on the other hand, utilizes the unlocalized *platea* space in service of the controller, gathering information and temporarily supervising and manipulating other characters in the drama. It should be pointed out that mobility is not, in itself, sufficient for successful execution of a master's orders. While figures like Puck and Ariel are given much power in the *platea* space—an investment they usually repay—many other servant characters in Shakespeare prove less successful.

The two Dromios in *The Comedy of Errors,* Launcelot Gobbo in *The Merchant of Venice,* Viola/Caesario in *Twelfth Night,* and *Cymbeline's* Pisanio are only a few of the servant figures in Shakespeare's drama who act in a less than fully instrumental capacity.

In several plays, the Shakespearean *poeta* assumes this agency within his or her own character; in this apparent self-sufficiency, the *poeta* most approximates the independence usually accorded the Vice/Machiavel, the "antic," "practicer," and "trickster." In Richard III, Aaron, and Iago, for example, Shakespeare combines master and servant into one character: they answer, finally, to themselves and cross boundaries with relative ease. Surely it speaks to Shakespeare's fascination with the "hidden aristocrat" trope that he has Richard III mention this ploy after rising from his prophetic dream the night before Bosworth Field. There Richard turns to Ratcliffe and says:

'Tis not yet near day. Come, go with me,
Under our tents I'll play the ease-dropper,
To see if any mean to shrink from me.
   (5.3.220–22)

The image of Richard sneaking by his soldiers' tents is at once humorous, pathetic, and terrifying. It reminds us that much of Richard's power has depended on surveillance. At the same time, Richard's vow to "play the ease-dropper" speaks to the comedic side of his character, the cunning manipulation he practices throughout the play, which often has us laughing against our better judgments.

Other disguised comedians are more benign in their intentions. Such characters as Hal/Henry in *1 Henry IV* (1597) and *Henry V,* Duke Vincentio in *Measure for Measure,* King Polixenes in *The Winter's Tale* (1611), and Lord Lysimachus in *Pericles,* for instance, attempt to gain geographic and social mobility through disguising themselves as anonymous members of a middle or lower class. Hal's exploits near Gadshill (2.2), the "little touch of Harry in the night" (4.Chorus.47), Polixenes' (and Camillo's) "not appearing what we are" (4.2.47–48), Vincentio's disguising himself as a friar and Lysimachus as an anonymous citizen—all show an appropriation of high and low, near and far, centralized *locus* and dispersed *platea.* Lysimachus's "disguise," it should be pointed out, is less than effective, as the Bawd in the brothel at Mytilene tells her companions: "Here comes the Lord Lysimachus disguis'd" (4.6.16–17). The immediate response here of Boult, Pander's servant, however, is significant: "We should have both lord and lown, if the peevish baggage would but give way to customers" (4.6.18–19). Boult's exasperated comment (he, like Bawd and Pander, wishes Marina would submit to the brothel's customers) incidentally defines the range of disguise afforded the *poeta*. That is, concealing their political identities allows characters like Hal/Henry, Vincentio, and Lysimachus to move from high ("lord") toward low ("lown" [i.e., "low fellow"]) and, in doing so, to travel in areas of society most accessible to figures of lesser social rank.

Portia in the Court

One of these normally inaccessible areas is delimited by gender. For this reason, perhaps, Portia, who disguises herself as "Doctor Bellario" in *The Merchant of Venice,* is most often connected by critics with Shakespeare's other cross-dressed heroines, with such characters as Rosalind in *As You Like It,* Viola in *Twelfth Night,* and Imogen in *Cymbeline.* These characters find a freedom in disguise that they do not enjoy when dressed as women. But in directing the events of the courtroom drama within the drama (and what transpires in the following act), Portia functions also as a *poeta* figure. Bertrand Evans touched on Portia's relation to other Shakespearean producer figures when he acknowledged that, although structurally "Portia replaces Oberon she does not replace him early or completely."[55] Evans continued his comparison in wondering

> how it can be that [Antonio's] three argosies—which we were first assured would be lost and then informed were lost in fact—"Are richly come to harbour suddenly." Portia is only the bearer of the good news and can of course have had no actual part in saving the ships: *yet the effect is as though she had saved them.* The sudden, surprising announcement, coming from her after we have been assured that they were lost, makes it seem almost as if she had wrought the miracle. Fabulous when we first hear of her, dazzling in the casket scene, all-knowing and seemingly all-powerful in the court scene, nowhere does she more truly prefigure the ultimate Prospero than in the effect of this closing moment.[56]

To similar effect, Marc Shell, discussing Portia's cross-dressing, suggests that she "is at once a *deus ex machina* (Balthasar in the court) and a disguised *dea in machina* (Portia in the courtship)."[57] But in magically restoring Antonio's ships ("*the effect is as though she had saved them*"), Portia in the courtship undeniably retains some of the *ex machina* power that had characterized her in the court. As Evans pointed out in his analogy with "the ultimate" Prospero: unlike Rosalind, Viola, and Imogen, Portia takes an extremely active—even dominant—role in determining the outcome of the comedy.

We can see the power of this role in her orders to Balthazar, one of her servants. Her commands remind us of Oberon even as they anticipate Vincentio and Prospero:

> Now Balthazar,
> As I have ever found thee honest-true,
> So let me find thee still. Take this same letter,
> And use thou all th' endeavor of a man
> In speed to Padua. See thou render this
> Into my cousin's hands, Doctor Bellario,
> And look what notes and garments he doth give thee,
> Bring them, I pray thee, with imagin'd speed
> Unto the traject, to the common ferry
> Which trades to Venice. Waste no time in words,
> But get thee gone. I shall be there before thee.
> (3.4.45–55)

The breathless compression of language here (one might notice the determined monosyllables in "Waste no time in words, | But get thee gone. I shall be there before thee") combines with parallel enjambment in the preceding lines ("man | In," "this | Into," "speed | Unto," "ferry | Which") to underscore a general quickening of pace and intensity in the play as the trial scene (4.1) approaches. Portia's instruction to Balthazar to use all "imagin'd speed" (that is, speed as quick as the imagination) also brings the mobility of Puck and Ariel to mind.

By donning Bellario's "garments," Portia takes on the role of actor and director, controlling the confrontation at law even as she controlled Balthazar. Her success in this legal confrontation, bringing about a change of dramatic venue from the commercial, litigious world of Venice to the green, poetic world of Belmont, signals a partial victory of the upper orders over those to whom money is not a given. No less than her gender, Portia's social status would seem to hinder her from entering into the practical—that is, male and commercial/legalistic—world of the comedy as an equal participant: how could a lord or lady be expected to know the subtleties of the law or courtroom protocol? Taking on the garments and professional attributes of Doctor Balthazar, she exchanges her passive role as one *chosen* from the three caskets for a more active, directorial part. Like Oberon/Theseus, Vincentio, and Prospero, Portia averts a tragic ending by altering the social alignments of character and fortune from above.

We have seen that Shakespeare's relation to the Plautine *poeta* and the master-servant dynamic transcends categories of genre. Rather than deploying the *poeta* trope in opposition to generic classification, however, we may read it alongside character and genre for a deeper understanding of Shakespeare's dramaturgy and of the nature of his quotation of Plautus. By way of example, we might turn to *Romeo and Juliet*'s Mercutio: an energetic and verbally sophisticated character much like the Plautine *poeta*. Mercutio's potential as *poeta* becomes clear during his well-known "Queen Mab" speech (1.4.53–103), in which he imaginatively details the activities of "the fairies' midwife" (1.4.54), who races through the night performing mischievous acts like those of Puck (MND 2.1.32–57). In the middle of Mercutio's speech, Romeo interrupts him with a telling remark: "Peace, peace, Mercutio, peace! | Thou talk'st of *nothing*" (1.5.95–96, emphasis mine). Mercutio responds:

> True, I talk of dreams,
> Which are the children of an idle brain,
> Begot of nothing but vain fantasy,
> Which is as thin of substance as the air,
> And more inconstant than the wind, who woos
> Even now the frozen bosom of the north,
> And, being anger'd, puffs away from thence,
> Turning his side to the dew-dropping south.
>   (1.4.96–103)

Romeo's insistence on the *nothing*ness of Mercutio's dream oration precedes the latter's admission that his words are indeed "nothing but vain fantasy," a fantasy that ranges over the natural world in a manner typical of the comedic *poeta*'s ubiquitous imagination.

Mercutio's relation to the drama and its genre is exceedingly problematic, for the tragedy of *Romeo and Juliet* cannot proceed with a potentially controlling *poeta* figure involved in its plot. Here Dryden's somewhat casual remarks in his "Essay on the Dramatique Poetry of the last Age" are illuminating:

> *Shakespeare* showed the best of his skill in his *Mercutio,* and he said himself, that he was forc'd to kill him in the third Act, to prevent being kill'd by him. But, for my part, I cannot find he was so dangerous a person: I see nothing in him but what was so exceeding harmless, that he might have liv'd to the end of the Play, and dy'd in his bed, without offence to any man.[58]

To Dryden, Mercutio's skillfully drawn character came to an unjust and untimely end. What Dryden failed to realize, however, is that, while not harmful or "dangerous" to any person, Mercutio remains anathema to tragedy. We can perhaps feel in the overwhelmingly tense Queen Mab speech a generic conflict between comedy and tragedy, staged in language. And as witty, empowered *poeta,* Mercutio can discern and act in a way inimical to tragedy. He is killed, therefore, not because he would be the death of Shakespeare but because he would be the death of the *tragedy* of *Romeo and Juliet.* In the words of Richard Hillman, "the generic destiny of the text is logically related to the elimination of a genuine agent of disruption and the assumption of responsibility for the plot by a would-be engineer of comic closure."[59] That is, Mercutio is replaced by the well-meaning but inept Friar Lawrence, comedy giving way to tragedy in the process. But Hillman makes no attempt to explain *why* these characters should be different generically and why Mercutio is an "agent of disruption"—or, if so, how that distinguishes him from such disrupting characters as Puck, Portia, Vincentio, and Prospero.

Friar Lawrence is only a "would-be engineer of comic closure," I believe, because he is lower on the social ladder than most of Shakespeare's *poetae.* As *Measure for Measure* suggests, a friar can better write and direct plays when he is not really a friar but a duke. To be sure, Friar Francis in *Much Ado About Nothing* (1598) helps brings about a comedic ending to that play. But his efforts are only part of the play's successful resolution, and he is by no means a sufficient controller: he lacks the ability to determine why Hero has been unjustly accused and to punish those responsible. When in the tragedy of *Romeo and Juliet,* Shakespeare sought an engineer of comic closure whose efforts would go awry, he looked lower on the social ladder than Prince Escalus, the ostensible governor of Verona. Here

Mercutio's social status may offer a clue to why he is dangerous to the play as tragedy. Mercutio is a Veronese aristocrat. We are also told, in an otherwise extraneous passage, that he is "kinsman" to Prince Escalus, the ruler whose inability to end the feud between the play's rival families leads to the tragedy of *Romeo and Juliet* (3.1.145). Mercutio is in this way a stand-in for the Prince and his absent authority: "kin" by generic function as well as blood. With Mercutio's death, the Prince as well as his stand-in are absent. As in *A Midsummer Night's Dream,* where the potential tragedy of Hermia and Lysander (burlesqued by the Mechanicals' play of *Pyramus and Thisby*) is averted by Oberon, Puck, and Theseus, with Mercutio alive, *Romeo and Juliet* might well have turned out to be a romantic comedy. The difference between the two plays is the presence, in the comedy, of *poeta* figures. And one qualification for such figures seems to be positive social difference: rank, class, degree. Although Dogberry possesses the information needed to help solve the central dramatic problem of *Much Ado About Nothing,* his class-related "tediousness"—the lack of the right words at the right time, compounded by the malapropisms that his rhetorical aspirations produce—brings his dramatic world closer to tragedy. Ultimately, one of the play's practicing villains, not Dogberry, delivers the incriminating information to the authorities.

Thus if, as the example of the various versions of *King Lear* reminds us, playwrights are the chief movers of a play's genre, character can strongly affect how a playwright comes to establish dramatic kinds. As we have seen, Shakespeare was especially sensitive to social class when he came to consider the resources a character could offer. His quotation of Roman New Comedy entails a significant revision of the master-servant dialectic—or, at the very least, a temporary alteration of the duke figure through costume and disguise. Changing the social relations of the comedic model he inherited, Shakespeare consistently pushed agency upward on the social scale. He was called a "*Johannes fac totum*" by Robert Greene in 1592, a phrase which, as we have seen, can be translated as "John Mend-all" or "Jack-of-all-trades."[60] Perhaps Shakespeare, actor and playwright, soon to be poet and gentleman, wrote what he wanted to be—a well-governing individual from the upper orders—and avoided what he was—a jack-of-all-trades who dreamed of better things. Revising his Plautine model, Shakespeare exhibits a deference to benign political authority; the consistency of such revision speaks to a traditionalism in his dramaturgy. By changing the male *poeta* of Plautus into female characters such as Portia and Helena, Shakespeare performs another displacement, one perhaps harder for us to read as traditionalistic. In chapter 5 of this study, we will see Shakespeare lend an equally significant importance to a seemingly marginalized figure, that of the Jailer's Daughter in *The Two Noble Kinsmen* (1613). With Prospero in *The Tempest*, however, he would perhaps most fully express a model of power relations that had always been present to his dramatic practice.

CHAPTER 4

Quoting the Playhouse in *The Tempest*

If all the year were playing holidays,
To sport would be as tedious as to work.
HAL, in *I Henry IV* (1597)

We have seen that, throughout his career, Shakespeare tended to change a dramatic model he had inherited, rewriting the Plautine slave as a controlling aristocrat. The preceding chapter explored the ways in which Shakespeare incorporated elements from his reading into his plays, emphasizing, in this way, the quotation of books. If we define quotation more liberally, however, understanding it to encompass not just printed matter but other elements in the world, we broaden the range of things that may be seen as having contributed to Shakespeare's plays, hence putting ourselves in a better position to recognize their complexity. I will employ this broader definition of quotation in suggesting that one late play in particular, *The Tempest* (1611), draws on Shakespeare's feelings concerning not a classical but a real-life clown, one with whom he had worked.

The Tempest is often seen as Shakespeare's allegory of colonial relations. But as much as it uses the theater to talk about colonialism, *The Tempest* uses colonialism to talk about the theater—particularly about authority and work in certain early modern playhouses. I have argued in the preceding chapter that we must turn to books to understand the significance of Shakespeare's controlling figures—and, by doing so, avoid using an amorphous theatricality to explain this character type in his plays. My emphasis on theatrical elements in what follows does not contradict that argument, for my remarks here concern actual playhouses. Traditionally, when critics have spoken of the theater in *The Tempest,* it has been as an abstraction. In contrast, I take Shakespeare's theatrical experience to be a practical, not an abstract, matter. It is not enough to say *The Tempest* is about the theater.

We need to ask: "Which theater or theaters?" and "Who and what *in* those theaters may have shaped the play?"

My primary claims are twofold, though related. First, that *The Tempest*, commonly acknowledged as a play without a major literary source, looks to the Globe and Blackfriars playhouses—and to the realities of working in those structures—for its most salient sources. Its portrait of playhouse labor and experience includes not only Prospero as a playwright/director but also Miranda as figure of an idealized spectatorship and Ariel as boy actor. My second major claim, one that builds on this playhouse allegory, is that Caliban derived from Shakespeare's experiences with Will Kemp, the celebrated Elizabethan clown known for his physical, even priapic comedy, his independent spirit, folk ethos, and intrusive ad-libs. In this reading, Kemp's tendency to ignore the lines that playwrights had written translated into Caliban's animosity toward Prospero's powerful books. Rewriting the relation of, among others, Theseus to Bottom as one of Prospero to Caliban, Shakespeare quoted an apparently unwelcome relation between himself, as playwright and actor for what were then the Lord Chamberlain's Men, and the company's famous if unruly clown.

In situating *The Tempest* locally, I call into question a thoroughly colonialist interpretation of the play—an interpretation, that is, set in and about only the New World.[1] The play, in this familiar reading, concerns European exploitation of the New World and its inhabitants. Here critics typically survey Montaigne's "Of Cannibals," Strachey's "True Repertory," Jourdain's *Discovery of the Bermudas,* and various passages from the extensive literature of European exploration. The play's island becomes Virginia, Ireland, or the Bermudas, Prospero a colonialist master, and Caliban an oppressed native. Perhaps not surprisingly, this reading, while available in general outline since Hazlitt, gained widespread acceptance in Anglo-American criticism during the governments of Thatcher and Reagan—themselves manipulative dramatists who, for this reason and others, may have increased empathy for such an interpretation in politically alienated critics at the inauguration of postcolonialist studies.

Since the rise of a colonialist *Tempest*, a number of voices have challenged the foundations on which such an interpretation rests. Meredith Skura, Frances Dolan, David Kastan, and Jerry Brotton, among others, have offered reasons to be wary of reading the play as a straightforward allegory of European domination of the New World. Skura points out that the play remains a "notoriously slippery" document and contains much that an intensively postcolonialist hermeneutics cannot account for. The word "discourse," Skura demonstrates, has licensed many arguments even as—perhaps because—it fails to account for the variety of ideological positions about the New World available in Jacobean England. These positions varied not only from person to person and text to text but even from year to year, something that a nebulous "colonialist discourse" does not acknowledge.[2] Similarly, Dolan has changed the way we see the drama by arguing for an inherently small *Tempest,* one in which the crime of petty treason steers a counterplot in this "shrunken, enclosed world . . . in which Prospero's household is the commonwealth."[3] By reminding us that Prospero governs a household and that the drama's plot is more domestic than critics have acknowledged, Dolan gives us reason to think of the play in more homely terms. In contrast David Kastan, suggesting that "the Americanization of *The Tempest* may be itself an act of cultural imperialism," reads the play in terms of "European dynastic concerns rather than European colonial activities," placing focus on James's negotiations with the Palatine in the years preceding *The Tempest.*[4] Likewise Jerry Brotton seeks to return a Mediterranean context to *The Tempest,* arguing that English interests in the eastern Mediterranean were as important an influence on Shakespeare's romance as were issues connected with the Americas.[5]

However corrective these voices seek to be, a colonialist *Tempest* still holds sway in many classrooms and critical journals and is the reading this chapter attempts to revise. Some scholars might claim that arguing for a local *Tempest* evades the political—political here meaning the intercultural, if not the transatlantic. As will become clear, however, my interpretation does not evade "the" political but rather argues that much of *The Tempest's* politics are strongly local. We need to consider that elements of this play may represent the very structures and relations that produced it. Inasmuch as the activities of any theater are intensively social in nature, such elements bear examination for what they may tell us about the arrangements of power and the distribution of resources in and among the diverse group of workers who labor to provide dramatic fantasies to their audiences. This situation certainly applies for the workers who made up the acting companies of Shakespeare's time. Only when we think seriously about Shakespeare's lived history of performing and writing, in fact, can we better understand the political energies of *The Tempest.*

The Tempest Question

A "theatrical" *Tempest* is hardly new. Many who write on the topic agree that Prospero is a playwright or director—whether symbolic or real, Machiavellian or benevolent. Fewer, however, have agreed as to the nature and location of the world that this directing figure oversees, leading to what we might call the "*Tempest* question." The *Tempest* question is actually two intertwined questions: Where is the play set? and Who or what is Caliban? Historically, where readers have believed *The Tempest* to be located has influenced what they thought the play was about. Similarly, who or what readers have believed Caliban to represent—whether Native American, Caribbean, African, "missing link," or British wild man—has greatly affected their readings. Each of these decisions—location of the action and the significance of Caliban—bears on the other: a Virginian *Tempest,* for example, asks for one kind of Caliban; a Caribbean Caliban, another kind of *Tempest.* Despite disagreement about the local geography of the play, many of those who have written on *The Tempest* in the last two decades have answered the *Tempest* question in relation to the New World. So strong is this impulse, in fact, that one critic who fixes *The Tempest* in a tradition of utopias purposefully located "nowhere" insists on seeing this as underwriting the play's New World discourse.[6]

Yet *is The Tempest* about the New World? Neither the play nor its near contemporaries say so. This "notoriously slippery" play believes itself to take place in the Mediterranean. The "still-vex'd Bermoothes," where Ariel has traveled to fetch dew, is a place elsewhere (1.2.229). Commenting on this aspect of the play, Frank Kermode suggests that "the fact that Shakespeare is at pains to establish his island in the Old World may be taken to indicate his rejection of the merely topical."[7] Certainly there is nothing "mere" about the topical. As criticism of early modern literature has shown with startling force during the last few decades, the topical is almost always complex in nature. Even if we accept Kermode's definition of the topical, however, we can learn about the situation of *The Tempest* in relation to these topical pamphlets by examining their lack of effect on the play's afterlife. It is significant, surely, that none of the playwrights who commented on, quoted, revised, and otherwise paid homage to *The Tempest* before the closing of the theaters seems to have been any more interested in colonialism than Shakespeare—or, for that matter, showed that he believed Shakespeare in *The Tempest* was talking about the New World. From Jonson's *Bartholomew Fair* (1614), his Folio *Every Man In His Humour* (1616), Tomkis's *Albumazar* (1615), and Fletcher's *Sea Voyage* (1622), to John Kirke's *Seven Champions of Christendom* (1635) and Suckling's *The Goblins* (1638), drama that quoted Shakespeare's romance in the three decades following *The Tempest* saw it as a play about magic and illusion, not about the other end of English exploration.

In fact, decidedly local aspects of *The Tempest* were suggested in a later version of the story—a burlesque, in part, of Davenant's revision. This play locates the story in London. Thomas Duffett's *Mock Tempest; or, The Enchanted Castle* (1674) opens with a tempestuous conflict in a brothel before moving to Bridewell prison, where Prospero, once "Duke of my Lord Mayor's Dog-kennel," has become Keeper. Duffett's burlesque not only insists on the essential homeliness of *The Tempest* but does so by reproducing, with slight variation, lines from that play, examples of which include:

> This Miscreant, so dry he was for sway, betray'd me to *Alonzo,* Duke of Newgate; and in a stormy and dreadful Night open'd my Kenell Gates, and forc'd me thence with thy young Sister, and thy howling self. (Prospero: 1.2)

> More toil—I pri'thee now let me mind thee of thy promise then—where is my Two-penny Custard? (Ariel: 4.1)

The Mock Tempest restages the opening storm of Shakespeare's play as an assault by a Quaker and his friends on a brothel. Duffett's burlesque mocks the enchantment of Davenant's "Enchanted Island" by choosing to see the story's locale as London, its urban characters immersed in the politics of their place and time. Duffett's mockery, his vision of *The Tempest*'s homeliness, was itself close to home, for what he recognized in Shakespeare's story was waiting to be seen. Unlike Duffett's play, though, Shakespeare's drama seems to concern not a brothel or Bridewell prison but rather other structures of early modern London: the playhouses that Shakespeare worked in and for.

"Playhouses" is in the plural here, for in 1608 Shakespeare helped lease the Blackfriars Theater and by 1611 had routinely divided his time between the Blackfriars and the Globe playing spaces. Because *The Tempest* relies on elements of and working histories associated with each theater, it is important to keep both in mind. To begin with the beginning: the opening scene of *The Tempest* appears to incorporate Shakespeare's experiences of the

Blackfriars playhouse, a private theater known for its elite, sometimes pretentious clientele. The confusion of authority and division of labor on the deck of the ship seem to respond to the probable reality of working as an actor on the Blackfriars' stage.

Why should a ship remind us of a playhouse? By 1611 the trope of "theater-as-ship" had become commonplace for dramatists. Jonson would inveigh against this simile in the Prologue to the Folio version of *Every Man In His Humour*. In lines preceding his sneer at the sound effects of "roll'd bullet heard | To say, it *thunders*; [and] *tempestuous* drum [which] | Rumbles, to tell you when the *storm* doth come" (emphases mine) and his equally caustic remark about his audience having "grac'd monsters" (presumably Caliban) (lines 18–20, 30), Jonson speaks disparagingly of plays where the "*Chorus* wafts you o'er the seas." Both *Pericles* (1608) and *Henry V* (1599) feature these shiplike choruses, able to transport audiences overseas and back without wetting their clothing, as Ariel in *The Tempest* makes possible for that ship's passengers. Dekker's eighteen-line Prologue before *The Shoemakers' Holiday* (1599) is perhaps the most characteristic unfolding of a popular trope:

> As wretches in a storm, expecting day,
> With trembling hands and eyes cast up to heaven,
> Make prayers the anchor of their conquered hopes,
> So we, dear Goddess, wonder of all eyes,
> Your meanest vassals, through mistrust and fear
> To sink into the bottom of disgrace
> By our imperfit pastimes, prostrate thus
> On bended knees, our sails of hope do strike,
> Dreading the bitter storms of your dislike.
> Since then, unhappy men, our hap is such
> That to ourselves ourselves no help can bring,
> But needs must perish, if your saint-like ears,
> Locking the temple where all mercy sits,
> Refuse the tribute of our begging tongues:
> Oh grant, bright mirror of true chastity,
> From those life-breathing stars your sun-like eyes,
> One gracious smile: for your celestial breath
> Must send us life, or sentence us to death.[8]

This speech is titled "The Prologue as it was Pronounced Before the Queen's Majesty," and refers to a production at court (on 1 January 1600) rather than at a public or private playhouse. But the metaphor of stage and ship remains apparent in a cluster of words and phrases including "anchor," "sails," "sink into the bottom," "storms," and even, perhaps, a pun in "vassals" (i.e., "vessels"). The Queen's potential disapproval is like a storm, which would sink the ship of their production along with the actors, who resemble sailors manning the ship. A more compressed version of the metaphor that Dekker explores appeared in a play the year before Shakespeare's romance, when the Prologue of Robert Daborne's *A Christian Turned Turk* (1610) held "Our Ship's afloat, we fear nor rocks nor sands, | Knowing we are environ'd with your helping hands" (lines 23–24)—"hands," of course, used for applause as well as for handling ropes and sails. The metaphor is in every way a natural one.

As Dekker, Daborne, and Shakespeare realized, playhouses are like ships in many ways. Both are wooden structures packed with people. Both are sites of labor where work is usually concentrated and frantic. Both rely on intensive cooperation: ships and their sailors' hands; actors and their audiences' hand clapping—and, in a common trope, windy shouts of acclaim. Both can give one the impression of learning "what is happening abroad," as Thomas Platter said of English plays and playhouses in the 1590s, commenting on how the English "do not travel much, but prefer to learn foreign matters and take their pleasure at home."[9] In early modern London, people took boats to playhouses: to the Blackfriars as well as to the Globe. Middleton plays on this mode of travel in *Father Hubburd's Tales* when he says that, after dinner, a gallant "must venture beyond sea, that is, in a choice pair of Nobelman's Oars, to the Bankside."[10] And plays (including *Hamlet*) were sometimes acted on seagoing ships. When Prospero says to the audience in the Epilogue of *The Tempest* that he will be "confin'd" to his "bare island" without "the help of your good hands," and that the "Gentle breath of yours my sails | Must fill, or else my project fails, | Which was to please" (lines 4, 8, 11–13), he thereby conflates the present, empty stage with the "bare island" of *The Tempest* and the playhouse proper with the ship that is to return him to Naples in a metaphor of unusual force.

At The Playhouse

But what was it about the Blackfriars that may have shaped this scene? A hallmark of the private theaters, and of the Blackfriars in particular, was the habit of sitting on stage—gallants perched on stools more to display themselves and their clothing than to gain better view of the play. In the famous sixth chapter of *The Gull's Horn-book* (1609), Thomas Dekker advises "How a gallant should behave himself in a playhouse," suggesting, among other things, that "By spreading your body on the stage and by being a Justice in examining of plays you shall put yourself into such true scenical authority that some poet shall not dare to present his Muse rudely upon your eyes without having first unmasked her, rifled her and discovered all her bare and most mystical parts before you at a tavern, when you most knightly shall for his pains pay for both their suppers."[11] Dekker pictures a gallant's body spread egregiously over the stage, dominating the performance with "true scenical authority." This intrusion upon the players' space and authority did not pass without comment. Many resentful asides about stage sitting survive in plays of the period; playwrights and actors appear to have greatly disliked the practice.[12] As a dramatist subject to this form of criticism, Dekker recognizes that playwrights of the Blackfriars compete with these voyeuristic, stage-sitting gallants for "authority."

Such competition appears to have been an important source of *The Tempest's* opening scene. This scene frames the conflict between the laboring mariners and the Italian aristocrats and courtiers in terms of both "labor" and "authority." "You mar our labor," the Boatswain says to Antonio, "Keep your cabins; you do assist the storm" (1.1.13–14). When Gonzalo interrupts him, this Boatswain responds "if you can command these elements to silence, and work the peace of the present, we will not hand a rope more. Use your authority" (1.1.21–23). The annoyance that actors undoubtedly felt when spectators at the Blackfriars marred their theatrical labor probably underlies a relevant statement of Heminge and Condell in the First Folio (1623). The epistle "To the great Variety of Readers" says that "though you be a Magistrate of wit, and sit on the Stage at *Blackfriars,* or the *Cockpit,* to arraign Plays daily, know, these Plays have had their trial already, and stood out all Appeals; and do now come forth quitted rather by a Decree of Court, than any purchased Letters of commendation." Pitched to censorious stage sitters, this passage is also about them. With its opening storm scene, *The Tempest* is the first Shakespearean work in the First Folio. In the context of the epistle's chastisement, the scene suggests that the conflict between playhouse laborers and unappreciative stage sitters was much on the mind of the King's Men from 1608 forward.

Thus if the scene is about a ship at sea, it may also be about working in a crowded playhouse. The Boatswain expresses his annoyance at the interference of a group of gazers who impede the working men in the performance of their roles. The ship's deck, like a stage circled by gallants, seems crowded. As the Boatswain apostrophizes the gale: "Blow till thou burst thy wind, if room enough" (1.1.7–8). In his insightful response to an earlier version of this argument, Robert Weimann traces the language that "those who are in charge of doing the job of running the ship-stage" use to "answer back" the "abuse from their represented betters":

I pray now keep below (11)

What cares these roarers for the name of king? (16–17)

You are a councilor . . . Use your authority (20–21, 23)

Out of our way, I say (26–27)

As Weimann concludes, "In this opening scene, the thrill of liminality, especially viable at the play's beginning and ending, may well have inspired a playful way of dealing with the nuisance of a notorious privilege."[13]

Significantly, when Alonso gives unhelpful advice to the mariners, he tells them to "*Play* the men" (1.1.10, emphasis added), as though he, like a stage-sitting gallant, is offering the judgment of his "true scenical authority." It is relevant here that, in the same section of *The Gull's Horn-Book*, Dekker imagines such intrusive authority precisely in terms of the theater-as-ship metaphor: "By sitting on the stage you have a signed patent to engross the whole commodity of censure; may lawfully presume to be a girder; and *stand at the helm to steer the passage of scenes.*"[14] Alonso, Gonzalo, and the other passengers are analogous to these stage-sitting gallants who "stand at the helm to steer the passage of scenes." Dekker's gallants are in 1609—two years before *The Tempest*—already described as interfering with the ship-theater of a private playhouse very much like the Blackfriars. We can see in the tension between the laboring mariners (represented by the Boatswain) and the ship's higher-status passengers a translation of the experience that Shakespeare and the King's Men had in the handful of years that they had been playing at the Blackfriars. Dekker sees these gallants as "girder[s]"—that is, sneering wits. On them, the message of *The Tempest*'s opening scene, with its call for self-awareness and for room in which to work, may well have been lost. But to those on stage doing the work of the performance and to those in the audience who, like Dekker and many others, resented these stage sitters, the point may have been unmistakable: plays are hard work and are hindered by nonlaboring, intrusive stage sitters.

The arrogance of these stage sitters—whom the epistle calls "Magistrate[s] of wit," and Dekker "girder[s]"—is likely to have been the underlying source of another sequence in *The Tempest,* the otherwise inexplicable "widow Dido" passage in 2.1. There Gonzalo, the old counselor, a type of character Shakespeare appears to have played, slips and says that Tunis had not been graced with such a queen as Claribel since "widow Dido's time" (2.1.77). The following exchange occurs:

Antonio. Widow? a pox o' that! How came that widow in? Widow Dido!

Sebastian. What if he had said "widower Aeneas" too? Good Lord, how you take it!

Adrian. "Widow Dido," said you? You make me study of that. She was of Carthage, not of Tunis.

Gonzalo. This Tunis, sir, was Carthage.

Adrian. Carthage?

Gonzalo. I assure you, Carthage.

Antonio. His word is more than the miraculous harp.

Sebastian. He hath rais'd the wall, and houses too.

Antonio. What impossible matter will he make easy next?

Sebastian. I think he will carry this island home in his pocket, and give it his son for an apple.

Antonio. And sowing the kernels of it in the sea, bring forth more islands.

This passage is, arguably, one of the strangest in all of Shakespeare's plays. Heather James speaks for a long line of readers when she describes the "annoying jokes" of this sequence as offering a "quirky allusion" both "aggressive and under-motivated." Before admitting (as most readers have) that the passage "refuses to disclose how that widow came in," James usefully observes that this sequence "unleashes a derisive and bawdy revision of the *Aeneid* and a traditionally optimistic reading of Vergil's epic, the island, and the court's prospects for survival."[15] James foregrounds, in this way, *The Tempest*'s larger debts to the *Aeneid* and to a host of issues that subtend Vergil's epic. Other critics have been less willing to try to explain the passage. Most have resigned themselves to admitting that it is a puzzle. Anne Barton, for instance, declared that it "may well have held a meaning for Shakespeare's contemporaries that is lost to us."[16] And, likewise, Frank Kermode suggested that "our frame of reference is badly adjusted, or incomplete, and that an understanding of this passage will modify our image of the whole play."[17]

While James is clearly right to argue that a Vergilian subtext dominates *The Tempest* and that the *Aeneid* provides the raw material—perhaps even the "logic"—of the exchange, both Barton and Kermode seem correct as well in offering that the passage contains a further, coterie implication that may help us better understand the play itself. We might start uncovering that implication by observing that Dido was, of course, a widow. Stephen Orgel has made this point in his edition of *The Tempest* and further comes to the aid of Gonzalo by citing an Elizabethan source that sees Tunis and Carthage as sharing a geographical location.[18] But Orgel's research, in proving Gonzalo somehow "right," inadvertently leaves the passage even less clear than it was before, when Gonzalo's "errors" seemed to be the basis for the mockery. For if Gonzalo is right, why does Shakespeare have Sebastian, Adrian, and Antonio make so much fun of him? I would offer that Gonzalo is both right and wrong, and in a Shakespearean way. That is, what happens in the "widow Dido" exchange is a version of what happened to Shakespeare's works in the marketplaces of print and theater in early modern London. Shakespeare, that is, has cast himself as Gonzalo and contemporary detractors as the mocking aristocrats who question his authority.

Gonzalo remains a figure for jests because the epithet "widow Dido" would have sounded indecorous if not incorrect to many in the play's Jacobean audience. For, *contra* Orgel, Dido was not a widow—if being a widow means being called so by Vergil. Nowhere in the *Aeneid*, for example, does Vergil apply available words for "widow/ed" to Dido—or even to women, for that matter. And nowhere in Ravisius's collection of classical epithets for literary and mythological figures is Dido called a widow. Ravisius's list runs as follows:

> *Dido.* Sidonia, pulcra, dives, elisa, infelix, candida, sidonis, miserabilis, sanguinolenta, misera, profuga, advena, tenera, furiata, tyria, lacrymosa.

Which we could translate as:

> *Dido.* Sidonian, beautiful, rich, Elissa, unlucky, fair, of Sidon, wretched, stained with blood, pitiable, fugitive, a stranger, delicate, frenzied, Tyrian, tearful.[19]

What I am suggesting is that, in offering their intrusive commentary on another's speech, the mockers in the "widow Dido" exchange are so much like Dekker's stage-sitting girders that they beg to be understood as Shakespeare's *version* of what it meant to play to a Blackfriars audience. The mockers talk about Gonzalo's utterance as though he were not a part of their group, as though he were an actor standing a few yards away and speaking the lines of a playwright whose authority they question. Dido a widow? Carthage Tunis? The "impossible matter" Gonzalo makes easy is the illusion of the theater—moving place and object, transporting and reproducing, in the manner of a playwright, fantasies like the present island.[20]

Yet we might see Gonzalo standing in for a particular playwright—Shakespeare himself—for these impossible matters are uncannily like the errors that at least one contemporary, Jonson, would identify as quintessentially Shakespearean. To Jonson, Shakespeare was often poetically incorrect. Two statements by Jonson support this view: the first from his *Conversations* with Drummond of Hawthorndon, the second in his *Timber, or Discoveries.* I quote both here in the order mentioned:

> Shakespeare in a play brought in a number of men saying they had suffered Shipwrack in Bohemia, where there is no Sea near by some 100 Miles. (vol. 1: lines 208–10).

> Many times he fell into those things, could not escape laughter: As when he said in the person of *Caesar,* one speaking to him; *Caesar, thou dost me wrong.* He replied: *Caesar did never wrong, but with just cause*: and such like; which were ridiculous. (vol. 8: lines 661–66)

In these lines we hear Jonson the girder snickering at Shakespeare's infelic-ities. Many scholars have pointed out that nowhere in the *Julius Caesar* (1599) we have does Caesar say what Jonson alleges; this discrepancy may be an instance, it is further argued, of Jonson's critique affecting the ver-sion of the play ultimately printed. In any case, what Jonson says here about "those things" that for him characterized Shakespeare—the impossi-ble matters his rival insisted on raising, the violations of decorum and fact—are played out in Gonzalo's calling Dido a widow and Tunis Car-thage. In Jonson's view, such were typical of Shakespeare: "He flowed with that facility," Jonson wrote in the *Discoveries,* "that sometime it was nec-essary he should be stopped: *Sufflaminandus erat*; as *Augustus* said of *Hat-erius*. His wit was in his own power; would the rule of it had been so too" (vol. 8: lines 658–61). Like the Shakespeare of Jonson's *Discoveries,* whose wit flows so freely that others wish it might be stopped, Gonzalo's mouth and imagination flow from "widow" to the awkward rhyme of "Dido," from an error of place to geographical impossibility.

Like Jonson, the critics within *The Tempest* step forward to mock this flow. It is as though Shakespeare wrote both himself (as Gonzalo) and Jon-son (as the kind of competitor we see in Sebastian, Antonio, and Adrian) into *The Tempest.* To be sure, actors and poets within the worlds of Shake-speare's plays are invariably at the mercy of their audiences and patrons. But where the nobles in *A Midsummer Night's Dream* (1596) seem physi-cally distanced from the errors and actors they censure—though within earshot, they appear part of a great hall or the select boxes behind a public theater's stage—*The Tempest* imagines these Jonsonian girders as within arms' reach of the actor whose impossibilities they criticize. Within, that is, a distance equivalent to that between stage sitters and actors. The space as well as the aesthetic politics of the scene speak strongly of the Blackfriars.

Yet however much *The Tempest* draws from the Blackfriars, Shake-speare's career at the Globe must also have been a resource for the play. To examine Shakespeare's use of this resource, we might turn here to the char-acter of Prospero, who remains in every way the culmination of the asser-tive, controlling figures examined in the previous chapter. As playwright figure, Prospero is widely held a double of Shakespeare—his version of the abilities and responsibilities of the dramatist written into and writing a dramatic plot. If Prospero stands in at times for Shakespeare, we need to remember that Shakespeare's associate, Richard Burbage—leading actor of the King's Men, and, arguably, of the early modern theatrical scene in London itself—is most likely to have played Prospero, just as he is likely to have played Vincentio, Macbeth, Lear, Hal, Othello, Hamlet, and Richard III. The controlling impulse and ability that Shakespeare lends Prospero, then, may have much to say about Burbage's history as a senior member and shareholder of their acting company. As Charles Wallace first pointed out, Burbage's role in *The Tempest* was doubtless shaped by a directing role in the city pageant for Prince Henry on May 1, 1610, where Burbage played "Amphion, the Father of Harmony or Music," a figure described as "a grave and judicious prophet-like personage, attired in his apt habits, every way answerable to his state and profession."[21] Burbage's abilities as a leading actor dovetailed with Shakespeare's image of a playwright figure leading characters through plays—from Richard III and Thomas More through Hamlet and Vincentio, a favorite Shakespeare type.[22]

Miranda and Ariel

Prospero the playwright casts Miranda as an ideal and idealized audience in the second scene of the play, which is a scene of exposition. Faced with narrating the complicated background of the plot, Shakespeare breaks up Prospero's exposition into units of less than twenty lines—in contrast, for instance, with the opening of his early comedy with "unity of time," *The Comedy of Errors* (1592), where Egeon's rambling, sixty-five-line exposition tends to bore audiences now. *The Tempest*'s exposition is remarkably skillful. The difference between narration in *The Comedy of Errors* and in *The Tempest* might be ascribed in part to Shakespeare's increased sophistication as a playwright. But there are other differences as well. Prospero's relation to Miranda during this famous exposition also works against a Jacobean trend toward the spectacular in drama—evidenced, for example, in the Masque of Ceres that Prospero arranges.[23]

For obvious reasons, we associate Miranda with the visual—she is both gazer ("O brave new world | That has such people in't!" [5.1.183–84]) and object of gazes ("Admir'd Miranda, | Indeed the top of admiration!" [3.1.37–38]). Her relation to Prospero-as-director, grounded both in the etymology of her name (from Latin *mīranda,* "wonderful") and in an inequality of knowledge and control, is that of spectacle to spectator. That is, in *The Tempest* she represents the seen, seers, and seeing itself. These positions were shaped by the play's historical moment. During Shakespeare's lifetime, the early modern theater in England increasingly relied on the visual, as opposed to the aural. The linguistically copious writing habits of the late 1580s and 1590s (we might remember Middleton's "huge bombasted plays, quilted with mighty words") gradually gave way after 1600 to a spectacular, masque-influenced practice—what Samuel Daniel called "Punctillos of Dreams and shows."[24] Shakespeare's descriptions of playgoers changed accordingly. "From 1600 onwards," Andrew Gurr notes, "Shakespeare abandoned the idea of an auditory in favour of spectators."[25] Such may not have been a welcome change, however, for it is Prospero's task in the play's second scene to get his spectators—represented on stage by Miranda—to follow a story with their ears, to become, that is, an *audience* again. That this effect is more difficult to achieve here than in *The Comedy of Errors* is evident in Prospero's eight, apparently impatient interjections: "I pray thee mark me" (67); "Dost thou attend me?" (78); "Thou attend'st not!" (87); "I pray thee mark me" (88); "Dost thou hear?" (106); "Mark his condition" (117); "Hear a little further" (135); "Sit still, and hear" (170). Clearly this impatience corresponds with Prospero's disagreeable behavior in the first half of this play, and it also seems to respond to the sleepiness that the island seems to induce in all but Prospero, Ariel, and Caliban—the primary "actors" of the island. Yet it also seems to embody the impatience of a playwright describing spectators grown restless over a story he is intent on telling. As such, it may speak to certain historical changes in the early modern theater. Perhaps what we have in the twenty years between *The Comedy of Errors* and *The Tempest*, then, is less Shakespeare learning to vary narration than it is Shakespeare's audiences losing the patience to listen.

Where Miranda's relation to Prospero is, in part, that of an idealized spectatorship to what is perhaps an equally idealized playwright, Ariel relates to Prospero as boy actor to adult dramatist or stage director. Like Puck and Oberon, Ariel and Prospero collaborate in directing. Prospero's actors, we are told, are inept, misguided, and lazy. Prospero calls Ariel, in contrast, "my industrious servant" (4.1.33). When Ariel successfully tantalizes Alonso, Sebastian, and the other hungry newcomers with the magical banquet during 3.3, Prospero sounds exactly like an older actor, one who has spent a life in the theater, praising a boy actor: "Bravely the figure of this harpy hast thou | Perform'd, my Ariel; a grace it had, devouring. | Of my instruction hast thou nothing bated | In what thou hadst to say; so with good life, | And observation strange, my meaner ministers | Their several kinds have done" (3.3.83–88). Throughout *The Tempest,* the relations between Prospero and his industrious servant are deeply analogous to the relations among mature players and boy actors in the early modern playhouse. We often find these playhouse relations embedded in plays: for example, in Lord and Bartholomew, his Page, in *The Taming of the Shrew* (1592); the aristocrats and Moth in *Love's Labour's Lost* (1595); Oberon and Puck in *A Midsummer Night's Dream;* and Clerimont and the Boy in *Epicoene* (1609). It matters to Prospero that his spirit is a particularly good actor. Ariel's acting talents, in fact, are consonant with—even a sign of—his closeness to the human in *The Tempest.* Indeed, when Ariel teaches Prospero charity ("Mine would, sir, were I human," he tells his master [5.1.20]), the difference between them is simultaneously suggested and questioned.

Caliban and Kemp

In contrast to Ariel, Caliban is both a bad actor and—at least to Prospero—decidedly nonhuman. These attributes appear connected in the theatrical logic of the play. Could Shakespeare really have seen the difference between good actors and bad actors as equivalent to the difference between the human and the nonhuman? We can see that such a belief was at the very least available to him in Hamlet's injunctions to the Players, often thought to represent Shakespeare's opinions on the contemporary acting scene:

Hamlet. O, there be players that I have seen play—and heard others praise, and neither having th' accent of Christians nor the gait of Christian, pagan, nor man, have so strutted and bellow'd that I have thought some of Nature's journeymen had made men, and not made them well, they imitated humanity so abominably.

I. Player. I hope we have reform'd that indifferently with us, sir.

Hamlet. O, reform it altogether. And let those that play your clowns speak no more than is set down for them, for there be of them that will themselves laugh to set on some quantity of barren spectators to laugh too, though in the mean time some necessary question of the play be then to be consider'd. That's villainous, and shows a most pitiful ambition in the fool that uses it.

(3.2.28–45)

What Harold Jenkins calls Hamlet's *excursus on acting* appears to change directions with the First Player's interjection, when the genre under discussion seems to switch from tragedy to comedy.[26] Yet we can see that Hamlet's critique is continuous. Hamlet begins by saying that some players are such bad actors that, though they have drawn praise from others, they seem nonhuman when on stage. The descending hierarchy of these actors' "gait" runs from Christian to pagan, to "man" and then to not "man." The punning phrase "they imitated humanity so abominably" relies, of course, on an Elizabethan understanding of "abominable" as deriving from Latin *ab homine*, "away from man(kind)." The word is always spelled with the medial "h" in Shakespeare. (The quotation above modernizes this spelling.) That Shakespeare was aware of these valences—in the air whenever the word was used—is perhaps shown in Holofernes' pedantic insistence on the aspirate form in *Love's Labour's Lost*: "This is abhominable—which he would call 'abbominable'" (5.1.24–25). The allegation that certain actors possess a gait that is neither Christian nor pagan nor human spirals down to the word *abhominable*: to act badly is to be less than, and other than, human.

Hamlet only appears to change topics when he inveighs against the clown who speaks more than has been written in the playbook. For when he uses the adjective "villainous" (line 44), calling upon a word that could imply moral or ethical corruption, and (from "vilein") lower class and rank as well, he continues to associate bad acting with the nonhuman. Thus Caliban says that Prospero can turn the subplot's conspirators "to apes | With foreheads villainous low" (4.1.248–49). Not surprisingly, perhaps, Shakespeare several times uses "abominable" with "villain." In *King Lear* (1605), for instance, we hear Gloucester call Edgar a "brutish villain!" then "worse than brutish!" until finally settling on "Abominable villain!" (1.2.76–78)—indicating that "abominable" is "worse than brutish." Playacting in *1 Henry IV* (1597), Hal calls Falstaff "That villainous abominable misleader of youth" (2.4.462–63). Because Hamlet's remarks on the nonhuman nature of certain gaits jibe ethically with his critique of the villainous behavior of the bad clown, these apparently separate statements work to form a single diatribe. Turning from tragedy to comedy, this diatribe is based on the conviction that bad actors—whether egotistical improvisers or bellowing stompers—are something less than human.

The improvising clowns that Hamlet decries were undoubtedly suggested by Will Kemp, famous comedian of the Lord Chamberlain's Men. In *An Almond for a Parrat* (1590), Nashe calls Kemp "That Most Comical and Conceited Cavalier *Monsieur du Kemp, Jestmonger and* Vice-gerent general to the Ghost of Dick Tarlton."[27] As this figurative kinship with Tarlton might suggest, Kemp was known for, among other things, the folk obscenity of his nonrepresentational jigs and merriments and for breaking the illusional boundaries of the plays in which he acted by directly addressing audiences with ad hoc banter.[28] His reputation for ignoring the authoritative *locus* areas of the dramatic action to engage the audience from the imaginary *platea,* the no-man's-land between spectacle and spectator, lived long after him.[29]

In *The Antipodes* (1638), for instance, Richard Brome has characters recall Kemp and Tarlton in an argument about theatrical decorum:

Letoy. But you, sir, are incorrigible, and
    Take license to yourself to add unto
    Your parts your own free fancy, and sometimes
    To alter or diminish what the writer
    With care and skill compos'd; and when you are
    To speak to your coactors in the scene,
    You hold interlocutions with the audients—

Byplay. That is a way, my lord, has bin allow'd
    On elder stages to move mirth and laughter.

Letoy. Yes, in the days of Tarlton and Kemp,
    Before the stage was purg'd from barbarism,
    And brought to the perfection it now shines with.
    Then fools and jesters spent their wits, because
    The poets were wise enough to save their own
    For profitabler uses.
       (2.2.39–53)[30]

To Letoy, Byplay's "elder stages" immediately suggests Tarlton and Kemp, actors he associates with misspent wits and such theatrical barbarism as holding "interlocutions with the audients." Thus Hamlet's clowns who "will themselves laugh to set on some quantity of barren spectators to laugh too, though in the mean time some necessary question of the play be then to be consider'd." Kemp left the Chamberlain's Men under mysterious circumstances sometime in 1599, after becoming one of the seven original shareholders in the new Globe playhouse. Even if he had not done so, the preceding passage from *Hamlet* (1601) would suffice to show a tension between Shakespeare and Kemp, one perhaps partly responsible for Kemp's departure from the company.

This tension between what Kemp represented in the economy of work in the Globe playhouse and what Shakespeare imagined as an ideal seems to surface in *The Tempest* in the relation between Prospero and Caliban. Shakespeare invokes the human/nonhuman distinction in his representation of the differences between these characters. In an infamous phrase, Prospero calls Caliban "this thing of darkness" (5.1.275). Elsewhere he uses the animalistic to describe Caliban in recounting for Ariel how uninhabited the island was before they came: "Then was this island | (Save for the son that she did litter here, | A freckled whelp, hag-born) not honor'd with | A human shape" (1.2.281–84). Jonson would be equally blunt, speaking of "a *Servant-monster*" just before slighting "*Tales, Tempests,* and such like *Drolleries*" in the Induction to *Bartholomew Fair* (lines 127, 130). Like Hamlet the playwright, who contrives to interpolate "a speech of some dozen lines, or sixteen lines" as part of his rewriting of *Hamlet,* Prospero consciously "directs" the island world of *The Tempest.* He owns the "trumpery" and "glistering apparel," steers the actions of Ariel, his boy actor, cues the weather effects that Jonson would sneer at, and controls the shape and pace of the plot generally.[31] The word Shakespeare uses here is "project," one that, as we have seen, typically referred to plots and intrigues within plays: one might note Ariel's "My master . . . sends me forth | (For else his project dies) to keep them living" (2.1.297–99), his description of the subplot's conspirators "always bending | Towards their project" (4.1.174–75), and the Epilogue's "my project . . . was to please" (lines 12–13). Most important to Caliban's improvised project, however, is Prospero's "book."

Prospero is defined by books, speaking early of how Gonzalo, "Knowing I lov'd my books," had stored several prized volumes in his boat (1.2.166–68). Caliban is in every way outside Prospero's book, and books in general, from the parody of kissing the Bible/bottle at 2.2.130–57 to his repeated injunctions to Stephano and Trinculo to seize and destroy Prospero's books: "There thou mayst brain him, | Having first seiz'd his books . . . Remember | First to possess his books; for without them | He's but a sot, as I am; nor hath not | One spirit to command: they all do hate him | As rootedly as I. Burn but his books" (3.2.88–95). Caliban's animosity to Prospero's books and language contrasts with Prospero's reliance on them. Yet where Caliban resents Prospero's *books,* Prospero speaks of "book" in the singular. "I'll to my book," he says; later, "I'll drown my book" (3.1.94, 5.1.57). It is as though Caliban, like an actor prone to interpolation, is thinking of a cache of playbooks—a collection of oppressive (and flammable) works owned by an acting company and stored in their "house." In contrast, Prospero, like an actor/writer/director/producer focused on the production at hand, seems to refer to the actual prompt book of the current performance. In making Caliban resent books and having him speak of spirits who hate working for Prospero, Shakespeare may well have been describing the local relations of actors at the playhouses with which he was associated and his theatrical experience over the past several decades.

From at least 1599, when Kemp left the Chamberlain's Men, Shakespeare and Burbage would have been in a position over the junior and part-time actors at the Globe and Blackfriars playhouses similar to that of Prospero over the theatrical "spirits" and others on "his" island. Even as Kemp apparently stepped outside the scripts of Shakespeare's plays, Caliban has ideas and desires of his own that run contrary to the plot Prospero writes. In this aspect, Caliban differs from Ariel, the "industrious servant" who follows the orders Prospero gives. To Prospero's "Thou shalt be as free | As mountain winds; but then exactly do | All points of my command," Ariel replies: "To th' syllable" (1.2.499–501). Besides his machinations within the play to murder Prospero and burn his books, Caliban's improvised plots include the attempted rape of Miranda before the action of *The Tempest* begins. Kemp's notorious obscenity, his lewd jigs and songs, may have contributed to this narrative. If Prospero relates to Miranda in the way that a playwright and leading actor imagined themselves relating to their spectators, so may have Kemp's theatrical praxis, his lewdness, and his willingness to violate theatrical decorum functioned as an underlying source of the narrated rape in *The Tempest.* Called "An abominable monster!" by Trinculo (2.2.158–59), Caliban, by trying to take the plot his way, embodies the abominable and villainous acting that Hamlet complained of shortly after Kemp left Shakespeare's company.

Caliban is linked to Kemp through Kemp's physical habits as well. Caliban's joy upon conspiring with the bad actors Stephano and Trinculo, for example, is capped with a song—"Sings drunkenly" is the stage direction:

> Farewell, master; farewell, farewell!
>
> . . . .
>
> No more dams I'll make for fish,
> Nor fetch in firing
> At requiring,
> Nor scrape trenchering, nor wash dish.
> 'Ban, 'Ban, Ca-Caliban
> Has a new master, get a new man.
> Freedom, high-day! high-day, freedom! freedom, high-day,
> freedom!
>
>   (2.2.178–87)

"O brave monster! lead the way," Stephano rejoins, and Caliban's song is surely a song and dance, a jig with which he leads Stephano and Trinculo offstage. The "high-day!" that closes his song is almost never glossed by editors but is crucial to understanding what the passage is about. "High-day" is a variant of a folksy exclamation, which appears variously as *hey day, hey-day, heyda, hayday, hay day, hoighdagh, hoy day, hoyda, hoida, hay da, ha day, heigh-day*. Added to this complex was *hey-day guise* (sometimes *hay-de-gay*), a rural folk dance for which, Nares suggests, the "hay" (a synonym for jig) "was only an abbreviation."[32] That such were interchangeable to Shakespeare can be seen, perhaps, in the use of "hoy-day" in both *Richard III* (1592, 4.4.459) and *Timon* (1607, 1.2.131) and "hey-day" in *Troilus* (1602, 5.1.66). Defined by the OED as "An exclamation denoting frolicsomeness, gaiety, surprise, wonder, etc.," the "hey-day"/"high-day" complex was often used in jigs and morris dances.

Will Kemp, of course, was famous for his jigs; in fact, he danced a celebrated, marathon morris from London to Norwich the year he left the Chamberlain's Men. When he wrote his account of this stunt in *Kemp's Nine Days' Wonder* (1600), he punned on the Globe in mentioning that some have alleged he had "danced myself out of the world." In this pamphlet Kemp calls himself "High Headborough of heighs," dancing his "hey de gaies" to Ilford, and interjects both a "hey" and a "*hey de gay!*" into his songs.[33] It is impossible, of course, to establish that Shakespeare was "quoting" Kemp when he gave Caliban the "high-day"s of this sequence. It *is* clear, however, that the genre of lusty self-assertion was an important part of Kemp's character. And this quality seems precisely what Shakespeare sought to make suspect in lending Caliban the "high-day"s of his song.

Despite the celebratory picture of folk culture we get in the work of such critics as C. L. Barber and François Laroque, Shakespeare displays some suspicion toward the traditionalistic *homo gloriosus* throughout his plays.[34] By *homo gloriosus*, I mean the hearty, loud, and aggressively social man we encounter swearing oaths and rubbing elbows in the plays: the Host of the Garter in *The Merry Wives of Windsor* (1597), Bottom the Weaver in *A Midsummer Night's Dream,* Falstaff himself. Certainly there are things to like about all of Shakespeare's clown figures. Yet if one looks closely at Bottom—almost certainly a portrait of Kemp—and Peter in *Romeo and Juliet* (1596)—where textual evidence (in Q1 and Q2, respectively) suggests that Kemp acted the part—it is difficult not to recognize an uneasiness regarding Kemp's style of humor.[35] However much he enjoyed Falstaff (perhaps also played by Kemp), Shakespeare ultimately endorses the more calculating Hal. The sentiments behind this choice ran deep in Shakespeare. Empson was surely right, in his reading of the word "honest" in *Othello* (1604), to suggest that "what Shakespeare hated in the word . . . was a peculiar use, at once hearty and individualist," and that "honest" eventually "came to have in it a covert assertion that the man who accepts the natural desires, who does not live by principle, will be fit for such warm uses of *honest* as imply 'generous' and 'faithful to friends', and to believe this is to disbelieve the Fall of Man."[36] Significantly, the other characters in Shakespeare who use "hey-day" and "hoy-day" are Thersites, Apemantus, and Richard III. This group of characters strongly suggests that Shakespeare may well have had the same impatience with its untrustworthy folkishness that he had for words like "honest" in *Othello.*

Giving Caliban a song that ends with "high-day, freedom!" suggests carnival and the unrestrained. This reference may also have included energies associated with the lower orders and may not be too distant from the specter of rioting apprentices in early modern London—apprentices who routinely vandalized theaters during moments of drunken holiday (compare "freedom").[37] With his implied hearty individualism, Caliban displays an aggressive and questionable ethos that may have called upon these social formations. In any case, Kemp embraced this ethos and made it his public persona. We can see it as something akin to the expression of a folk id. Thus in Caliban, I believe, Shakespeare quotes less the New World, which he never saw, than he does Will Kemp, of whom he appears to have seen too much.

Topicality

Why, we may ask, should this portrait appear in *The Tempest* and not earlier? Some current notions of the "topical" would lead us to believe that Kemp would have been positively untopical by the time Shakespeare wrote *The Tempest*. Likewise, the New Historicism's penchant for the synchronic would emphasize the years immediately preceding and following the first performance of *The Tempest*. Why reach so "far," then, in an attempt to understand this play? There are perhaps three relevant answers to such a question.

First, it seems clear that current ideas of the "topical" differ greatly from early modern understandings of time and notable events. Our notions of topicality have been unduly influenced by the rapid rate of social change today and by our access to electronic oceans of information; correspondingly, our sense of what is "in" and "out" alters at a feverish pace. Most Elizabethans, in contrast, thought about time in relation to the life and rule of their monarch. Thus while we often think an event or personality hopelessly "dated" after being out of the spotlight for as little as two years, early modern persons had a more supple imagination regarding time. We can see this endurance of memory, to give one example, in relation to the satirical play *Pedantius,* originally written around 1581. This dramatic lampoon sends up Gabriel Harvey, who had taught at Cambridge, where the play was originally performed. But *Pedantius* remained in manuscript for a full fifty years, until after the death of Harvey, when it was immediately published. It is hard to imagine such being a coincidence, although the alternative—the idea that this play would be thought noteworthy so long after Harvey had retired from public view—seems just as startling. To *Pedantius* we might join the long-distance topicality of *Twelfth Night*

(1601); as Eric Mallin has argued, *Twelfth Night* appears to incorporate a constellation of issues and relations involved in the proposed Anjou match of the 1570s as well as the social and doctrinal conflicts of that decade and those following.[38]

Where New Historicism has accustomed us to thinking about topicality and the political in terms of conjuncture, of the temporally adjacent, Shakespeare's definition of the topical appears to have been much more elastic. The second answer one might give to the question of apparent anachronism, then, involves Shakespeare's elastic sense of time. The "birth" of Elizabeth in *Henry VIII* (1613), a decade after her death, stands as a metaphor of how Shakespeare's personal references most often come at a safe distance. For whatever reason, he waited before mocking his dead contemporaries. Shakespeare waited six years to deal with Marlowe's memory through an unfortunate joke in *As You Like It* (1599, 3.3.12–15), for instance, and with Burghley as Polonius in *Hamlet,* he waited barely three. We are not certain when Kemp died. In any case, such was his impression on Shakespeare that he appears to have remained present to the playwright's mind when he wrote *The Tempest,* "long" after Kemp had left the company.

A third answer to this question might return to *Hamlet*—along with *The Tempest,* the play in which Shakespeare appears to have thought most seriously about playing. For it is in this play, which focuses so often on theatricality, that Hamlet gives us another opinion about a comedian. When the First Gravedigger identifies a skull as "Yorick's skull, the King's jester," Hamlet remembers his jests with a mingled fondness: "Alas, poor Yorick! I knew him, Horatio, a fellow of infinite jest, of most excellent fancy. He hath bore me on his back a thousand times, and now how abhorr'd in my imagination it is! My gorge rises at it. Here hung those lips that I have kiss'd I know not how oft. Where be your gibes now, your gambols, your songs, your flashes of merriment, that were wont to set the table on a roar?" (5.1.181–91) Earlier Hamlet has complained about improvisation by a company's clowns; here he describes a courtly fool licensed to sing, dance, and improvise at will: one might note both "flashes of merriment" in the above quotation and the First Gravedigger's complaint that Yorick "pour'd a flagon of Rhenish on my head once" (5.1.180). One of the differences between a stage clown and a court fool is that the latter is not responsible to other performers, whereas a stage clown, in Hamlet's view, remains responsible both to a script and to his fellow players. And while it is not necessary to see Yorick as representing the famous comedian Richard Tarlton, who had died in 1588, Hamlet's thoughtful recollection of Yorick so many years after that fool's fictional death offers us a version of what Shakespeare may have done in *The Tempest*. Where Hamlet understands the passage of time through the body of a comedian, Shakespeare's late romance seems to attempt to understand a comedian through, and after, the passage of time.

Even more than *Hamlet*, perhaps, *The Tempest* is a play about Shakespeare's life in the theater. From individual actors to specific stages and rival playwrights, London's local scene appears to have shaped *The Tempest* in important ways. The playhouse relations uncovered here ask us to reconsider a critical trend that has made Shakespeare, variously, the anthropologist, chronicler, critic, jingoist, prophet, and poet of colonialism. Granted, *The Tempest* is interested—even invested—in the relations of power associated with what we have come to call colonialism. Although this chapter has responded to *The Tempest* question with a local answer, we have learned too much from colonialist readings of the play and from histories of colonialism to deny that the play at times quotes issues and social formations associated with the New World. But *The Tempest* also—and, I believe, to a greater degree—concerns itself with a more homely topic: the theatrical experiences of Shakespeare and his company. Much of its content seems to be Shakespeare's lived history of work in the Globe and Blackfriars playhouses. We need to take into account how this history affected the drama in order to understand it adequately.

The tension between Prospero and Caliban, I have argued, embodies the tension between Shakespeare (and perhaps Burbage) and Will Kemp. It is perhaps not surprising to find Shakespeare suspicious of the uncontrolled, traditionalistic energy of Will Kemp and the potentially anarchic aspects of the folk structures Kemp represented. Shakespeare resembled the type of the calculating, legal-rational individual in early modern England: a man who made considerable money from using and inventing words, from lending money, speculating in real estate, and engaging in entrepreneurial activities in the early modern playhouse.[39] To Shakespeare, as to Prospero, dramatic projects are serious work. However much he endorsed the vital, Shakespeare was, in matters of business, puritanically thrifty. As E. A. J. Honigmann puts it, to his contemporaries Shakespeare was not only "ungentle" but "sharp and businesslike" as well.[40] Thus *The Tempest* reverberates with Prospero's endorsements of obedience, discipline, and patience. Of waiting to have one's toil and suffering rewarded. Of doing things, literally, by the book. *The Tempest* is a play about Art, but it is also about the work that Art requires. As such, it was perhaps the right play with which to open the First Folio. For if this 1623 magnum opus of Renaissance England is a collection of Shakespeare's theatrical labors, *The Tempest* is among the deepest of his meditations on laboring in the theater and the latest of his serious thoughts about the business of playing. As Shakespeare's double, Prospero haunts the island world like a playhouse director. If *The Tempest* allegorizes Shakespeare's life and work in the theater, then Prospero is the phantom of his opera.

CHAPTER 5

Quotation and Madwomen's Language

The previous three chapters have examined figures who have an almost dictatorial relation to the world: Marlowe's seductive Shepherd; the Shakespearean controlling characters; Prospero's theatrical governance. All of these figures are assertive and controlling in some way, and the chapters that focused on them have attempted to foreground the politics of their assertiveness. The theater is an important part of these figures' assertiveness as well. We have seen how in *The Tempest* (1611) and other plays by Shakespeare such characters are strongly related to the bridge between theater and world. Whether using theatrical forms of behavior to manipulate action in their playworlds or foregrounding the theatrical nature of everyday life, these characters help us understand the reflexive quality of plays during this time—that is, how plays themselves came to represent the theater and the relation of playhouses to the world. But while characters like Prospero raise metatheatrical issues in an unmistakable manner, they are far from the only ones who do so.

Mad characters, for instance, offer an instructive metaphor for the quoting practices of early modern drama. Critics have always regarded the speech of these characters as important; such is the theatrical power of madness, perhaps, that it is difficult to ignore them. Because this mad speech can seem frustratingly random, an apparently loose gathering of materials, however, critics have typically been content to discuss the relevance of individual fragments of such speech: what it means, for instance, for Ophelia to make a certain reference or for a character in Lear to borrow from a particular pamphlet.

An exception to this tendency comes with a recent essay on madness and gender in Shakespeare's tragedies by Carol Thomas Neely. Neely compares Lear with Ophelia and observes that "The construction of Lear's mad discourse, like that of Ophelia's, involves fragmentation, formula, depersonalization, the intersection of communal voices, and secularized ritual. Like Ophelia, he uses tags of social formulas incongruously."[1] Neely calls this process *quotation*:

> Shakespeare's language of madness is characterized by fragmentation, obsession, and repetition, and most importantly by what I will call "quotation," which might instead be called "bracketing" or "italicization." The mad are "beside themselves"; their discourse is not their own. But the voices that speak through them are not (even in the case of Edgar's parody of possession) supernatural voices but human ones—cultural ones perhaps. The prose that is used for this mad speech (although it includes embedded songs and rhymes) implies disorderly shape, associates madness with popular tradition, and contributes to its colloquial, "quoted" character. These quoted voices, however, have connections with (or can be interpreted to connect with) the mad characters' pre-mad gendered identity and history, their social context and psychological stresses— as well as with larger themes of the plays and of the culture. The alienated speech allows psychological plausibility, thematic resonance, cultural constructions, and social critique.[2]

Neely observes that such quoted voices connect with "larger themes of the plays and of the culture." But however pertinent the quotation that Neely describes, the precise nature of the connections it forges is left unclear: "cultural ones perhaps." We could ask, therefore, what this culturally evocative madness means and how it does so.

Another question we could ask in relation to this observation involves the apparent exceptionality of quotation in Neely's description. As the previous chapters of this book have argued, quotation was the norm, rather than the exception, in early modern plays. The difference in the speech of mad characters resides in the seams visible among the various quotations. Neely describes this difference in referring to such quotation as "italicization." To see and hear the speech of mad characters is to feel a purposeful disjunction, often one that asks us to relate its various quotations in new ways. Both Hamlet's and Ophelia's mad speech, for instance, obviously relate to larger themes in *Hamlet* (1601), though it can take concerted thought to understand those relations. In comparison with the speech of such characters, however, most of the material in early modern plays feels relatively *seamless*: quotations that do not feel like quotations. Thus as the introduction to this book pointed out, reading *Hamlet* is reading a play full of quotations. We "see" these quotations primarily in the play's mad speech, but, upon closer inspection, the rest of the play might be seen as equally mad. If the speech of mad characters can be said to foreground the way in which early modern plays were composed, it only does so because it presents this mode of composition in an exaggerated, even parodic way. Thus where Prospero has often been seen as Shakespeare's portrait of the artist, this chapter offers another candidate—one much less powerful in appearance but whose quotations perhaps more accurately capture the working realities of an early modern playwright.

The Individual and the Social

The Jailer's Daughter in Shakespeare and Fletcher's *The Two Noble Kinsmen* (1613) remains a pivotal figure in Jacobean drama. More than any other character in Shakespeare's late plays, she embodies changes in both dramatic representation and the larger culture of early modern England. As if testifying to the social and dramatic difference of this important character (not, it should be pointed out, in the source materials from which the play's more familiar plot derived), Shakespeare and Fletcher work to isolate her from the rest of the drama's action and characters.[3] Grounded in a pathetic madness, she stands outside the play's self-definition of the social and is not recognized as politically significant by any character in the drama. We will see here, however, that it is precisely the mad language of this otherwise disempowered character that provides the richest picture of the arrangements of power in the play, of the social relations in the early modern playhouse, and of the transformations in the Jacobean culture that produced *The Two Noble Kinsmen*.

The play came into existence as a collaboration of two dramatists and two dramatic traditions at a transitional moment in the early modern theater. On the one hand, the rise of melodrama and the courtly were augmenting the power of female roles; on the other, folk strains in the drama were dwindling as urban and courtly plots and characters replaced the rural. Correspondingly, it became increasingly difficult to imagine community, folk and otherwise; indeed, the attempt to do so in *The Two Noble Kinsmen* is awkward and tense. The play both coincides with and, through the Jailer's Daughter, expresses truths about this twofold transition in the history of London's stage. As we will see, her voice is not only culturally thick but historically telling, for she is uniquely situated between a Shakespearean tradition that emphasized folk culture and Fletcher's commitment to strong female characters and dramatically striking episodes, irrespective of social class. If an immediate inheritance from the drama of the late Elizabethan era was a complex literary model of subjectivity and individuality, only with the Jailer's Daughter would this model be translated—and, significantly, translated downward—to a member of those lower orders without which the definition of social community had once been impossible.

Because she is isolated from the play's community, the Jailer's Daughter acts more as a choric figure than as an agent in its plot. Yet she remains a chorus with a difference. As we will see, her "private" language of madness works in several directions at once. First, in the through-line of its style, it establishes her as an individualized character. In contrast to a recent focus on the disintegration and radical self-estrangement of character in Shakespeare, this interpretation stresses the deeply continuous character of the Jailer's Daughter as it unfolds in her speaking style.[4] To read and hear the play is to perceive her as a character because of the way she speaks. Even as it establishes an individuality of character, her speech insistently directs one's attention to the worlds inside and outside the playhouse. The private, in her case, is oddly public, for the rich sociolinguistic textures of her speech lend it a significance inversely proportional to her social status.[5] If she is the least powerful figure in the play—power here understood to mean both self-determination and the ability to affect one's environment—the Jailer's Daughter nonetheless retains a powerful significance *for* the play; what she says and how she says it are crucial, in fact, to our understanding of the place of *The Two Noble Kinsmen* in its time and culture.

The dramatic idiolect of the Jailer's Daughter is remarkable because it appears to transcend the particularities of authorial style—that is, to retain a stylistic integrity despite the two playwrights' own compositional idiolects. She appears in nine scenes in *The Two Noble Kinsmen,* two of which were probably written primarily by Shakespeare (2.1 and 4.3), the rest primarily by Fletcher (2.4, 2.6, 3.2, 3.4, 3.5, 4.1, 5.2).[6] How she speaks depends less on who is writing, however, than on who the playwrights imagined her to be.

Her role in the play continually foregrounds her difference from other characters—social and psychological as well as linguistic. Daughter of the jailer charged with keeping Palamon and Arcite (the "two noble kinsmen"), she soon falls in love with what she sees as Palamon's gentility, frees him, and, once in the forest, finds herself alone, her love unrequited. Suffering from lack of food and sleep as well as from unrequited passion, she goes mad and is temporarily taken up as a morris dancer. She eventually returns home to her father and to her long-time Wooer—neither of whom she recognizes, and who, under the advice of a Doctor, pretend to be Palamon and other courtiers to cure her of her delusions within the context of her fantasy. This fantasy and its dramatic complications dominate the play's underplot.

The Jailer's Daughter is marked as an underplot character, and as a character of the lower orders, in that she is never shown in the company of Palamon—or even in the company of any of the "noble" characters in the drama. Her freedom is restricted to spatial movement and linguistic facility; the former appears in her journey into the forest and her return, the latter in ballad singing and an unconstrained, though stylized, "mad" discourse. Four scenes in the middle of the play consist entirely of her speech; it should be noted as well that in 2.4, 2.6, 3.2, and 3.4, she appears alone and shares her speech only with the audience.

Separated from the speech of characters in the main plot, the language of the Jailer's Daughter is also distinguished from that of the predominantly lower-class figures in the underplot through an ensemble of signature phrases, topics, and images. For instance, the Jailer's Daughter is individualized in ending sentences with "else"; in the idiosyncratic use of the phrase "like a top" in various scenes and contexts; in sporadic but concentrated alliteration; and in her frequent use of "all," a word occurring nineteen times in her speech, often in clusters.[7] Despite Shakespeare and Fletcher's different modes of literary representation (Shakespeare at 2.1 and 4.3 employing prose, Fletcher typically preferring verse throughout his scenes), similar concerns and images infuse both playwrights' versions of the speech of the Jailer's Daughter, indicating a mutual conception of her character. Both playwrights emphasized sounds and noise, the sea and sailing, gentility, martyrdom, animals (especially birds), festivity, clothing, flowers, her maidenhead, and the "law" as oppositional force.

The influence of gender on this idiolect can be seen initially in the character's tension with the law and in her emphasis on virginity. Like

147

Hermia in *A Midsummer Night's Dream* (1596), the Jailer's Daughter loves someone whom the paternalistic order of her society hinders her from marrying. In contrast to Hermia, however, her problem runs deeper than wanting the wrong member of a pair of similar men. Although Palamon and Arcite are doubles like Lysander and Demetrius, their play advances the problem of cross-class desire in a way *A Midsummer Night's Dream* does not.[8] The Jailer's Daughter sees her desire as dependent on freeing Palamon: "What should I do to make him know I love him?" (2.4.29). Her desire is blocked by the "law" and her family: "Say I ventur'd | To set him free? what says the law then? | Thus much for law or kindred!" (2.4.30–32). After setting Palamon free, she imagines her role as one of martyr to an ambiguous law: "If the law | Find me, and then condemn me for't, some wenches, | Some honest-hearted maids, will sing my dirge, | And tell to memory my death was noble, | Dying almost a martyr" (2.6.13–17). The "law" she keeps mentioning seems ambiguous; it is difficult to discern exactly what she has in mind. This ambiguity is the case, I would aver, because the powers that affect her are more properly "law *and* kindred"; as a jailer's daughter, she is part of a family whose social role is to penalize. This family is without a mother—part of a Shakespearean pattern of gender relations.[9] "Kindred" for her, therefore, is her father (the Jailer) and his brother. It is significant, then, that when she violates the "law," she creates a female community by imagining female voices chronicling her martyrdom to this penalty of law and kindred: "some wenches, | Some honest-hearted maids, will sing my dirge." The choric virgins she imagines are given voice through the songs she herself will sing.

The influence of gender on the speech of the Jailer's Daughter also includes the increasingly conventional, sexually frank language of her madness. This language derives from a familiar subgenre, one that perhaps originated in Ophelia's mad discourse. Representations of madness were themselves subject to gendered conventions during the early modern era. "Beliefs about gender and sexuality influenced conceptions of madness in sixteenth- and seventeenth-century England in complex ways," Michael MacDonald notes. "It could hardly have been otherwise."[10] Theaters both depended on and dramatized these beliefs in their portrayals of madwomen. It has been argued about madwomen on the Renaissance stage, for instance, that "their madness is interpreted as something specifically feminine, whereas the madness of men is not specifically male."[11] This claim is borne out formally in early modern plays. The pathetic madness manifested in song, for example, was gender-specific in the Elizabethan and Jacobean theaters. As one scholar notes about the dramatic lyric during the English Renaissance, "Male characters whose madness is meant to be pitied do not sing."[12] The pathetic mad singer in early modern drama is always female.

This pathetic madness sometimes had liberating aspects. For instance, along with the mad speech of the She Fool in Fletcher's *The Pilgrim* (1621) and Isabella in Middleton and Rowley's *The Changeling* (1622), the mad discourse of the Jailer's Daughter points to an emerging convention of the early modern theater, one that licensed sexually explicit language by female characters when they were "mad." Of course, sexual language is not confined to the Jailer's Daughter in this play. In referring to her maidenhead twice (2.4.13, 4.1.112), for instance, she might appear merely to extend the prologue's (in)famous trope of play-as-maidenhead (Pro. 1 ff.). But in her mad discourse, virginity is both a real and more serious thing. Where the speaker of the prologue strikes a courtly, even dilettantish tone, the Jailer's Daughter speaks from a decidedly embodied position.

Precisely how embodied this position is becomes apparent when we trace differences, as well as similarities, between the speech of the Jailer's Daughter and that of Ophelia. The bawdy language of the Jailer's Daughter has clear intertextual links with Ophelia's. One might compare, for instance, the latter's "How should I your true-love know | From another one? | By his cockle hat and staff" (*Hamlet* 4.5.23–25) and "Young men will do't if they come to't, | By Cock, they are to blame" (*Hamlet* 4.5.61). The Jailer's Daughter uses similar words, and words containing them: "Close as a cockle" (4.1.131), "I must lose my maidenhead by cocklight" (4.1.112), "Then would I must make | A carreck of a cockleshell" (3.4.13–14), and "O for a prick now . . ." (3.4.25). While some of these are not bawdy in themselves, it seems significant that no other character in *The Two Noble Kinsmen* uses either "cock" or "prick" or any words that contain them. Ophelia's bawdy has formed the basis for the speech of the Jailer's Daughter. But located in an intertextual relation with Ophelia, the Jailer's Daughter nonetheless asserts sexual desire more directly than her predecessor, whose statements are often enigmatic and riddling. Hence the Jailer's Daughter's "Sirrah tinker, | Stop no more holes but what you should" (3.5.82–83) and "I must lose my maidenhead by cocklight"—lines difficult to imagine

Ophelia speaking.

Why should the bawdy of the Jailer's Daughter be more direct than Ophelia's? Initially their situations appear identical: each loves a man who does not return her love; each appears motherless; each engages a pathetic language of madness that draws heavily on the natural world and popular forms of representation. One reason the madness of the Jailer's Daughter registers more "coarsely," I would argue, is her social class.[13] We are not surprised to find her speech prosaic and direct because she comes from a lower order of society; as has been mentioned, she never shares the stage with members of the higher orders. Her speech is more directly about her body and bodies generally because it comes from a social stratum of dramatic representation where neither madness nor bawdy is typically phrased in decorative poetry.

We can also see the class valences of her idiolect in an unusual place: her speech's strange emphasis on numbers. Following her early statement that " 'Tis odds | [Palamon] never will affect me" (2.4.1–2), the Jailer's Daughter shows a marked, almost obsessive concern for numbers and counting. One might consider the following: "When fifteen once has found us"; "I lov'd my lips the better ten days after"; "Tell ten—I have pos'd him"; "I can sing twenty more"; "at least two hundred now with child by him—| There must be four"; "and at ten years old | They must be all gelt"; "he had not so few last night | As twenty to dispatch. He'll tickle't up | In two hours"; "a whole million of cutpurses"; "He'll dance the morris twenty mile an hour"; "Some two hundred bottle, | And twenty strike of oats"; "and two coarse smocks"; "And twenty?"[14] What is the significance of this trait? Her emphasis on figures locates her character in a quotidian, ledger-centered sphere; full of numbers, her speech is the language of reckoning, of the shop and tavern tally. These numbers also relate her to the play's main plot, where the plural of the epic and romance traditions is a sign of narrative as well as of cultural wealth: three kneeling queens, two noble kinsmen. This play appears to need someone to reckon this wealth, someone to keep the score. If in counting things that the main plot does not require she count—imaginary boys and provisions—the Jailer's Daughter comes close to parodying this need, her devotion to Palamon shows that she has counted something that matters to the play's traditional narrative. By thematizing her as the play's counter, this obsession with numbers establishes her as an audience figure within the play—someone, like us, impressed by the powerful figures of the main plot.

But the most striking *difference* of the Jailer's Daughter in *The Two No-ble Kinsmen* lies in the complexities of her mad discourse. Music is an important part of this madness: her songs are closely linked to it, even advanced as its product. She does not sing or refer to songs or singing until after she goes mad and begins to dream, in her father's words, "of another world and a better" (4.3.5). Like her music, madness sets her apart from other characters in the play; this separateness, in turn, allows Shakespeare and Fletcher to show the audience how and what she is thinking, as she is thinking. However stylized their portrayal of her mental process, we are left with an early modern, dramatic stream of consciousness.

We can best begin to understand how this stream of consciousness registers the cultural and historical by examining a characteristic sample of her mad discourse. The following soliloquy comprises the whole of act 3, scene 4:

> I am very cold, and all the stars are out too,
> The little stars and all, that look like aglets.
> The sun has seen my folly. Palamon!
> Alas, no; he's in heaven. Where am I now?
> 5 Yonder's the sea, and there's a ship. How't tumbles!
> And there's a rock lies watching under water;
> Now, now, it beats upon it—now, now, now!
> There's a leak sprung, a sound one. How they cry!
> Open her before the wind! you'll lose all else.
> 10 Up with a course or two, and tack about, boys!
> Good night, good night, y' are gone. I am very hungry:
> Would I could find a fine frog! He would tell me
> News from all parts o' th' world. Then would I make
> A carreck of a cockleshell, and sail
> 15 By east and north-east to the King of Pigmies,
> For he tells fortunes rarely. Now my father,
> Twenty to one, is truss'd up in a trice
> To-morrow morning; I'll say never a word.   [*Sing.*]
>   "For I'll cut my green coat a foot above my knee,
> 20   And I'll clip my yellow locks an inch below mine e'e.
>   Hey, nonny, nonny, nonny.
>   "He s' buy me a white cut, forth for to ride,

> And I'll go seek him through the world that is so wide.
> Hey, nonny, nonny, nonny."

25   O for a prick now, like a nightingale,
     To put my breast against! I shall sleep like a top else.

The Jailer's Daughter is alone throughout this twenty-six-line scene. Probably because of her solitary position (both in the context of the dramatic fiction and theatrically, on the empty stage), her soliloquy contains many deictic markers; besides many pronominal references, there are many spatial and temporal indices: "yonder's" (5); "there's" (5); "there's" (6); "now, now, . . . now, now, now" (7); "there's" (8); "tomorrow" (18); "now" (25).

Her speech here is unusually condensed and varied. Questions give way to exclamations; quiet introspection to noisy description and shouted, slangy advice; realism to fantasy; and blank verse to ballad. The relative brevity of its periods joins sudden, disjunctive transitions of thought and subject to mark it as an instance of remarkable poetic compression. The soliloquy's images oscillate between large and small, diminutive and expansive, as the Jailer's Daughter unfolds her solitary state against the nocturnal background of the natural world in noun pairs, some of which contrast: "I/stars"; "stars/aglets"; "sea/ship"; "ship/rock"; "I/frog"; "carreck/cockleshell"; "prick/breast"; "[I]/nightingale"; "I/top." Her distress is exacerbated, in the logic of the play, by her lack of sleep and by her hunger, both of which she indicates with sentences beginning "I am very" (1, 11)—the kind of repetition that creates her individualized speaking style throughout the play. In the poetry of this scene, she shows a heightened sensitivity to both internal and external stimuli; her soliloquy acts as an almost unmediated voice, revealing thoughts and feelings.

The soliloquy also bears certain idiolectal marks we have come to expect of her speech, such as her tendency to end sentences with "else" (9, 26); concentrated alliteration ("carreck of a cockleshell" [14], "Twenty to one, is truss'd up in a trice | To-morrow" [17–18]); the signature simile "like a top" (26); fondness for animal imagery ("frog" [12], "cut" [22])—especially birds ("nightingale" [25]); her emphasis on numbers ("Twenty to one" [17]); and repeated use of "all" (1, 2, 9, 13). None of these features occurs in the quoted language of the ballad, which possesses a speech genre, or register, of its own. Of different meter and rhetorical form, it embraces a separate pattern of images and themes, among the former a concern with colors ("green" [19]; "yellow" [20]; "white" [22]) and among the latter an emphasis on cutting—stressing, again, the theme of diminution: "I'll cut" (19) and "I'll clip" (20) anticipate the "white cut" (22), that is, the cut-tailed horse of the song. Though differing from the language of the rest of the soliloquy, the ballad also harmonizes with it in several areas. For example, the "white cut" joins "frog" preceding it (12) and "nightingale" following it (25) in referring to the natural world. The "nonny, nonny, nonny" refrain (seen twice in the ballad) recalls with repetition and its initial "n" sound the almost ritualized "now, now, now!" of line 7. Perhaps most important, though, is how the scenario of the heroine that the ballad describes—its narrative speaker cross-dresses, altering her dress and hair to gain the social freedom to seek her absent lover "through the world that is so wide"—concretely articulates the fantasy to "make | A carreck of a cockleshell, and sail | By east and north-east to the King of Pigmies" (15).

While these ballad lines underscore the real position of the Jailer's Daughter in the world—she is cold, hungry, and blocked in her desires—they offer by way of compensation "another world and a better." Playwrightlike, the Jailer's Daughter imagines such a world through folk narratives. Here and elsewhere, she represents the folk world of *The Two Noble Kinsmen*—and of the culture beyond the stage on which it was originally performed—in a play within and apart from the mythological narrative of the main plot. Along with her ballads, the language of work is important to this folk texture; her shouted instructions to the sailors, for instance— "Open her before the wind! you'll lose all else. | Up with a course or two, and tack about, boys!" (9–10)—display a strange familiarity with the vocabulary of their occupation. The emphasis on animals and on nature imagery in her speech, however, implies that this folk world is increasingly associated with the countryside rather than with work practices or groups in the countryside. What she imagines is full of fantasy: the utopian freedom of the ballads she sings is only imaginary. She nonetheless carves out an important space of imagination and possibility and does so at a shift in the history of the drama.

From Shakespeare to Fletcher

With Shakespeare's retirement as playwright, a move toward less popular forms of drama—a move that had been occurring for several years and had left its mark on his romances through the influence of tragicomedy—became apparent. This development corresponded to larger changes in literary culture and culture generally during the seventeenth century, when the gap between the patrician and the plebeian steadily widened.[15] In the words of R. Malcolm Smuts, striking stylistic changes during the early Stuart period in particular "were symptomatic of a . . . fundamental reorientation of attitudes, values, patterns of conspicuous consumption, and modes of thought and feeling."[16] While this reorientation was inherently courtly and urban in nature, folk elements far from disappeared. Certainly in the work of Herrick and others we see an attempt to preserve, even recreate, traditional patterns of life.[17] Jonson's "To Penshurst," among other works, comes immediately to mind. But however serious such efforts were, their very attempts to preserve testify to the larger forces of cultural transition affecting literary representation in early modern England. Because it had traditionally spoken to heterogeneous audiences in various registers of discourse, the drama was especially sensitive to such changes.

The pull of city and court altered the politics of seventeenth-century plays. In relation to the latter, the rise of a more aristocratic aesthetic worked to change drama and other literary modes during James's first decade of rule. We can see this evidenced in the leasing by the King's Men of the Second Blackfriars as a private theater in 1608, something that coincided with Fletcher's adaptation of Guarini's *Il pastor fido* as *The Faithful Shepherdess* (1608), published a few years later. These actions show a commitment to a more aristocratic vision and audience as well as the changes in moral and ethical directions implied by that commitment. Jonson, for example, would later describe the author of Fletcher's source as someone who "in his Pastor Fido kept not decorum in making shepherds speak as well as himself could"—someone, that is, who effectively erased sociolinguistic difference by elevating dramatic speech regardless of the characters' class backgrounds.[18] At the same time that the influence of the court worked to change the drama, the rapid growth of London made this city increasingly popular as a source of inspiration and setting for imaginative works.[19] "With time," King James himself declared, "England will be only London."[20] London-born playwrights like Jonson and Middleton felt at home in this urban environment. In contrast, Shakespeare's interest in what we would call folk culture—in the language of games, occupations, animals, and nature—drew from the countryside and often saw him take the action of plays outside cities to the rural world.[21]

The important difference between Fletcher and Shakespeare was that between the court and the country.[22] The folk basis underlying Shakespeare's plays had temporarily produced, Robert Weimann argues, a "scene indivisible," which ultimately "gave way to a divided scene where the universal perspective found itself forever compromised. Seen either from the court or the City, the growing tensions could no longer be apprehended in their entirety and incorporated in a poetic vision of society. The register of dramatic values and attitudes would henceforth cease to be as broad and as vital as the social organism itself."[23] Customarily stretched during the Elizabethan period to encompass various social groups and visions, drama during the early Stuart era no longer possessed this suppleness. The social integration that an Elizabethan tradition had imagined in the country is lacking in the plays of later dramatists like Beaumont and Fletcher, whose social visions are more aristocratic than folk. The chief avenues of dramatic development following Shakespeare—the court (Beaumont and Fletcher) and the City (Heywood and Middleton)—were not directed, as the Elizabethan theater had been, toward the mingling of social classes, attitudes, and values: the "kings and clowns," which Sidney loathed to see together but evidently did see together. One might note how the business of a cross-class, play-within-the-play performance, executed without friction—albeit condescendingly—in *A Midsummer Night's Dream,* is harder to duplicate after the dissolution of what has been called the "Elizabethan compromise."[24] While this compromise implied an acceptance of the hierarchies of the prevailing Tudor order, it also recognized the need for criticism of that order and of those who abused privilege.

Lear's railing, for instance, can be seen as the culmination of a theatrical tradition that had been much more interested in social justice than later drama would be: "see how yond justice rails upon yond simple thief. Hark in thine ear: change places, and handy-dandy, which is the justice, which the thief?" (4.6.151–54).[25] When, nearly a decade later, the Jailer's Daughter voices similar criticism in *The Two Noble Kinsmen,* it is less connected with an object: "Alas, 'tis a sore life they have i' th' tother place, such burning, frying, boiling, hissing, howling, chatt'ring, cursing! O, they have shrowd measure! take heed: if one be mad, or hang or drown themselves, thither they go—Jupiter bless us!—and there shall we be put in a cauldron of lead and usurers' grease, amongst a whole million of cut-

purses, and there boil like a gammon of bacon that will never be enough"
(4.3.31–39). The Doctor observing her responds "How her brain coins!"
(40). Because the overplots of the play do not touch on the issues that the
Jailer's Daughter raises, and because she is not integrated into any of the
plots, this mad coinage floats within the play. Like those she mentions, she
is "thither," in another place.

We might take "usurers' grease" as an example. This reference undoubtedly figured into an intensification in the early seventeenth century of a
longstanding debate on usury in early modern England.[26] Around 1612 an
anonymous author penned an apology for the infamous usurer Thomas
Sutton, who had died the preceding year.[27] On March 7, 1613, the eloquent Puritan Thomas Adams preached at Paul's Cross a sermon against
usury titled "The White Devil; Or, The Hypocrite Uncased."[28] During the
same year William Pemberton inveighed against greed in financial affairs
in *The Godly Merchant, or the Great Gaine.*[29] Norman Jones tells us that
Francis Bacon perhaps prepared his famous tractate on "Usury and the
Use Thereof" in relation to a 1612 committee for the "Repair of the King's
Estate and Raising of Monies."[30] While her reference to "usurer's grease"
gestures toward the debate these texts represent, little in the traditional social satire of the Jailer's Daughter attaches to anything in the play itself.
Unlike Lear and Lear's Fool, she is positioned by Shakespeare and Fletcher
in a part of the drama that prevents her language from finding an object.

The shift in dramatic representation that I have been describing—a
shift away from mingling social spheres—ensures this lack of connection,
for it underwrites the general separation of the Jailer's Daughter from the
characters of the play, and the fact that she is even silenced in the presence
of the aristocratic characters. This failure to connect is part of what we
consider the weakness of the Fletcherian pattern toward which drama
moved. Formally, this shift produced flatter characters, less-motivated action, and an emphasis on conveying emotion immediately through situation, rhetoric, and condensed scenes, in contrast to the rounder characters and the larger, tableau-oriented practice of the Shakespearean play.
Aesthetically, this shift strikes us as an unfortunate one. But it was nonetheless a shift that provided Fletcherian playwrights with strengths and
possibilities that Shakespeare lacked.

Strong female roles were part of this shift. Shakespeare's Cleopatra, har-
binger of things to come, was followed by such characters as the Duchess

of Malfi, Vittoria Corombona, Bonduca, Livia, and Beatrice-Joanna. Partly in the tradition of the pathetic, often powerless heroine of Shakespearean tragedy and romance—characterologically the Jailer's Daughter seems somewhere between the literary traditions of the Renaissance *inamorata* and the Dickensian "angel of the hearth"[31]—she also enjoys some of the strengths of these more powerful characters. Her madness, for example, licenses speech freer than that of any other female character in Shakespeare's plays. Where *The Tempest* begins with the cries of mariners aboard a sinking ship, *The Two Noble Kinsmen,* in the soliloquy examined above, channels such cries through the voice of the Jailer's Daughter. She also uses, as we have seen, the biting language of social satire: something previously relegated to male fools and cynical choric figures. Shakespeare's practice of keying characters' speech to their social position along the general division of prose for the lower classes and verse for those of a higher social station—what Jonson would have called his *decorum*—also implies limits on the Jailer's Daughter that Fletcher's drama refused to impose.

To Shakespeare, the social origins of characters determined how they could speak. In turn, how they spoke often determined their dramatic possibilities. This constraint, for example, gave madness certain class valences. Brian Vickers has observed that "If we establish a hierarchy of psychological normality, those characters who predominantly speak verse can fall down into prose when they lose their reason: Ophelia, Othello, Lear, Lady Macbeth. (Characters from the prose domain never go mad—their dramatic status would not warrant it.)"[32] If we look at plays written before *The Two Noble Kinsmen,* Vickers is right. In an earlier Shakespeare play, the Jailer's Daughter would not have gone mad: her social status would have precluded it. Yet in this collaborative effort Fletcher's tendency to give every character blank verse, albeit with various textures, levels a prejudice inherent in the Shakespearean pattern and helps make madness—until this time, as Vickers indicates, the psychic property of the aristocracy—available to a member of a lower class. If the honor initially seems dubious, we should remember that, with madness, the Jailer's Daughter inherits a complex subjectivity typically associated with tragic, often male aristocrats of the late Elizabethan stage. Thus if we compare her to Mopsa in Sidney's *Arcadia* (pub. 1593)—a probable model for the Jailer's Daughter—we can see the significant changes in what their authors imagined for women of the lower orders.[33] Sidney's Mopsa is a cruel caricature lacking the depth and the affective power of the Jailer's Daughter. The differences between these female characters are not just an expression of authorial idiosyncrasy; such differences have a historical cause as well. The drama changed significantly during Shakespeare's career, losing some of its vitality and some of its ability to represent diverse social values and attitudes; the Elizabethan compromise also limited social possibilities that later dramatists—ironically, through the absence of the very element that had made Shakespeare's drama so powerful—would be able to explore. Decorum of character, to which Shakespeare adhered and for which Fletcher would later be renowned for violating, reminds us that the social integration of Shakespeare's theater often came at a great price.[34]

Madness and Society

The madness of the Jailer's Daughter is remarkably social, yet its content has an importance not immediately apparent. If initially her madness seems a dustbin of materials randomly deposited, closer examination shows it to explore topics outside the sphere of the play's traditional plot. With an emphasis on folk culture, what is inside her mind turns out to be the outside world. That it happens to be the world outside London follows from the increasing pull of court and city that marked the transition from Shakespeare to Fletcher.

This pull marks madness as a resistance to the historical pressures of the modern. It was precisely in terms of such pressure that C. L. Barber explained a new emphasis in late Elizabethan literature on folk pastimes and festivals: "During Shakespeare's lifetime, England became conscious of holiday custom as it had not been before, in the very period when in many areas the keeping of holiday was on the decline. Festivals which worked within the rhythm of an agricultural calendar, in village or market town, did not fit the way of living of the urban groups whose energies were beginning to find expression through what Tawney has called the Puritan ethic."[35] Indeed, it seems a sign of the changes the festive underwent that Barber chose in *Shakespeare's Festive Comedy* not to follow out his claims in relation to plays after *Twelfth Night* (1601). Along with *Bartholomew Fair* (1614), which emphasizes the thoroughly "contagious" commercialism of that traditional environment, *The Two Noble Kinsmen* shows how subordinated the country had become to the city and the court.[36]

For example, the morris dance in which the Jailer's Daughter is used remains on the surface similar to the Mechanicals' performance in *A Mid-summer Night's Dream*. Coming thirteen years after Will Kemp's commercializing stunt of dancing the morris from London to Norwich,[37] however, the episode is darker, even menacing. One might note the joy of the countrymen at having found her:

> *3. Coun.* There's a dainty mad woman, master,
> Comes i' th' nick, as mad as a March hare.
> If we can get her dance, we are made again.
> I warrant her, she'll do the rarest gambols.
> *1. Coun.* A mad woman? We are made, boys!
>   (3.5.72–76)

To be "made" here is to succeed at putting on a good morris dance and receiving, like the Mechanicals, a reward for their performance from the aristocratic spectators. But the Jailer's Daughter is given no lines to speak in the performance before Theseus. It is as though Shakespeare and Fletcher did not know what she could say to Theseus, or Theseus to her. Unlike *A Midsummer Night's Dream,* there is no dialogue between and among the various levels of society: Bottom hears the nobles talking about him and responds; the Jailer's Daughter does not, perhaps cannot.

Yet the word "made" in the above exchange (lines 74, 76) puns as well on "maid"—as in the "Maid Marian" figure central to the tradition of morris dances. An important part of the May games in many English villages, the morris dance was perhaps the most resonant symbol of an older way of life outside England's cities and towns. "The Hobby-horse is Forgot," the seemingly omnipresent ballad to which Shakespeare refers in both *Love's Labour's Lost* (1595, 3.1.29) and *Hamlet* (3.2.135), alludes simultaneously to a popular fondness for the morris dance (in which the hobby-horse had traditionally been a figure) and nostalgia for a time when its vitality was better appreciated. Significantly, much of the morris dance in which the male characters of the underplot employ the Jailer's Daughter appears to have been borrowed from a courtly document, Francis Beaumont's *Masque of the Inner Temple and Gray's Inn,* performed at Whitehall on February 20, 1613, in honor of Princess Elizabeth's wedding to the Elector Palantine. In this performance, the morris dance was an antimasque. Philip Edwards aptly captures its function in describing it as "a parody of the traditional country dances at the ancient may-games, or summer 'may-ing' festivals."[38] The appropriation of this traditional celebratory dance for a performance at Whitehall is in line with the growing separation of court and city from the countryside that we have seen represented in *The Two Noble Kinsmen*. This play's awkward revision of *A Midsummer Night's Dream*, whose portrait of social integration is based on the old calendar, also shows that the rituals of the countryside and the related myths of the Elizabethan compromise were increasingly displaced by the power of the court and city.[39]

The Jailer's Daughter represents the country. We can see the country basis of the Jailer's Daughter in an important strain of her idiolect: her use of rural words and phrases. Such words as "whoobub," "reak," and "mop'd," for instance, survived in northern England and even in 1613 marked her speech as rural; they work with other words of dialectal valence—for example, "char'd," "rearly," "ken'st," "shrowd," and "cut" (i.e., "horse")—to ground her language in the country.[40] This dialect and the ballads in which it is frequently found evoke rural culture. That the Jailer's Daughter was followed on London's stages by Constance, *The Northern Lass* of Brome's 1629 play—a character based strongly on the Jailer's Daughter—indicates that the latter may already have seemed provincial to urban and courtly audiences.[41]

By 1613 the rural undoubtedly held associations of the past for many audience members in London playhouses. Journeying to London in the genre of cony-catching pamphlets, for instance, is a process of gaining experience; the geographical movement of its simpler characters doubles as an educational one. For London readers, such narratives would assure them not only of the sophisticated complexity of their city but also of the backwardness of the country. When she took the stage in 1613, the Jailer's Daughter must have represented both the countryside and the Elizabethan past, even as in the twentieth century jokes about "farmers' daughters" created a naive and simple past set in the country.[42] Three plays and entertainments written before *The Two Noble Kinsmen* help to reveal how belated the Jailer's Daughter would have seemed in 1613: *The Painter's Daughter* (1576), *The Blacksmith's Daughter* (1578), and *Fair Em, the Miller's Daughter of Manchester* (1590).[43] While only the last of these plays has survived,[44] their titles alone speak to the potential belatedness of and nostalgia connected with the dramatic "type" of Jailer's Daughter. All these titles identify their heroines with their fathers' occupations. Only *Fair Em*, however, specifies the location of its action; significantly, it is set in Manchester, in the north. As past is to present, so is the northern to London. As part of a dramatic tradition that had found expression during the Elizabethan period, the Jailer's Daughter thus signifies what Leah Marcus has called "survivalism"—the symbolic representation in early modern England of "communal economic activities" and "the maintenance of old collective customs and collective village order."[45] But the survivalism of the Jailer's Daughter is inflected through a complex psychology. Where Barber describes England as being newly "conscious" of traditional customs, we must invert this observation for *The Two Noble Kinsmen:* this play is conscious of folk culture primarily in the unconscious language of the Jailer's Daughter.

Far from being a random collage of materials, the unconscious that her mad discourse vents has direction as well as expressive modes. As for the latter, we have already seen that the Jailer's Daughter frequently sings ballads. In *The Two Noble Kinsmen* she sings, alludes to, or is described as singing almost a dozen different songs, even boasting at one point "I can sing twenty more" (4.1.106). Both as topic and as practice, such songs as "The George Alow" (3.5.59–71) and "O fair, O sweet" (4.1.114 ff.) connect her to a tradition of oral folk culture even as they lend her character a sentimentalized, pathetic aura. Popular ballads represent in the drama sources and limits of the social realm as conceived in Jacobean London. They traditionally took country themes, incidents, and characters as their subject. But ballads changed in important ways during the Jacobean era. As Tessa Watt indicates, "Although early Elizabethan ballads were sometimes billed as 'A warning to London' or addressed to 'London dames', by the second quarter of the seventeenth century they were much more commonly given titles like 'The cooper of Norfolke' or 'A pleasant new northerne song, called the two York-shire lovers.'"[46] We can see in this shift a chiastic change in audience and subject matter: early Elizabethan ballads about London were addressed to country folk, whereas Jacobean ballads about the country were more often addressed to urban dwellers. The shift from Elizabethan to Jacobean saw ballads latch on to and emphasize the country in a survivalistic way.

Ballad singing also associates the Jailer's Daughter with the politics of that form. Inexpensive and ephemeral, ballads were often despised as mere commodities, too easily fashioned and too publicly sold. Contemporary critics repeatedly described the ballad as "ribald," "lascivious," "common," and "base."[47] In *A Defense of Poetry* (1579), Thomas Lodge stated: "Believe me the magistrates may take advice (as I know wisely can) to root out those odd rhymes which runs in every rascal's mouth, savoring of ribaldry."[48] Here ballads ("odd rhymes") have a promiscuous life of their own, running "in every rascal's mouth": they remained popular because rhythm, music, rhyme, and patterned theme combined to ensure memorability. Lodge's description highlights the fact that songs can "sing" people, filling their empty moments with what seems a will of the songs' own. Occupying an important place in the madness of the Jailer's Daughter, popular ballads work to place her on the social scale, both vertically— that is, in a hierarchy of power and rank—and horizontally—her agency and mobility within those places. As we have seen, they also provide the folk content of her madness.

The dramatic space of her madness forms a charged register. This register is at once dynamic, thick with the worlds inside and outside the playhouse, and yet carefully demarcated from the rest of the drama. The madness of the Jailer's Daughter works like an unconscious of the play —hidden yet present, unseen and at the same time powerful. Indeed, her madness remains relatively inaccessible to the traditional narrative of the drama while continually suggesting the cultural and historical forces that drive her play. In Fredric Jameson's view, the political unconscious of literature is the "repressed and buried reality" of once vital cultural struggles, practices, and beliefs.[49] History—to Jameson "the experience of Necessity" or, in a phrase almost poetic in its frankness, "what hurts"—is articulated positively in literature through antagonistic class voices and the dominant's "management" of social and political impulses.[50] In a manner that speaks to Jameson's notion of the reality buried in texts as well as to the coercive nature of historical forces, the madness of the Jailer's Daughter explores topics that elude the rest of the play. As no other character can, she foregrounds through her mad speech the increasing separation of court and city from the countryside in early modern England.

Throughout *The Two Noble Kinsmen*, the Jailer's Daughter's speech is an emblem of difference; embodying an oral, folk, and desiring world, she labors both in and for a dramatic community relatively unconscious of her existence. Through the fullness of her speech, she voices truths about what brought that drama into being. We have seen that the content of her mad speech, with its survivalistic emphasis on folk culture, foregrounds the pull of court and city, and it highlights the corresponding differences in dramatic representation between Shakespeare and Fletcher. But this madness is also acutely concerned with relations of work and gender inside the playhouse, relations that are presented in a way that accentuates their place in a larger history of cultural performances.

The Jailer's Daughter functions as both audience and playwright in this drama, albeit a less dictatorial playwright than Prospero or the controlling figures examined in earlier chapters. Her obsession with Palamon embodies—even offers a pattern for—an audience's own desires toward the aristocratic characters. One of her most insistent themes, however, involves the figure of the boy actor. The play opens with a boy *"singing and strewing flow'rs"* (1.1.2 stage direction) for the wedding procession. The Jailer's Daughter repeats this action in a more homely fashion when she enters later and remarks "These strewings are for their chamber" (2.1.21). Obeying her father's orders to care for their two prisoners, she brings new rushes for the floor of their cell. She thus mimics, with a difference, the custodial role of the boy who opens the play.

Her relation to the boy actor is much more complicated, though, for the play places special pressure on the boy's body behind her role. Significantly, in *The Two Noble Kinsmen* she both mentions and is mentioned in context with singing boys. The latter occurs when her Wooer describes to a group of her concerned friends and relatives, all males, how he accidentally found her next to a lake:

> As I late was angling
> In the great lake that lies behind the palace,
> From the far shore, thick set with reeds and sedges,
> As patiently I was attending sport,
> I heard a voice, a shrill one; and attentive
> I gave my ear, when I might well perceive
> 'Twas one that sung, and by the smallness of it,
> A boy or woman.
>
> (4.1.52–59)

The Wooer emphasizes the *difference* of the voice he heard ("a shrill one," "smallness"), something that tells him it belongs to "A boy or woman." Like the chorus of maids that the Jailer's Daughter has fantasized, this voice registers the body behind it: to the Wooer, to be "A boy or a woman" means to sing with a small, shrill voice.

What does not register to him in this "woman's key," however, is the difference between boy and woman. In this lack of recognition he is like the third "fool" in a ballad stanza that the Jailer's Daughter has already sung in her madness:

> There was three fools fell out about an howlet:
> The one said it was an owl,
> The other he said nay,
> The third he said it was a hawk,
> And her bells were cut away.
>
> (3.5.67–71)

To one fool an owl, to another the howlet is a female hawk—without bells. These cut-away bells point to a trope of cutting that underlies how the Jailer's Daughter explains gender difference. For example, when she fantasizes about the four hundred children Palamon has fathered with "All the young maids | Of [the] town" (4.1.125–26), she speaks of the need for them to be castrated: "at ten years old | They must be all gelt for musicians, | And sing the wars of Theseus" (4.1.132–34). For these boys, to keep the woman's key means to be gelded. In the pas de deux of the "woman's part" in the theaters of Jacobean England, the image of the castrated boy must have seemed a logical figure with which to foreground the tension between female role (as with the Jailer's Daughter) and adolescent male actor. But there remains something critical in her otherwise offhand remark about the compulsory gelding of these boys—all boys, for "He has the trick on't"—at ten years of age.

Coming from the mouth of a boy actor, part of this criticism can be seen to concern what it meant to be a boy in the early modern playhouse, where a boy actor's lack of power in the acting company was exacerbated by an impending change of voice and body. At the same time, however, this remark seems concerned with what it meant culturally to have boys play women on the stage. The "maids" she has once imagined singing her martyrdom are, in this passage, merely the potential mothers of boys who will sing Theseus's wars. Where the cutting dynamic of the ballad we examined in the soliloquy above—clipping the hair, cutting the coat, riding a cut-tailed horse—offers her character a freedom she would not otherwise possess, gelding the four hundred boys removes even the possibility of representing such freedoms in the theater. In this emphasis on the boy behind the role, the mad speech of the Jailer's Daughter examines critically the social arrangements of London's theaters and what it means for them to take boys for women. Athenian society, like that of London's stages, employs boy "musicians" to "sing the wars of Theseus"—to accompany, admire, sing for, and strew flowers in front of its heroes. And, most important, to play its women.

Unlike the traditional morris dance, the early modern stages had no place for real Jailer's Daughters. Although the Maid Marian character in the morris dance was sometimes played by a cross-dressed male during Shakespeare's lifetime, there are many indications that women had typically taken the role and were a welcome part of the morris dance performance.[51] When Kemp performed his morris to Norwich, for example, he danced with several women on separate occasions—one of whom he calls his "Maid Marian"—and shows great respect for their abilities.[52] Yet the purpose-built playhouses of early modern London shunned the inclusiveness of the folk tradition that Kemp evidenced in dancing with these women. There the all-male acting companies appropriated female roles. If *The Two Noble Kinsmen* is about a growing separation of the court and city from the countryside, one of the differences defining this separation lied in the business of playing. In using boy actors for female roles, London's professional theaters denied women the freedom to perform that they would enjoy in more traditional environments. The morris dance in *The Two Noble Kinsmen*, then, remains a formal irony. For even in the appropriative employment of the (mad) Jailer's Daughter in their morris dance, the underplot males display a respect for the woman behind the role that early modern acting companies did not share. We can perhaps see Theseus's "trick"—begetting only boys on the "maids" of Athens—as a metaphor for the all-male acting companies themselves. As is the case with many social relations in the play, though, the politics of Theseus's "trick" is something for which the main plot of the drama shows no concern. The mad language of the Jailer's Daughter, in contrast, raises these otherwise ignored issues by foregrounding the material relations of the theaters that brought it into being.

The Talking Cure

Giving voice to certain cultural topics in a separate part of the play, the

Jailer's Daughter remains analogous to its unconscious. But if her mad emphasis on the rural world and its folk culture implies a tension between the courtly idealism of the overplot and the decidedly nonheroic lives of those in the underplot, her allusions to the politics of playing remind us that she is separated from others in that plot. *The Two Noble Kinsmen* marks her discourse as different not only in the surplus of individualizing features but also by rendering it, and her, the object of analysis by other characters, many of them male. Like Ophelia, Cassandra, and Lady Macbeth, the Jailer's Daughter, in her madness, comes under scrutiny. The burden of her gendered madness, like theirs, is to be watched and analyzed.

Portrayed as almost transparent, in fact, her mad language becomes the focus of a crude psychotherapy. The Doctor hired to heal her sets out his diagnosis and proposed cure in a forty-one-line, darkly farcical disposition. Its beginning and end are quoted here:

> That intemp'rate surfeit of her eye hath distemper'd the other senses. They may return and settle again to execute their preordain'd faculties, but they are now in a most extravagant vagary. . . .

> I will, between the passages of this project, come in with my appliance. Let us put it in execution; and hasten the success, which doubt not will bring forth comfort.

> (4.3.70–73, 98–101)

The Doctor's love of Latinate words ("execute," "faculties") and redundant phrases ("intemp'rate surfeit," "extravagant vagary") adds to the tone of authority, however parodic, in his speech. Later this intensifies when he talks about the physical administration of a cure. After the Wooer relates that the Jailer's Daughter had asked him (as Palamon) to kiss her and sing for her, the Doctor urges him to do so, concluding: "If she entreat again, do any thing, | Lie with her, if she ask you" (5.2.17–18). Here the doctor touches on a belief common in early modern medical theory. As Michael MacDonald puts it: "When women were deprived of sexual satisfaction, [it was believed] they were prone to illness and insanity."[53] Reading a similar "cure" from Robert Burton's *Anatomy of Melancholy,* Juliana Schiesari refers to "the phallic subservience of women."[54] This subservience works linguistically in *The Two Noble Kinsmen* through the gendering of languages.

When the Jailer, listening to this conversation, objects with equal vehe-

mence—"Ho there, doctor!" (18)—the physician insists the Wooer sleep
with the Jailer's Daughter as necessary to the "cure": "Cure her first this
way; then if she will be honest, | She has the path before her" (22–23). Af-
ter the Jailer departs, the Doctor turns to the Wooer and conspiratorially
remarks:

> What e'er her father says, if you perceive
> Her mood inclining that way that I spoke of,
> *Videlicet,* the way of flesh—you have me?
>
> .   .   .   .
>
>   Please her appetite,
> And do it home; it cures her *ipso facto . . .*
>   (5.2.33–37)

The Doctor uses Latin tags to accompany his prescription and intrudes
authoritatively on familial space, his "professional" advice taking prece-
dence over the Jailer's paternal concern. Like the Doctor, the Schoolmaster
who enlists the Jailer's Daughter for his morris dance uses Latin when he
speaks of influencing her behavior. "Go take her," he instructs his men,
"and fluently persuade her to a peace. | '*Et opus exegi, quod nec Jovis ira, nec
ignis*'—| Strike up, and lead her in" (3.5.86–89). The slight misquotation of
Ovid here (*Metamorphoses* XV, 871: "And I have completed a work that
neither the wrath of Jove nor fire [shall undo]"), and his Latin quotations
generally, support the audience's perception of him as a pedant in every
sense of the word. Like the Doctor's Latin, however, his Latin tag has implications beyond characterization, for it reveals an implicit gendering of
speech and language in the underplot of the play. Latin, known to and
used by the authoritative figures who oversee, evaluate, and direct others,
becomes a male language, with the "mother" tongue of colloquial English—the language of the countrymen and of the Jailer's Daughter—gendered female.[55] Even as the Schoolmaster's (false) etymology of the word
"morris" (3.5.118–20) testifies to a clumsy, inadequate, and academic relation to the morris dance tradition, the Latin he and the Doctor employ in
relation to the Jailer's Daughter signal a harmfully wrong "fit" with her situation and the cultural forces she represents.

Using Latinate language as framing discourse, Fletcher and Shakespeare
foreground the Doctor's early modern psychotherapy as authoritative even

as they further isolate the speech of the Jailer's Daughter. This isolation is also an objectification, one that hinges on the gendering of mad language. We have seen how the pathetic mad singer is always female, her musical mad language always strongly gendered. The reciprocal nature of this relation expresses more than an accident of form. The pity accorded such mad singers as Ophelia and the Jailer's Daughter depends on an acknowledgment of their relative powerlessness. Their madness, in turn, appears to result from conflictive pressures. As a woman and as a daughter, the Jailer's Daughter lacks the autonomy enjoyed by adult male figures in the play. As the daughter of a jailer—and thus a member of a lower class—she cannot gain the attention or affection of the aristocratic Palamon. So while she represents a pattern of historical pressures in early modern England, the Jailer's Daughter also stands between forces that have a more personal implication. The contradictions between her social position and her personal desires, in fact, find recurrent expression in images of pressure and division throughout the play. Sometimes such images explicitly concern the Jailer's Daughter; at other times she uses them.

These images of pressure go deeply to our understanding of her character, dramatic situation, and the politics of her speech. In her first scene, for instance, she describes how Palamon and Arcite occasionally express frustration over their captivity:

> Sometime a divided sigh, martyr'd as 'twere i' th' deliverance, will break from one of them; when the other presently gives it so sweet a rebuke that I could wish myself a sigh to be so chid, or at least a sigher to be comforted.
> (2.1.40–44)

The "divided sigh" she refers to is half uttered. Her description of it as repressed, "martyr'd . . . i' th' deliverance," and as meeting an almost dialectical "rebuke" joins her desire to be either that sigh or "at least a sigher" in prefiguring her pathetic speaking position later in the drama. Two scenes later she ascribes such pressures to her sex and age: "What pushes are we wenches driven to | When fifteen once has found us!" (2.4.6–7). "Fifteen" is her approximation of social as well as sexual maturity. Still later, she utters a desire for a pain that will keep her from sleeping:

> O for a prick now, like a nightingale,
> To put my breast against!

(3.4.25–26)

The "martyr'd" sigh, the "pushes" that "wenches are driven to," and the "prick" against which, like a nightingale, the Jailer's Daughter desires to press her breast—all these images contribute powerfully to a sadistic model of speech. This model is connected in this play and in many others with women's speech.

Like the mad language of Ophelia, the songs and mad speech of the Jailer's Daughter result from pressure. Not surprisingly, then, what is literally her final word in the play responds to pain:

Doctor. Let's get her in.
Wooer. Come sweet, we'll go to dinner,
    And then we'll play at cards.
Daughter. And shall we kiss too?
Wooer. A hundred times.
Daughter. And twenty?
Wooer. Ay, and twenty.
Daughter. And then we'll sleep together?
Doctor. Take her offer.
Wooer. Yes, marry, will we.
Daughter. But you shall not hurt me.
Wooer. I will not, sweet.
Daughter. If you do, love, I'll cry.
    (5.2.107–12)

The Wooer and the Doctor take the parts of Palamon and Arcite while maintaining a separate, if equally theatrical, space for their discourse of "reality." The Jailer's Daughter explores her fantasy within the context of their obliging conspiracy. Yet significant in this sequence is how her final line conveys an image of the body in pain. "If you do, love, I'll cry" comes as an unsettling last word, testifying to how she has been alternately frustrated and manipulated throughout the play.

It is important to heed the situation of the Jailer's Daughter as an individual because formally her pathos is tightly linked to how she expresses the cultural and historical. Without the madness prompted by what seems initially a personal situation, the more public valences of her speech would not be so concentrated. While signaling the cultural and the public, for instance, the ballads she sings in her madness depend on the individual and the private for their existence. The drama's individuation of the Jailer's Daughter—a process that includes her personal manner of speech—leads first to the production of an unconscious responding to her pain; that unconscious, in turn, embodies both her individual state and the conditions of the worlds around her.

The Jailer's Daughter is a pivotal figure in Jacobean drama; her character, richly synthesizing Fletcherian and Shakespearean traditions, was perhaps unrepeatable. Although her role was not to be duplicated in the drama of the time, its significance merits an expansion of the areas in which we look for cultural content in early modern drama. Materialist criticism, for instance, has traditionally emphasized the choric speech of male characters like fools and gravediggers. It is the Jailer's Daughter, however, who provides the richest portrait of the cultural in *The Two Noble Kinsmen*. Where female characters in Shakespeare's history plays have been described as "antihistorians," in this late play the Jailer's Daughter remains the character with the clearest and most meaningful relation to the historical.[56] If her speech makes little happen in the drama's political world, it nonetheless represents the worlds inside and outside the playhouse and formulates their truths. The speech of the Jailer's Daughter records things that other characters and other speech genres in *The Two Noble Kinsmen* do not. Through her special way of speaking and through what she says, we see that her mad language in this play registers the increasing separation of court and city from the country. *The Two Noble Kinsmen* is culturally and historically thick in and through the quotations of her mad speech.

CHAPTER 6

A Renaissance of Quotation

So far, this book has looked at selected patterns of quotation in various texts of the sixteenth and seventeenth centuries. The intention throughout has been to demonstrate the value of a "writerly" intertextuality to our understanding of literature, especially in relation to questions of culture and history. Inasmuch as the term "quotation" has been used in its general, early modern sense—one that encompasses a material borrowing or repositioning—this book has until now run the risk of disappointing those readers who might have expected a full-length study of Shakespearean quotations in our contemporary sense of the word: individuals deploying bits of Shakespeare in speeches, literary works, and other publications.

I will now address such an expectation and at the same time extend the scope of my inquiry in two ways. The previous chapters have offered readings of intertextuality through the aid of a focusing text, author, or character; this chapter will survey the quotation of the historical and literary period known as the English Renaissance. That such quotation is not during but after—quoting the Renaissance rather than the Renaissance quoting—brings us to the second way in which I will now extend the implications of this study's argument. By examining the manner in which texts and persons from the sixteenth and seventeenth centuries were quoted in the first half of the twentieth, the following discussion will show the necessity of understanding how quotation operates in modern cultural and critical discourses as well as those of the early modern era.

Scholars commonly agree that the intensive *bricolage* of modernist art frequently turned to the sixteenth and seventeenth centuries for its material; this quotation affected our reception of those works and the era from which they came. Recent studies by Hugh Grady and by Richard Halpern, for instance, have demonstrated how crucial the modernist movement was to the formation of our critical and aesthetic assumptions about the English Renaissance.[1] Such was the direction of this quotation that by the 1940s an English "Renaissance" was a given. This conceptualization of the period had not been the case several decades earlier, when other terms and concepts had been used to describe the period. Ironically, whereas the *bricolage* that led to the sixteenth- and seventeenth-century Renaissance was a messy, laborious thing, the twentieth-century notion of Renaissance (formed by a pattern of quotation only slightly tidier) was elitist in orientation. This viewpoint had important critical as well as cultural implications, for the scholars affected by this period concept aligned English authors less with domestic sources than with foreign and classical ones. Instead of ballads, English-language primers and catechisms, and Sternhold and Hopkins, English writers would be associated with, for example, Sannazaro, Castiglione, and Boccaccio.

To be sure, English authors of this time read widely, and their reading obviously included Continental and Classical authors—to suggest otherwise would be to fly in the face of reality. Just as surely, however, the notion of an English Renaissance has led us at times to focus too selectively upon the rarefied rather than the ordinary quotations of English writers. It is not at all clear, for instance, that Petrarch was a more important resource for Shakespeare's Sonnets than was Thomas Tusser's *Five Hundreth Points of Good Husbandry,* although criticism invariably turns to Petrarch and almost never to Tusser when acknowledging the framework of values in those poems. To work with a Renaissance as a model is to be tempted to embrace *imitatio* at the expense of *bricolage,* to gaze toward the light in Troy at the expense of closer, English flames. Obviously, we need to retain the lessons of such criticism and to recognize the stunning variety of texts and resources that English writers drew upon when constructing their own. But we also need to realize that the notion of an English Renaissance was itself constructed at a certain time and that this construction was accomplished through a cultural pattern of *bricolage*—quotation that pieced together an elevated period myth that has sometimes obscured our vision of reality. That this myth effectively denied its own origins is a story less of England than of America.

Parallel Lives

The handicraftsmen of democratic ages not only endeavor to bring their useful productions within the reach of the whole community, but strive to give to all their commodities attractive qualities that they do not in reality possess. In the confusion of all ranks everyone hopes to succeed in this object. This sentiment, indeed, which is only too natural to the heart of man, does not originate in the democratic principle; but that principle applies it to material objects. The hypocrisy of virtue is of every age, but the hypocrisy of luxury belongs more particularly to the ages of democracy.

ALEXIS DE TOCQUEVILLE, *Democracy in America*

In 1930 readers who had made their way to the second volume of J. M. Keynes's *Treatise on Money* encountered a curious footnote. In a section treating the effects of New World gold and silver on the economies of Renaissance Europe, the English economist paused just long enough to imply a positive relation between a society's economy and the quality of its art. Shakespeare's career as a dramatist, according to Keynes,

> chanced to fall at the date of dates, when any level-headed person in England disposed to make money could hardly help doing so. 1575 to 1620 were the palmy days of profit—one of the greatest "bull" movements ever known until modern days in the United States. . . . I offer it as a thesis for examination by those who like rash generalisations, that by far the larger proportion of the world's greatest writers and artists have flourished in the atmosphere of buoyancy, exhilaration and the freedom from economic cares felt by the governing class, which is engendered by profit inflations.[2]

To Keynes, the greatness of art remains tightly linked to the "freedom from economic cares felt by the governing class." He makes no effort, however, to explain the underlying reason for and the exact nature of the relation between the "greatest writers and artists" and this governing class. Instead, looking back on the bull market of 1920s America and earlier, Keynes invites comparison between the putative "buoyancy" and "exhilaration" of the Elizabethan era and the atmosphere of apparently limitless possibilities that had characterized the financial scene in the United States during the previous few decades.[3] The first and last historical periods Keynes uses in illustrating his larger argument are labeled "Spanish Treasure" (from which the footnote is drawn) and "The United States,

1925–30." As if borrowing a chapter from Plutarch, Keynes suggests the parallel lives of "great" cultures.

Whether this aside is, as Harry Levin grumbled, "as crass an application of economic determinism as any Marxist has ever perpetrated," it clearly offers a malleable version of history consonant less with the economic theory of Keynes's day than with its literary Modernism.[4] One finds in Pound's *Cantos* and in Eliot's *The Waste Land,* for instance, both a complex pattern of allusions to and appropriations from the verse of previous eras.[5] Eliot's poem has been described as "like a parody of a Poem (capital P), which in the course of getting itself written . . . manages imitations of Jacobean verse, of Shakespearean set pieces, of Sappho, of Dante, of *vers libre,* of Hindu oracularisms, and of the multilingual play Hieronymo devised to trap the murderer of his son."[6] Modernist works, popular and otherwise, tend to quote; in so doing, they often align (in however invidious a way) the present with the culture of the past. As Malcolm Bradbury and James McFarlane argue, in its most general manifestation "What Modernism does is to raise in ferment the notion not only of form but also of significant time. . . . It illuminates the symbolist effort to transcend historical sequence by intersecting with it the timelessness of artistic revelation."[7] Of course, when this effort to transcend sequence joined an aggressive nostalgia (as it would, for example, in various fascistic movements of the 1930s), the brutal burden of such mythology became only too apparent. For various reasons, the mythology of the Renaissance proved less malignant in its twentieth-century reincarnations than that of the classical periods. Its storehouse of texts, themes, and figures exceeded the narrower interests of what has been called the project of "nativist modernism" in America during the 1920s and after.[8] In fact, what Keynes hinted at almost in passing in 1930—that is, a relationship, based on economic factors, between the Renaissance and the world of the present—formed a powerful yet supple cultural paradigm in the extended 1930s. Because its immediate economic basis would dissolve with the Great Depression, Keynes's model can be said to anticipate ironically the significance that Shakespeare and the English Renaissance assumed for America throughout the late 1920s and the whole of the 1930s. This irony did little, however, to diminish the attractiveness of the analogy, for nowhere at this time did the myth of the English Renaissance become more important.

Shakespeare's plays had long been considered somehow "American" in essence and import—considered American, that is, by Americans who used Shakespeare to define their cultural heritage.[9] Yet if Shakespeare seems always to have enjoyed a sacrosanct place in American notions of culture, one should remember that cultural perceptions of and familiarity with his plays have varied over time even as his overall reputation has remained strong.[10] These varying levels of familiarity pose a challenge for cultural criticism, for in glossing over them we contribute to the myth of a monolithic, ever-central Shakespeare—a myth that, however useful rhetorically, does not square with historical reality. A related error commonly made in this regard is focusing on the cultural presence of Shakespeare to the exclusion of other authors, works, and figures from early modern England. Surprisingly, our penchant for contextualizing Shakespeare's works in their own time has seldom extended in studies of their reception to the roles assumed by his contemporaries. That is, while Shakespeare's reputation in America has frequently been scrutinized, the story of his influence on American culture has too rarely been told in relation to the cultural visibility of the English Renaissance as a whole. By examining the mutual resonance of Shakespeare and the English Renaissance in America in the 1920s and 1930s, we can acquire a deeper understanding of how and why works of the sixteenth and seventeenth centuries—including Shakespeare's plays—came to assume such a lasting place in that part of the American public sphere relating to culture.

During this period Shakespeare and other Renaissance authors and figures began to appear with a novel regularity in venues from the academy to Hollywood and from Broadway to the popular press; as they did so, they took a more prominent place in America's definition of the cultural as well as changed how Americans would define their own domestic cultural heritage. The first efforts of Americanist scholars like F. O. Matthiessen and Willard Thorp, for example, concerned Elizabethan literature; their later success at exploring an "American Renaissance" depended greatly upon the creation of a prestigious English forerunner. This endeavor involved more than domesticating a foreign Renaissance, for until the 1920s it was not usual to speak of an "*English* Renaissance," and only during the 1930s would the term become standard for describing what had earlier been called, among other things, "Elizabethan," "Tudor," "pre-Restoration," even "Old English." Before America could sustain a Renaissance of its own, it needed to invent one for England.

American artists and scholars invented this Renaissance for a variety of reasons and did so through a conscious, even obsessive pattern of engagement with a time and culture to which they felt they were heirs, yet needed, somehow, to recreate. What resulted was a period image, canon, and style that—with our current emphasis on the "early modern"—we are perhaps only now able to put in context and to understand as a beginning of the Renaissance we know.

The Hamlet of A. MacLeish

I do not mean by this to commit myself to any foolish prediction that the movies have before them a future comparable to the career of Elizabethan drama from 1580 on, but only to emphasize what we can be sure of: that the movies are an art with amazing resources and a very considerable accomplishment already to their credit, and that they offer the critics, who have been looking so hard in other places for such a thing, the makings of a great popular art. ARTHUR MIZENER, "The Elizabethan Art of our Movies" (1942)

In the extended 1930s, the period between (ex-heavyweight champion of the world) Gene Tunney's lecture on Shakespeare at Yale in 1928 and Ernest Hemingway's nod to Donne in titling *For Whom the Bell Tolls* in 1940, Americans alluded to, quoted from, and used the Renaissance with increasing alacrity and sense of purpose.[11] Playing on the same popular fancy that had welcomed Lytton Strachey's *Elizabeth and Essex* in 1928, for instance, Maxwell Anderson answered the public's desire for stories about the English Renaissance with the verse dramas *Elizabeth the Queen* (1930) and *Mary of Scotland* (1933). That same year, 1928, Houghton Mifflin brought out *The Hamlet of A. MacLeish,* a poetic meditation that drew on Shakespeare's tragedy as template, and T. S. Eliot published his own book of homage, *For Lancelot Andrewes.* In 1929 something akin to an institutional watershed was reached, as Hebel and Hudson's poetry anthology (one that would become standard for generations of students) presented its selections as *Poetry of the English Renaissance*—as opposed to "Poetry of the Tudor" or "Elizabethan" periods, both, again, traditional ways of describing the 1500s and 1600s in England.[12] In an essay published in the April 1929 number of *The American Mercury* and titled "Renaissance in Hollywood," Robert E. Sherwood argued that "the revolution" that the "talkies" caused in Hollywood "will come to be known, in time, as a memorable Renaissance."[13] That same year Mary Pickford and Douglas Fairbanks enacted marital farce for the nation in a United Artists production of *The Taming of the Shrew,* which included the real-life marriage of its stars in the studio's publicity promotion and the film's popular appeal.[14] The following year, in 1930, the appearance of Alfred Lunt (as Essex) and Lynn Fontanne (as Elizabeth) in the stage production of Anderson's *Elizabeth the Queen* replicated this style of casting as, a few hundred miles south of Broadway, the cornerstone of the Folger Shakespeare Library was laid in Washington DC. In 1930 also Archibald MacLeish published his poems "You, Andrew Marvell" and "'Not Marble Nor the Gilded Monuments'" in his collection *New Found Land;* and in 1930–31 Eliot wrote both "Mariana" and *Coriolan.*

Nineteen thirty-two saw the publishing house of Noble and Noble bring out, under a single cover, two plays "for Collateral reading": Shakespeare's *Julius Caesar* and Anderson's *Elizabeth the Queen.* A year later *Macbeth* would be bound with O'Neill's *The Emperor Jones* in this series dedicated to "Comparative Classics," suggesting a literary "parallel lives" of the two cultures not unlike that implied by Keynes. In 1933 American audiences flocked to see *The Private Life of Henry VIII,* a roisterous farce for which Charles Laughton, as Henry, would receive an Academy Award for Best Actor. In 1934 the Chicago World's Fair developed and staged thirty-minute versions of Shakespeare's plays to compensate for the unseemly reputation that burlesque shows had brought the fair.[15] And in 1934, the year in which riots broke out over Piachaud's *Coriolan* at the Comédie Française, T. S. Eliot displayed in his *Elizabethan Essays* the same admiration for the high culture of England that had helped make him an expatriate in the first place. The next year saw the founding of the Oregon Shakespeare Festival at Ashland, Oregon—America's first Shakespeare festival (following only four years after the New Memorial Theater opened at Stratford-upon-Avon in 1931). It was in 1935 too that Jimmy Cagney (as Bottom) and Mickey Rooney (as Puck) appeared in Max Reinhardt and William Dieterle's celebrated production of *A Midsummer Night's Dream* (Warners), followed in 1936 by Leslie Howard and Norma Shearer in MGM's *Romeo and Juliet* and Katharine Hepburn and Frederic March in RKO's *Mary of Scotland.*

Across the Atlantic, this Americanization of Shakespeare on film occasioned a somewhat pointed exchange in the pages of *The Listener* during the first ten days of March 1937. In an essay titled "Alas, Poor Will!" Harley

Granville-Barker decried the recent Hollywood versions of *Romeo and Juliet* and *A Midsummer Night's Dream* on a variety of grounds before maintaining that radio Shakespeare was perhaps the only legitimate alternative to a theatrical performance. Yet even a broadcast Shakespeare, he argued, needed to live up to the spoken standards of the BBC, for Shakespeare represents English "culture" and "national character"; countless listeners, Granville-Barker held, understood "Shakespeare on the wireless" as "'England calling.'"[16] The snobbery manifest in this position was countered a week later by none other than Alfred Hitchcock, then director of drama at the BBC, who, baiting Granville-Barker, trumpeted film's superiority to the stage and observed that "The cinema can do without Shakespeare." Even so, Hitchcock went on to say, the film version of *Romeo and Juliet* "sugar-coated the bitter pill of literature" and popularized Shakespeare: "In one showing of *Romeo and Juliet* round the country, more people will see a work of Shakespeare than will ever attend stage Shakespeare in a year."[17]

Within four months of this exchange, the CBS radio network had begun to act upon Granville-Barker's preference for wireless Shakespeare even as it used Hollywood talent to do so. In July 1937, CBS inaugurated a weekly series of eight productions of Shakespeare's plays. Every Monday night, from 9 to 10 P.M., Eastern Standard Time, listeners could hear a one-hour version of such plays as *King Lear, As You Like It,* and *Hamlet* on approximately ninety stations coast-to-coast. One "draw" of these productions involved the use of Hollywood stars in prominent roles: Burgess Meredith performed Hamlet in the first program and was followed by Edward G. Robinson as Petruchio, Humphrey Bogart as Hotspur, Tallulah Bankhead and Orson Welles in *Twelfth Night,* and Claude Rains in *Julius Caesar.*[18] Competing with this CBS program, the National Broadcasting Corporation began its own annual series of "Great Plays" in 1937. The first three series all began with classical dramas and included several plays of the English Renaissance—among these, Marlowe's *Tamburlaine, Edward II,* and *Doctor Faustus*; Shakespeare's *A Midsummer Night's Dream, Julius Caesar, Othello, Romeo and Juliet,* and *Macbeth*; and Jonson's *Volpone*—before concluding each year with one of Maxwell Anderson's plays: *Valley Forge, Elizabeth the Queen,* and *Winterset.*[19] That summer NBC, on its less prestigious "blue" channel, also began its own "Streamlined Shakespeare" series, starring John Barrymore. Starting at the end of June, Barrymore presented forty-five-minute versions of *Hamlet, Richard III, Macbeth, The Tempest,*

Twelfth Night, and *The Taming of the Shrew.*[20] In 1937 also Orson Welles stunned the American theater scene with a production of *Doctor Faustus* and a now famous, anti-Fascist *Julius Caesar.* Welles, of course, had one year earlier produced the famous "voodoo" *Macbeth* at the Lafayette Theatre in Harlem, and his interest in Renaissance plays continued as he commenced 1938 with a New Year's Day opening of Thomas Dekker's *Shoemaker's Holiday.* The next year, 1939, Bette Davis and Errol Flynn appeared in *The Private Lives of Elizabeth and Essex* (Warners); Rodgers and Hart adapted Shakespeare's *Comedy of Errors* under the title *The Boys from Syracuse*; and Louis Armstrong starred as Bottom in a jazz version of *A Midsummer Night's Dream,* titled *Swingin' the Dream.*

It was during the Depression decade that specialized institutions like the Folger and Huntington Libraries (the latter of which published its first *Bulletin* in 1931) allowed scholars further access to the Renaissance's literary riches in rare books and manuscripts purchased from England. The character of the Folger's holdings had been transformed almost overnight when, in 1938, it bought the collection of Sir Leicester Harmsworth; his nine thousand volumes helped change the Folger "from a resource primarily for Shakespeare studies into a major research center where scholars could study almost any aspect of English-speaking civilization in the 16th and 17th centuries."[21] A larger concern with the English Renaissance also characterized the Huntington Library in these years. In August 1940 this interest led the Huntington to host a conference on "historical problems in the interpretation of the civilization of the English Renaissance"; among the approximately sixty scholars in attendance were such influential figures as Josephine Waters Bennett, Lily B. Campbell, R. F. Jones, Helen White, Ray Heffner, and Louis B. Wright.[22]

As the preceding paragraphs demonstrate, however, scholars were not alone in tapping the riches of the Renaissance. Producers, writers, and actors used its drama—both what had been written for performance (e.g., *Hamlet*) and what transpired in the pages of history (e.g., the events forming the basis of *Elizabeth and Essex*)—for revivals and "original" stories alike. Although blank verse had long been used in dramatic texts, it was taken up with new enthusiasm and with reference to its roots in earlier English culture by such playwrights as T. S. Eliot (cf. *Murder in the Cathedral* [1935]) and Maxwell Anderson. The latter's plots made explicit a felt relation between Elizabethan form and content.

Hemingway's quotation from Donne in *For Whom the Bell Tolls* in 1940 formally capped a decade that had frequently looked to Renaissance literature for resonant titles and themes—beginning shortly after Hemingway's own "In Another Country" (from Marlowe's *The Jew of Malta* [4.1.41–42]) in 1927. Although American authors had sometimes quoted from Shakespeare and other Renaissance figures in naming their works, with the publication of Faulkner's *The Sound and the Fury* (*Macbeth* 5.5.27) and Thomas Wolfe's *Look Homeward, Angel* ("Lycidas" l.163)—both issued in the ill-fated month of October 1929—the Renaissance emerged as a source of an apparently instant profundity that one could attach to a novel or play.[23] Thus the 1930s saw Philip Barry's *Tomorrow and Tomorrow* (1931, *Macbeth* 5.5.19), Maxwell Anderson's *Both Your Houses* (1933, *Romeo and Juliet* 3.1.91), S. N. Behrman's *Rain from Heaven* (1934, *Merchant of Venice* 4.1.185), *Paradise Lost* by Clifford Odets (1935), and John Steinbeck's *In Dubious Battle* (*Paradise Lost* 1.104), which, like Aldous Huxley's *Eyeless in Gaza* (*Samson Agonistes* 41), took its title in 1936 from a passage in Milton's poetry. (Huxley's *Brave New World* [*Tempest* 5.1.183] had been published four years earlier, in 1932.)

This concerted use of the English Renaissance came not only at a certain time but also with a specific generation. I have maintained that the widespread engagement with the English Renaissance that occurred in America during the late 1920s and 1930s was related to the larger Modernist tendency of quotation and allusion. And indeed, several American modernists had previously shown an acquaintance with English Renaissance texts.[24] During the teens, for instance, Edwin Arlington Robinson published his important poem, "Ben Jonson Entertains a Man from Stratford" (1915), and Robert Frost wrote "Out, Out—" (1916), based on Shakespeare's line from *Macbeth*.[25] In 1917, Pound began publishing his "Notes on Elizabethan Classicists" in the *Egoist* and would mention Caliban and Ariel in *Hugh Selwyn Mauberley* in 1920. Eliot's own "incessant effort to come to terms with Shakespeare" and the literature of that era would surface in three essays published in 1919: "The New Elizabethans and the Old"; "Hamlet and His Problems"; and "*The Duchess of Malfi* at the Lyric: and Poetic Drama."[26] While examples of this kind of engagement can be found across the works of various modernists, however, not all of these writers would continue to quote and allude to texts of the English Renaissance. As the *Egoist* remarks make clear, for instance, Pound was interested in the Elizabethans primarily as filters for classical themes. And such poets as Frost, Wallace Stevens, and William Carlos Williams devoted little attention to the period. Instead, it would be Eliot and a younger generation of writers that most aggressively took up the Renaissance as a legitimate, and legitimizing, period.

Most of the figures involved in this endeavor, in fact, were born in or after 1888, establishing what one might see as a generational project. One can trace a significant pattern in the following chronology of birth dates, which includes both writers and scholars:

E. A. Robinson	1869
Robert Frost	1874
Gertrude Stein	1874
Willa Cather	1876
Wallace Stevens	1879
William Carlos Williams	1883
Ezra Pound	1885
TRANSITIONAL PERIOD	
T. S. Eliot	1888
Maxwell Anderson	1888
Raymond Chandler	1888
Archibald MacLeish	1892
Philip Barry	1896
William Faulkner	1897
Ernest Hemingway	1899
Thomas Wolfe	1900
Langston Hughes	1902
F. O. Matthiessen	1902
John Steinbeck	1902
Ralph Ellison	1914

Eliot is clearly a transitional figure in relation to the use of the English Renaissance, as are Maxwell Anderson and Raymond Chandler. That these three writers, otherwise quite different in their styles and subject matter, would all quote, allude to, and use the English Renaissance is more than accidental. It is, instead, a habit determined by history: born in the same year, they would later engage the Renaissance as a source in a way that set them apart from older writers working at the same time. Eliot's

Elizabethan era, of course, seems worlds apart from that of Maxwell Anderson: *For Lancelot Andrewes* (1928) and *Elizabethan Essays* (1934) are rarely mentioned in the same context with the works of Anderson, and we still labor under a Modernism divided by the putative audiences to which various works seem directed. But the coincidence of these artists' births suggests that the apparent differences between their audiences are less important than the deep continuities of their works' historical visions. Like many who followed them, and in contrast to the modernists who preceded them, this generation of artists dedicated itself to the invention of a usable English past.

An Impermanent Nation

Harvard, I trust, will counter by asking Babe Ruth to tell the boys in Cambridge just what Milton has meant to him.

HEYWOOD BROUN, in the *New York World,* on Tunney's Shakespeare lecture at Yale

But why this dedication? Why was the English Renaissance so ubiquitous in America during this period and for this generation of artists and scholars? One answer concerns the way in which the English Renaissance formed a locus of intrinsic worth, a ready-made source of cultural value that could be used to remedy a perceived lack in the American scene. Even as scholars and students in the English Renaissance had turned to Greek and Roman texts for authority, so did artists and academics during the late 1920s and 1930s look to the Renaissance for words, stories, and themes that could confer distinction upon a culture apparently still undistinguished. Yet the Renaissance was most useful in this regard when it was cast as a progenitor of things American, when it formed part of what one could call a cultural "family romance." Freud coined this last term to describe the self-aggrandizing stories that children tell themselves as part of a delusive reinvention of their origins.[27] Like erotic and ambitious daydreams, these fantasies remedy actual life by allowing these children to persuade themselves that, rather than the offspring of ordinary individuals, they come from "grander people" and "aristocratic parents" and hence should return to better circumstances.

Much like the working of the family romance on the personal level, the myth of the English Renaissance allowed Americans to believe themselves the rightful inheritors of a rich and esteemed culture. Frequently this genealogy took on an uncanny aura, the Renaissance appearing both strange and familiar, present and absent. This phenomenon manifests itself nowhere as clearly as in Wolfe's 1929 novel, *Look Homeward, Angel,* a text in which the Elizabethan age literally haunts America. When the protagonist, a young Eugene Gant, ponders the reality of the ghost stories he has been reading, he wonders "did an old ghost ever come to haunt this land? The ghost of Hamlet's Father, in Connecticut." What follows—almost an essay in bathos—shows how Wolfe measures America against a more substantial Renaissance:

> "I am thy father's spirit,
> Doomed for a certain term to walk the night
> Between Bloomington and Portland, Maine."

> He felt suddenly the devastating impermanence of the nation.[28]

That Eugene's cultural angst must be phrased in terms of Hamlet's psychic preoccupations may initially tell the reader more about Eugene than about his culture: that is, Wolfe's alter ego can be seen as fearing his own "devastating impermanence" in relation to the literary canon. But Eugene's "sudden" feeling about his nation's impermanence also summarizes a cultural preoccupation with America's lack of tradition, which—however perennial—produced a special interest in the English Renaissance at this time.

Two years after the publication of Wolfe's novel, in an article in *The Atlantic Monthly* dealing with the still unfinished Folger Shakespeare Library, George Whicher would invoke a version of Wolfe's metaphor to similar effect. Observing that its holdings would make the Folger indispensable to scholars concerned with the Renaissance, Whicher went on to speculate what the library might mean for American letters generally: "Can an institution so dedicated, and supported by the most munificent bequest ever made for the purpose of literary study and progress, be directed to the encouragement of contemporary letters as well as to the stimulation of research and criticism? Can it serve to make evident that the sprit of Shakespeare is continued down to our own day by the work of original writers no less than by the activities of actors, editors, and commentators?"[29] To Whicher, the "spirit of Shakespeare" extends beyond the playwright's works, beyond works of his time, and even beyond works written in England, for what he later calls "the life blood of a master spirit" flows in the veins of American writers as well. Posing rhetorical questions of his own, Whicher seems to answer with hopeful affirmation Wolfe's query as to whether a Shakespearean ghost haunts an impermanent nation.

To ask the question at hand in a more pointed way: Why this ghost and this culture? Why should the works of Shakespeare and other English Renaissance authors, rather than those of writers from another place and period, have been so resonant at this time? Here a number of answers apply. One might begin by observing that Renaissance works had the paradoxical attraction of being in a common language that, owing to shifts in vocabulary and syntax, was decidedly uncommon in its orientation. To master these texts required a linguistic fluency that could mark one with distinction; such mastery brought distinction because it most often indicated higher education, which in turn indicated the finances necessary to support study at that level. Thus "back," in time, could imply "up" on the social ladder.[30] These texts' copiousness and eloquence also appealed to American audiences, as did their emphasis (most marked in the drama) on a potentially liberating theatricality and role-playing.[31] Much Renaissance drama was, in this regard, structurally well-suited to an American public, for in general plays had been written for performance by actors of the middle and lower orders, before heterogeneous audiences, and often concerned the otherwise little-seen affairs of rulers. One can see the voyeuristic aspect of Renaissance plays spilling over to the titles of such works as *The Private Life of Henry VIII* and *The Private Lives of Elizabeth and Essex* and in the focus in biographical plays and films of the 1930s on Elizabeth and her court. Making greatness familiar, plays by Shakespeare and his contemporaries offered Americans a glimpse at the "private lives" of the aristocracy and were the motivating documents behind these later historical dramas.

As much as it offered eloquence, *copia,* and a public window to these elusive private lives, however, the English Renaissance offered Americans a sense of purpose and a way of bettering themselves by claiming the larger cultural inheritance of a common language. The emphasis on role-playing and eloquence appealed to a nation that sought to transform itself through an attachment to something greater than itself. As patterns for a different, more elevated life, works of the Renaissance lent, in their openness to performance, a sense of community with a storied past.

This effect appears most clearly, perhaps, in a high-school teacher's account of an ongoing "radio theater party" she established during the summer of 1937, when NBC and CBS broadcast their competing productions of Shakespeare's plays. As the teacher, Elizabeth Carney, relates the story, what had begun as an informal recitation of *Macbeth* with a younger friend soon involved family and friends and turned into a weekly "Monday evening radio theater party": "The first one met at my apartment where at half-past five I served the first courses of a simple supper. The next act was the listening to the play as presented by the 'Lux Radio Theater.' After that came dessert. And what a dessert—a Shakespearean carnival of spontaneous discussion. Everyone jabbered at once about his likes and dislikes of the play presented. . . . While the play was in action a few students quoted along with the actor some famous passages."[32] The wording of Carney's account makes it difficult to separate the dinner and its "act[s]" from the production; the scene of the dinner party becomes finally indistinguishable from the play that they have gathered to hear. Students "quote" along with the actors on the radio, and dessert becomes a "Shakespearean carnival." Significantly, the words on the radio seem to free the voices of the listeners. Carney's students go on to hold weekly radio parties at their own homes on Monday evenings and start a creative-writing magazine based on the collective enthusiasm for literature sparked by these parties and the ensuing "Shakespearean carnival[s]." Broadcast into American homes, Shakespeare's works served as scripts to be repeated. Where Wolfe and Whicher had hoped that the spirit of Shakespeare might somehow be recognized in America, Carney provides us with a practical account of how, during the summer of 1937, Shakespeare's disembodied words encouraged a sense of culture and possibility in those who heard them on the ghostly medium of radio.

We might take the preceding three instances as indicative of various cultural sites—a novel, a library, a radio program—where a national séance was held, a gathering that called up Shakespeare's ghost in order to bring meaning to America and to Americanness. But as our previous survey of the 1930s indicated, Shakespeare's was not the only spirit so invoked. Like many other artists of the era, Wolfe saw the English Renaissance itself as a powerful literary and historical period toward which one could gesture in response to a felt insecurity about the lack of a national culture. Joan Shelly Rubin's history of the growth of "middlebrow" culture during this period underscores how important the category of "culture" had become and how energetically individuals and institutions sought to increase the status of literature—even as this literature was felt to confer distinction upon those who appreciated it.[33] And where many aspects of American culture in the 1930s could be fairly characterized in relation to what Jürgen Habermas has called "legitimation crisis," the long-developing emphasis on Renaissance texts and figures clearly indicates that this tendency between the late 1920s and the early 1940s is less a crisis than a fruition that coincided with the emergence of mass cultural forms and technologies.[34] To legitimate these demotic outlets, those involved looked toward the "high" culture of Renaissance England in a manner whose paradoxical nature was matched only by that of the modernists, who strove to construct a "new" poetics by looking backward. Another paradox arose in that America—a self-proclaimed democracy—determined its aesthetic registers by increasing its idolization of an extremely absolutist period in the history of a monarchical state that it had once fought to leave.[35]

These paradoxes revealed themselves in certain proaristocratic appropriations of the Renaissance during the 1930s, in instances where the Elizabethan era served as an epic or tragedic advertisement for the glory that was England. In this way, an approving emphasis on aristocracy and on the often capricious decisions of a ruler could seem to flirt with the idea of a "strong-man" or even fascistic form of government and suggested class divisions stronger than those that already obtained. Such appropriations, however, were also joined by comedic uses of the English Renaissance that sought to popularize and even deflate it for a general audience. These two strategies, one articulating a high Renaissance, the other a low Renaissance—strategies that would invariably merge in the commodity form of middlebrow, popular art—define the major means by which Depression-era America used the Elizabethan age as cultural capital. A third kind of appropriation, dealt with later in this chapter, is significant not only in its pessimism but also in its eschewing of Shakespeare to focus instead on one of his dramatic contemporaries.

"You're English, aren't you?"

And of Shakespeare's poetry two or three hundred lines—not I think more— and these not merely mutilated, but occasionally even re-written from Elizabethan English into plainer American (and quite needlessly: there is nothing in the play that a child may not sufficiently understand).

HARLEY GRANVILLE-BARKER, on Max Reinhardt's 1937 film version of *A Midsummer Night's Dream*

To many Americans the tragedic or high Renaissance—the Renaissance of *Hamlet,* Queen Elizabeth, and the Earl of Essex—promised an unlimited upward perfectibility. We can see this high Renaissance in the works of Wolfe, Eliot, and MacLeish, among others, as well as in the Comparative Classics series and its yoking of Renaissance tragedies with their 1930s counterparts. Central to this version of the Renaissance were the images of grandeur, talent, and wealth customarily associated with the Elizabethan era. As Ralph Ellison would later recall, the 1920s and 1930s cultivated the dream of the complete individual in terms of the Renaissance: "Interestingly enough, by early adolescence the idea of Renaissance Man had drifted down to about six of us, and we discussed mastering ourselves and everything in sight as though no such thing as racial discrimination existed. As you can see, quite a lot of our living was done in the imagination."[36] Ellison and his friends lived in Oklahoma City in the 1920s and 1930s; their conception of the self-fashioned Renaissance Man most probably came from reading in school, at the public library, or from such magazines as *Vanity Fair,* which Ellison remembers his mother bringing home from work. "These magazines," he goes on to say, "and the discarded books my mother brought home to my brother and me spoke to me of a life which was broader and more interesting, and although it was not really a part of my own life, I never thought they were not for me simply because I happened to be a Negro. They were things which spoke of a world which I could some day make my own."[37] Here the life Ellison imagines as "broader and more interesting" suggests what he and his young friends may have seen as valuable in their conception of Renaissance Man. The idea of "mastering ourselves and everything in sight" played a role in its attraction as well. Ellison cites as its opposite the phenomenon of racial oppression. To more than a few critics today, Renaissance Humanism seems to have been too much a part of such oppression; to young Ralph Ellison, however, it offered—by way of the myth of Renaissance Man—value and hope. Retrospectively noting that "a lot of our living was done in the imagination," Ellison underscores how, for many interwar Americans, the

Renaissance allowed an imaginative life of greater scope than things perceived as American.[38]

Indeed, for many Americans the English Renaissance represented everything the American should strive to be. The Renaissance thus remained a goal: the American could approach the English, elevating the domestic to the rarified foreign. Perhaps the clearest example of this viewpoint in the art of the 1930s came in the film *Morning Glory* (1933, RKO), where Katharine Hepburn, as aspiring actress Eva Lovelace, sets out to develop her talents to their highest level. This goal, of course, is synonymous with Shakespeare and moves toward a high Renaissance but is not obtained without a monitory acknowledgment of the process's artificiality. The film opens with Hepburn walking into a theater lobby and gazing with wonder on the portraits of famous actresses, one of whom is Sarah Bernhardt. Upstairs in the producer's office, she meets an elderly actor named R. H. Hedges (C. Aubrey Smith). After asking him a question—"You're English, aren't you?"—and getting an affirmative response, she compares herself to the actresses whose portraits hang in the lobby: "I suppose I shall never be wonderful—not wonderful like them. But I've something very wonderful in me, you see."[39]

Eva's chance to display that "something very wonderful" comes months later, when, escorted by R. H. Hedges to a party at the producer's home, she drinks too much champagne and declares loudly: "You're talking to the greatest actress in the world, and I'm going to prove it to you." Stripping away the reminders of the ordinary, alcohol lets her reveal her inner worth. Silencing the noisy crowd of revelers, she fixes herself on a couch in a pensive pose like that of Rodin's *The Thinker* and solemnly begins Hamlet's "To be or not to be" soliloquy. She gets through twelve lines (all the way to "mortal coil") before an equally drunken heckler cuts her off with an obnoxious comment: "I saw Charlie Chaplin do this in California, and he was never as funny as this kid." In an instant the high Renaissance meets the low, and two Americas converge: the patently aristocratic theater scene of New York is razzed by the cynical film world at the opposite end of the country; comedy confronts tragedy. Sensing as much, Eva responds with some indignation and surprise: "Funny? Why *Hamlet*'s tragedy!" To which the drunk rejoins, "Well it's always been comic to me." Angry, Eva yanks a tablecloth off a nearby table and ascends the stairs of a raised, railed landing, which commands the center of the room, a platform not unlike the sketches sometimes drawn of the Elizabethan theater's upper gallery. With the cloth wrapped about her shoulders, Eva begins anew: "Romeo, Romeo, wherefore art thou Romeo?" Assisted by an admirer who, from below on the floor of the living room, takes Romeo's lines, Eva somberly delivers her monologue. Again someone talks over her speech: a woman asks, somewhat densely, "What is she *raving* about?" To which R. H. Hedges, the English actor, responds: "*Romeo and Juliet.* She's playing Juliet. And, my dear, she's *playing* it." He continues this vein of admiration later in complimenting Eva on an "impossibly beautiful" performance. The crowd, however, remains indifferent, generally unaware of the greatness that has graced their gathering.

The kind words of her (English) mentor nevertheless remind both Eva and the audience that something special has happened: Eva does have "something very wonderful," and that something is the ability to deliver Shakespearean lines with an archly serious conviction. The thrust of the story, from the Bernhardt portrait in the film's opening sequence to Eva's success in an unexpected opportunity at its close, concerns the myth of an American theatrical aristocracy descended from Shakespeare and the English Renaissance. Hepburn's Academy Award for Best Actress in the role of Eva Lovelace (in the same year in which Laughton won for Best Actor for his portrayal of Henry VIII) conferred on Hepburn, the actress, the same prestige that Eva, the hopeful, won through her performance of Shakespeare. Because the film's argument rests on the myth of a theatrical aristocracy, its dramatic climax comes at the producer's party, where Hepburn, as Eva, performs Shakespeare in an "impossibly beautiful" way. Like the approving English actor (who later became in real life Sir C. Aubrey Smith), Hollywood saw in Hepburn's performance an epitome of the best.[40]

This liberating nature of the Renaissance was perhaps most famously articulated in relation to the Harlem Renaissance, a term that describes the vital, creative community of African American artists in and around Manhattan during the mid- to late 1920s and the appreciation of their works in the larger culture. As David Levering Lewis points out, the phrase "Harlem Renaissance" developed from an article in the *New York Herald Tribune,* May 7, 1925, titled "A Negro Renaissance."[41] Students of the period may be familiar with Langston Hughes's cutting observation regarding this "Renaissance," an observation made in his autobiography *The Big Sea* (1940): "The ordinary Negroes hadn't heard of the Negro Renaissance.

And if they had, it hadn't raised their wages any."[42] Hughes reminds us that period tags may seem to be just that: labels, often applied in retrospect, for something that no one can see or touch. It seems significant, however, that, like Keynes, Hughes connects "Renaissance" with wealth. Five pages earlier, in fact, Hughes had associated the Harlem Renaissance with economic vitality by observing that, when the boom economy of the twenties ended, so did the Renaissance: "The 1920s were the years of Manhattan's black Renaissance . . . that Negro vogue in Manhattan, which reached its peak just before the crash of 1929."[43]

What is not frequently mentioned in discussions of the Harlem Renaissance and Hughes's relation to it, however, is that in 1942 the writer grappled with the Renaissance metaphor in his book of poetry, *Shakespeare in Harlem*. His jazzy preface speaks of locations important to African American culture, and does so with yet another nod toward Shakespeare: "A book of light verse. Afro-Americana in the blues mood. Poems syncopated and variegated in the colors of Harlem, Beale Street, West Dallas, and Chicago's South Side. Blues, ballads, and reels to be read aloud, crooned, shouted, recited, and sung. Some with gestures, some not—as you like. None with a far-away voice."[44] What we might take as an allusion to *As You Like It* in the penultimate sentence is immediately qualified: "None with a far-away voice." These are, as Hughes points out, quintessentially American poems. Shakespeare in *Harlem*. Hughes as Shakespeare. We can ask if Hughes's repeated denials of indebtedness in this book amount to an anxiety of influence or perhaps a tense means of paying homage: *Shakespeare* in Harlem. The first section of *Shakespeare in Harlem*, for example, is titled "Seven Moments of Love" with the subtitle "An Un-Sonnet Sequence in Blues." And the collection's title poem, "Shakespeare in Harlem," is a composite of Elizabethan and blues lyrics:

Hey ninny neigh!
And a hey nonny noe!
Where, oh, where
Did my sweet mama go?

Hey ninny neigh
With a tra-la-la-la!
They say your sweet mama
Went home to her ma.[45]

Like Thomas Wolfe, whose Eugene Gant is simultaneously obsessed with and oppressed by the weight of a Shakespearean heritage, Hughes is here haunted by the cultural past—and by a more recent past, which, with the Harlem Renaissance, has defined the achievement of African American writers metaphorically. Metaphors, of course, both give and take; comparisons initially welcomed can ultimately give way to a feeling of subordination. And it may be the case that, with its frequent nods to Shakespeare, *Shakespeare in Harlem* is Hughes's attempt to literalize the metaphor of a Harlem Renaissance and, by literalizing it, to gain some kind of control over the comparison. Whatever the motivation, Hughes insists on a popular version of the Shakespearean and in so insisting remains closer to the heckler in *Morning Glory* than to Eva and her aristocratic goals. As we will see, this essentially comedic Renaissance would form a rebuttal to some of the cultural assumptions made in the more pretentious recuperations of the Elizabethan era and its texts.

Shakespeare and Mickey Mouse

Hollywood made a projectile, as it were, to break down the barrier of public prejudice. Briefly, the cinema condescended to make Shakespeare palatable.

ALFRED HITCHCOCK, responding to Harley Granville-Barker (1937)

If the high Renaissance—that is, the tragedic and epic employment of the myth—provided the 1930s with a model for cultural achievement, so did a more earthy, comedic conception of the Elizabethan era. This mode might be conceived of, with the heckling Californian, as a project of deflation, of making the Renaissance safe for American democracy by emptying it of pretense and sophistication while insisting on its direct, practical value. Sometimes this comedic vein involved a glib competitiveness. In this vein, Edmund Wilson's diary for "New York, 53rd Street, 1932–33" recalls one "Manning," a Wall Street broker whom Bill (Slater) Brown worked under: "Learned *The Taming of the Shrew* by heart on account of his dislike of his wife—also, the pornographic passages in *Venus and Adonis*—when he and Bill were riding uptown in the limousine, Bill would have to go through a thesaurus and pick out words—like abracadabra—and Manning would try to think of a line from Shakespeare with 'abracadabra' in it."[46] Where the tragedic Renaissance encoded ambition, the comedic Renaissance often betrayed aggression (even when it was not, as here, so openly displayed). This familiar, even cynical use of the past and its mythology, characteristic of what I call the low or comedic Renaissance, occurs most memorably, perhaps, in the musical lyrics of Cole Porter. In Porter's puckish handling, the Renaissance in general and Shakespeare in particular become the objects of witty, tongue-in-cheek parody.

In "Goodbye, Little Dream, Goodbye," from the 1936 musical *Red, Hot and Blue,* a character asks: "Was it Romeo or Juliet, | Who said when about to die, | 'Love is not all peaches and cream, | Little dream, goodbye.'?"[47] Porter's rhetorical question spoofs the high Renaissance with a romantic awkwardness, a mediocrity that an ostensibly populist nation uses to define itself.[48] In songs like this one, he provided a softer version of what the Chaplin admirer at *Morning Glory*'s cocktail party claimed had "always been comic to me." Two years earlier, in 1934's *Anything Goes,* Porter had explored this comic vision by including Shakespeare in the first verse of the refrain of "You're the Top":

> You're a melody from a symphony by Strauss,
> You're a Bendel bonnet,
> A Shakespeare sonnet,
> You're Mickey Mouse.[49]

Reno Sweeney and Billy Crocker assure one another that they are, respectively, "the top": the best, highest, and rarest—at the pinnacle of society. They do so by equating personal value with choice items. Significantly, their use of the "top" commodities here and throughout the song (Reno and Billy's grounds of comparison) works by a leveling process in which intellectual and marketplace culture alike offer their best. Thus a "melody from a symphony by Strauss" stands side by side with a "Bendel bonnet," a "Shakespeare sonnet," and "Mickey Mouse."

Porter tricks listeners who would hear an anticlimax in this stanza and others by carefully mingling apparently disparate registers of art: though the rhyme scheme is *abba,* a commodity scheme here is *abab.* Sandwiched between a Disney character and a lady's fine hat, however, Shakespeare's sonnets (the "top" of their kind) seem somehow at home, as if by being considered the best they join a special club and attain the status of a shop-window commodity in an upscale store. The question "How is Shakespeare like Mickey Mouse?" has a straightforward answer: Both are now American. Indeed, Porter's cataloguing lyric, which includes in its many refrains "Napoleon brandy," "Garbo's sal'ry," "cellophane," "an Arrow collar," "Pepsodent," "Ovaltine," and "a dress from Saks'," functions like an advertisement for the American way, an advertisement in which Shakespeare's sonnets have a cachet determined by the approval of the market.[50] It was a market, in turn, that could make (the imported) Napoleon brandy and Greta Garbo as American as Mickey Mouse—and William Shakespeare.

This same playful commodification underlies the deployment of the Renaissance in another comedy of the 1930s, Philip Barry's *The Philadelphia Story* (play 1939, film 1940). In a compelling study of selected Hollywood film comedies drawn mainly from the period between 1934 and 1941, Stanley Cavell locates *The Philadelphia Story* in a subgenre that he calls "the comedy of remarriage." This literary kind he sees beginning (in its twentieth-century reincarnation in film) with *It Happened One Night* (1934) and centering on the romantic (re)alignment of lovers distinguished from the average by their verbal and physical wit, by their willingness to learn and forgive, and by an acknowledged common past. Significantly, one of Cavell's fundamental claims about this subgenre is that it is "an inheritor of the preoccupations and discoveries of Shakespearean romantic comedy."[51] For Cavell, that inheritance is primarily modal: the remarriage subgenre captures the emphasis on experiment and transformation underlying the green-world romance of Shakespearean comedy.

Like its dramatic original, the film of Barry's play offers an insistent version of a particular Shakespearean comedy. Cavell sees *The Philadelphia Story* as recuperating *A Midsummer Night's Dream*'s "conjunction of dreaming and waking, and of apparent fickleness, disgust, jealousy, compacted of imagination, with a collision of social classes and the presence of the whole of society at a concluding wedding ceremony."[52] And although Cavell acknowledges that his primary interests lie not in providing evidence for the textual relationship between the two worlds but rather in "discovering, given the thought of this relation, what the consequences of it might be," he nevertheless touches on a number of buried allusions and one direct nod to *A Midsummer Night's Dream*. This reference occurs when C. K. Dexter Haven (Cary Grant) offers Tracy Lord (Katharine Hepburn)—his former (and soon-to-be new) wife—an alcoholic stinger made with "the juice of a few flowers."[53] Cavell notes the resemblance to *A Midsummer Night's Dream*, where, in his words, characters' "eyes are analogously closed and opened by what it calls the liquor or juice of certain flowers or herbs."[54]

Like Cole Porter's commercial Shakespeare, C. K. Dexter Haven's "juice of a few flowers" is a commodity to be manipulated, both on the level of plot and myth (where Barry's allusion helps strengthen his play's links to Shakespeare) and on the level of personal intelligence or sophistication. To be able to quote Shakespeare is strangely equivalent to being able to pour a good drink—both of which Haven can do. Throughout the drama Barry and the dramatis personae make coy reference to Shakespeare, mimic his dramatic language (or at least a version of it), and play on figures connected with the Renaissance literary scene and its heritage. Barry's choice of name for Tracy Lord's fiancé—George Kittredge—comes as playful homage to his Shakespeare professor at Harvard, George Lyman Kittredge (1860–1941). And "Uncle Willie," the inebriated pincher who wanders through the play offering comic relief, recalls Shakespeare himself. (Cavell points out that "Bottom is the name of what it is of which Uncle Willie is the pincher" and offers that "Certainly the pun between Bottom's name and his temporary ass's head is no less blatant in Shakespeare.")[55] That Tracy's father is a man who, we are told, spends his time in the big city backing shows instead of being with his family at their country house (and briefly switches personalities and names with his brother—for a moment becoming, in Tracy's fiction, "Uncle Willie") may allude to Shakespeare's having left Anne Hathaway in Stratford with the children while he lived in London "backing" shows. We also hear of Tracy's older brother, Junius, who lives in London. As Junius is a relatively unusual name, it is perhaps not too much to see it as reference to Junius Brutus Booth (1796–1852), the London-born actor who made his reputation there as Shylock, Richard III, Iago, and Edgar, then moved to America, and became one of this country's most famous Shakespearean actors. (Booth was well named: "Junius Brutus" is, of course, a tribune of the people in *Coriolanus*). Likewise the name of "Sidney Kidd"—an editor, as one character (himself named "Macaulay," presumably after the historian) remarks, of "cheap stuff for expensive magazines"—seems a compound of Thomas Kyd and Sir Philip Sidney. These names connote two classes that could be considered, respectively, cheap (Kyd) and expensive (Sidney).

Like C. K. Dexter Haven, other characters in *The Philadelphia Story* play with the dramatic language of the Renaissance. More often than not, their allusions are general rather than specific. That is, what they say only sounds Shakespearean: the point, however, lies not in any accuracy of quotation but in their ability to approximate, mimic, and parody. Perhaps the point is to *not* get it right; they are akin, in this way, to the intentional mediocrity of Porter's Shakespeare citations. When Sandy tells Tracy "Get thee to bed," when Tracy, intoxicated, says "Not wounded, sire—but dead," and when Mike, also intoxicated, declaims "No lightweight is balding, beetle-browed Sidney Kidd, no mean displacement, his: for windy bias, bicarbonate," they are, like *Huckleberry Finn*'s King and Duke, having a good time with hard and archaic words but also making a space for their "new" American Shakespeare.[56] One could, of course, take Mike's declamation as a parody of certain Shakespearean lines (e.g., Mercutio's "Here are the beetle brows shall blush for me" [*Romeo* 1.4.32 (themselves spoken in play)], and Polonius's "With windlass and with assays of bias" [*Hamlet* 2.1.62]). But in the end it is the general unnaturalness of Shakespearean diction—the fact that we recognize it is (and isn't) Shakespeare—that makes things funny. Barry follows Cole Porter's lead in having his characters engage the American Glib; that Barry himself relies on this glibness testifies to the thoroughly "literary" nature of the group identity his characters forge.

To the "real" George (Lyman) Kittredge, Shakespeare "had the ability to put himself in your place, and then—to speak."[57] In *The Philadelphia Story,* Barry and his characters speak by putting themselves in the various places they see as Shakespeare's. The film version of Barry's play tells us that everyone connected with the drama, from playwright to director to character, seems to know all about "Shakespeare," to have read him in college, and, further, to enjoy showing this off. So if, like the "juice of a few flowers," Shakespeare is a commodity one can use to make the hours pass more quickly, it is also the case that Shakespeare forms part of the acknowledged common past so important to the characters (and subgenre) of remarriage comedies: what Cavell calls "a past they can admit together."[58] These same characters use Shakespeare to fashion themselves in the present. The importance of the First Folio as symbolic capital to the central characters of *The Philadelphia Story* brings us, then, to the importance of another symbolic capital: Philadelphia. Not for nothing does this film, which is so preoccupied with how to live with one another, open with a shot of the Liberty Bell, for what Cavell refers to as "what happened in Philadelphia during the making of our Declaration of Independence and our Constitution" seems, like the Elizabethan theater, central to the movie. Central, but different. For while the Constitution and the Declaration of Independence are the object of the *text*'s direction of historical reference, the characters within its green world glibly work to make another document, the First Folio, equivalent on the level of action to the unarguably less playful words of American democracy.

While Barry and Porter are scarcely anyone's idea of populist authors, they do offer a popularized Renaissance more open to the public than the tragic Renaissance of such works as *Morning Glory* or *The Hamlet of A. MacLeish*. Porter's lyrics place Shakespeare within the market of commodities broadcast to a mass cultural audience; the radio stations that brought condensed versions of Shakespeare's plays to the American public during the late 1930s did so with the sponsorship of commercial interests, whose products were advertised in a manner much like that which Porter's singers use in "You're the Top." We can imagine such commercials framing the one-hour Shakespeare plays that Elizabeth Carney and her students gathered to hear on their radios during the summer of 1937. Similarly, George Whicher's hope that the "life blood" of Shakespeare was running in the veins of American writers appears to have formed part of the background of *The Philadelphia Story*. While the plot of Barry's play and film revolves around the doings of a wealthy and pedigreed Philadelphia family, both vehicles imply that a rising middle class is taking strength from Renaissance words. Sidney Kidd is a newspaper editor, and Mike Macaulay is both a reporter and sometime creative writer whose short stories Tracy locates in the public library. Her ardent approval of Macaulay's stories suggests that, like the character Hepburn played in *Morning Glory*, he has "something very wonderful" in him.

But the conclusion to *The Philadelphia Story* indicates that Macaulay is, unlike Eva Lovelace, firmly moored in, even dedicated to, his class position. If Shakespeare's words can communicate one's innate value, they do not, as in *Morning Glory*, allow one to transcend the blunt realities of social class. In this way the comedic Renaissance expressed a more honest understanding of American society: fine words alone were no magical passport from one's class. But in acknowledging the diffusion of Renaissance words through public education and in the marketplace of such mass cultural forms and outlets as advertising and radio, the comedic Renaissance of Porter and Barry implied an inclusive, rather than exclusive, cultural heritage. However accurately, they envisioned a language that could be spoken by and among members of various social classes.

Zounds, He Dies

> Bogart knew she was a murderess and he also knew that the first person out of that door would walk into a hail of machine gun bullets. The girl didn't know this. Marlowe [sic] also knew that if he sent the girl out to be killed, the gang would take it on the lam, thus saving his own life for the time being. He didn't feel like playing God or saving his skin by letting Carmen leave. Neither did he feel like playing Sir Philip Sidney to save a worthless life.
>
> Letter from RAYMOND CHANDLER to HAMISH HAMILTON, May 30, 1946, on a scene (ultimately unfilmed) of *The Big Sleep*

To this point, Shakespeare has taken a primary role in this chapter's cultural archaeology. But Shakespeare was by no means as exclusive a presence during this period as our histories might indicate. One use of the Renaissance that mediated the tragedic and comedic modes outlined above and, in so doing, constituted a special kind of cultural borrowing came in Raymond Chandler's *The Big Sleep* (1939), in which his detective takes the name of Philip Marlowe. As with "Sidney Kidd" in *The Philadelphia Story* (also 1939), Chandler seems, in naming his detective, to have fused the first part of "*Philip* Sidney" and the last name of "Christopher *Marlowe*." Originally named "Mallory" in Chandler's early *Black Mask* stories, the questing detective would indeed appear at first glance to be more aptly connected to an author of romances (i.e., [Sir] Thomas Malory, compiler of *Le Morte d'Arthur*) than to a Renaissance dramatist. *The Big Sleep* opens, in fact, with Marlowe staring at a stained-glass window over the doorway of the Sternwood mansion, a window "showing a knight in dark armor rescuing a lady who was tied to a tree and didn't have any clothes on but some very long and convenient hair."[59] A kind of "knight in dark armor himself," Chandler's detective is a modern version of the chivalric hero. In this sense, "Mallory" (or "Malory") would seem a more appropriate name for Chandler's detective. Why, then, did Chandler change it to "Marlowe"? As Jerry Speir argues, the world of *The Big Sleep* makes pure chivalry impossible. Marlowe himself later passes a chessboard and says: "The move with the knight was wrong. I put it back where I had moved it from. Knights had no meaning in this game. It wasn't a game for knights."[60] Glossing this passage, Speir suggests that "*The Big Sleep* might be read as a chronicle of the *failure* of romance."[61] Chandler's choice of "Philip Marlowe" as a name for his detective, then, seems—with Conrad—to acknowledge the failure of the romance world by associating his detective with a noir Renaissance.[62] Although there is no direct proof for Christopher Marlowe as a model or source for the noir detective, much circumstantial evidence argues for the Renaissance playwright as the ultimate origin of Chandler's detective.

First, one might consider the way later authors of detective fiction seem to have read the name and gone on to associate themselves and their fictions with similar names. The Harvard Shakespearean Alfred Harbage, for instance, wrote four detective novels in the late 1940s under the pseudonym "Thomas Kyd." Similarly, Robert Parker's "Spenser" makes no secret of the fact that he spells his name like the Renaissance poet. Harbage and Parker (both professors, at one time, of English literature) seem to have played off what they saw as Chandler's allusion to the Renaissance dramatist in choosing for their fictional detectives the names of two of Marlowe's contemporaries. Kyd, mentioned before in conjunction with *The Philadelphia Story,* had been Marlowe's roommate and reportedly gave evidence under torture against Marlowe. Next is Chandler's own predilection for the Renaissance. Consider, for example, the process of titling *Farewell, My Lovely* (1940): Chandler originally wanted to call the new novel *The Second Murderer,* after *Richard III,* act 1, scene 4. Next he settled on a phrase from that scene (*Zounds, He Dies* [1.4.125]), while Blanche Knopf submitted *Sweet Bells Jangle,* from Ophelia's speech at 3.1.158 in *Hamlet.* Although all these titles were rejected, at the end of *Farewell, My Lovely,* Chandler has Marlowe quote Shakespeare. Describing a character in the novel, Marlowe speaks of "An old man who had loved not wisely, but too well."[63] Calling up the end of *Othello* (cf. *Othello* 5.2.344), Marlowe moralizes the events of his own story alongside Shakespearean tragedy. (More recently, Robert Parker chose the title *Perchance to Dream* [1991] for his sequel to Chandler's *The Big Sleep.* A year earlier Colin Dexter, another mystery writer, titled a novel *The Wench is Dead,* borrowing—like Hemingway—from Marlowe's *The Jew of Malta.*)[64]

A suitable representative of late 1930s disillusionment, Philip Marlowe appeared on the literary scene when developments in literary scholarship had brought his ancestor to the front of critical debate. In 1925, a young instructor of English at Harvard University named Leslie Hotson published the tantalizing fruits of his research in the patent rolls and miscellany of the Chancery in London. There Hotson—adept at research and with a special talent for retrieving lost documents and information—found the pardon of Ingram Friser for the murder of Christopher Marlowe, a pardon that, in Hotson's words, "exactly rehearsed the terms of the Coroner's inquest, telling in detail the story of the fatal affray."[65] The "fatal affray" arose, the pardon tells us, over "*le recknynge*," that is, over the bill for a supper that Marlowe and some of his friends enjoyed in a tavern at Deptford Strand, outside London. The story of the murder itself is straightforward but becomes charged with complications when taken in the context of Marlowe's life: his reputed service as "secret agent" of Elizabeth's authoritarian government and his scandalous association with the blasphemy and offhand outrageousness of the "Baines document" (the record of scandalous remarks that Marlowe, it was alleged, had made against Biblical and secular authority).

Hotson's discovery in 1925 of the Friser pardon and its detailed account of Marlowe's bloody death produced a morbid interest in Marlowe among modern scholars and critics. The late 1920s and 1930s saw a flurry of books and articles about Marlowe: from *Marlowe and His Circle* (1929) by F. S. Boas and *The Life of Marlowe* (1930) by Tucker Brooke to Mark Eccles's *Christopher Marlowe in London* (1934) and Boas's later *Christopher Marlowe* (1940). George Lyman Kittredge, the indefatigable scholar, anticipated the aura of mystery that would surround the figure of Marlowe in so many of these works when, introducing Hotson's book, he claimed that "The mystery of Marlowe's death, heretofore involved in a cloud of contradictory gossip and irresponsible guess-work, is now cleared up for good." Likewise Hotson himself explicitly described his research in terms of detective work: "Armed with a presentiment, I set out on the path which (as I feared) had been followed so often before—that leading to some possible vestige of the official record of the Marlowe murder case."

As we have seen, Kittredge's declaration (reminiscent of a district attorney's) that the Marlowe murder case had been "cleared up for good" came prematurely. In fact, unearthing the account of the murder produced the opposite effect. Many scholars actively debated the subject of Marlowe's death; for them, Marlowe's status as a shadowy figure on the margins of Elizabethan society precluded any certainty about the manner of his death or even the fact *of* his death. In *The Assassination of Christopher Marlowe (A New View)* (1928), Samuel Tannenbaum (a kind of Jazz Age Oliver Stone) made the skeptic's case by describing Marlowe's death as "a contrived murder," a "premeditated assassination" arranged by Sir Walter Ralegh. To bolster his case even as he undermined the reader's faith in the Hotson document's account of the murder, Tannenbaum includes an appendix in which he quotes the solicited opinions of four "Medical Experts" (a "distinguished consulting neurological surgeon," a "professor of pathology," the "head of the department of pathology" at Johns Hopkins, and a "professor of pathology and medical jurisprudence") on their skepticism that a wound such as that allegedly received by Marlowe could have caused instantaneous death.[66] To Tannenbaum, as to others, Marlowe's death was an unsolved mystery and scholars the detectives who could solve the case.

Tannenbaum's book contributed to Christopher Marlowe's growing reputation in and out of the world of literature as a noir figure, a man of intrigue and danger who could cauterize the sores of what was seen as a sick society. Later Chandler would write: "[Marlowe] will at any time, because he is that sort of man, meet any danger, since he thinks that is what he was created for, and because he knows the corruption of his country can only be cured by men who are determined if necessary to sacrifice themselves to cure it."[67] Something about the real Christopher Marlowe's reputation made him especially suited to the atmosphere of pessimism and suspicion that such noir authors as Chandler, Dashiell Hammett, and James M. Cain captured in their stories of the violent underside of American life. And Marlowe surfaced in the larger public sphere as well. During the original House Un-American Activities Committee meetings under Martin Dies, a Congressman from Alabama named Joe Starnes found himself asking Hallie Flanagan (then head of the Federal Theatre project) a question about whom Flanagan would call "the greatest dramatist in the period immediately preceding Shakespeare." On December 6, 1938, citing a story Flanagan had written for *Theatre Arts Monthly* in 1931, Starnes went on to quote her praise for the workers' theater: "Unlike any art form existing in America today, the workers' theaters intend to shape the life of this country, socially, politically, and industrially. They intend to remake a social structure without the help of money—and this ambition alone invests their undertaking with a certain Marlowesque madness."[68] Starnes turned directly to Flanagan: "You are quoting from this Marlowe," he (incorrectly) noted. "Is he a Communist?" Flanagan answered politely: "I am very sorry. I was quoting from Christopher Marlowe." The following exchange ensued.

Starnes: Tell us who Marlowe is, so we can get the proper reference, because that is all we want to do.

Flanagan: Put in the record that he was the greatest dramatist in the period immediately preceding Shakespeare.

Starnes: Put that in the record because the charge has been made that this article of yours is entirely Communistic, and we want to help you.[69]

Ludicrous as it may have appeared then, and as it may appear in retrospect, the HUAC inquiry into the Federal Theatre project that day foreshadowed the era when Joseph McCarthy and Richard Nixon would destroy many lives and careers under the banner of patriotism. The secretive caprice of governmental witch-hunting, in fact, had found expression in an illuminating metaphor in a statement Martin Dies gave to reporters about the House committee inquiry earlier that year. "This is not going to be any 'shooting in the dark' inquiry," he said. "We want the facts only and when the hearings start we will know where to go to get them. While the hearings will probably not be open to the general public, this does not say they will be star-chamber proceedings."[70] Dies's turn to this metaphor by way of denial seems uncanny, for, like the historical Star Chamber—a medieval creation best known, perhaps, for its ominous influence over Tudor and Stuart politics (when it often used torture to root out "treason")— the HUAC wielded an inordinate sway over thousands of people during its tenure. Dies's mention of the Star Chamber, then, was not only the right metaphor for the situation but also one that formed part of a larger cultural context. It was a context that found the Renaissance eerily analogous to the present. That the Star Chamber, "the proper reference" to Christopher Marlowe, and the English Renaissance figured so uncomfortably in the kind of paranoid world of distrust that Chandler's Marlowe would attempt to negotiate comes not, I would argue, as an accidental conjuncture but as an almost expectable occurrence.

One might have been led to expect such a pattern of allusions from the developing interest in Marlowe and his works. The "Marlowe Renaissance" of the late 1920s and 1930s led to five separate productions of *Doc-*

tor Faustus in 1937 alone. Such interest obviously traced its roots to events and activities of an earlier time. Flanagan's mention of "Marlowesque madness" in her article for *Theatre Arts Monthly,* for instance, probably derived in part from exposure at Radcliffe to George Pierce Baker, the dramatist and director of Elizabethan revivals whose famous "47 Workshop" on dramatic composition had included Philip Barry and Thomas Wolfe, among others. Baker himself had acted in a play called *Marlowe* at Radcliffe in 1905—he played Christopher Marlowe—and, writing his last scholarly monograph on "Dramatic Technique in Marlowe," remained a champion of Marlowe's drama throughout his life. If Flanagan's acquaintance with and interest in Marlowe in her 1931 essay drew on her experience at Radcliffe, so too did the larger interest in Marlowe during the 1930s depend, like the flourishing concept of the Renaissance itself, on a prior cultural investment. It was an investment that returned an impressive, if ambiguous, dividend throughout the Great Depression.

"The, er, stuff that dreams are made of"

She should have called me Christopher.

PHILIP MARLOW, in Dennis Potter's *The Singing Detective*

The importance of Renaissance themes to the 1930s spoke to a perceived lack in American culture even as it reflected the differing levels of wealth, both real and symbolic, that America had enjoyed over the past few decades. The Folger Library, the education of such authors as Ralph Ellison (who probably used the "Dunbar Colored" branch of the original Oklahoma City Carnegie Library, funded, like so many libraries, by Andrew Carnegie's millions), the founding of the Ashland Shakespeare Festival: all involved the expenditure of capital, much of it literal, accrued during the economic expansion of the late nineteenth and early twentieth centuries. The profits of Keynes's bull markets, for instance, gave Henry Folger— president of Standard Oil of New York from 1911 to 1923, and whose profession is listed in a dictionary of American biography simply as "lawyer, capitalist"[71]—the money to purchase the rare books he later donated to the library he had funded especially for research into the Elizabethan era. In much the same way, the artistic scene of the 1930s spent cultural capital that decades of economic dynamism had helped generate.

This expenditure had the eventual and ironic effect of enhancing America's cultural self-image. F. O. Matthiessen, who in 1931 had published a study of English Renaissance translations (*Translation: An Elizabethan Art*), was able by 1941 to domesticate the Renaissance in a monumental study titled *American Renaissance,* a work that would prove central to the foundation of the American literary canon. Matthiessen began this study, significantly enough, by stressing the richness of the literature written in America from 1850 to 1855, suggesting that the period could be seen as a "*rebirth*": "Not as a rebirth of values that had existed previously in America, but as America's way of producing a renaissance, by coming to its first maturity and affirming its rightful heritage in the whole expanse of art and culture."[72] Through its bold yoking of apparent unlikes, Matthiessen's two-word title communicates a newfound confidence in American culture. In retrospect, his emphasis on "America's way of producing a renaissance" reflects tellingly on the decade between his earlier critical study of Renaissance translations and his translation of the Renaissance into a model for classic American literature. That Matthiessen was part of a larger movement can be seen in the career of Willard Thorp, a professor of English at Princeton University. Thorp's doctoral dissertation was titled *The Triumph of Realism in Elizabethan Drama, 1588–1612,* accepted in 1926 and published in the "Princeton Studies in English" series in 1928. Over the next decade, however, Thorp's interest in the English Renaissance gave way to his interest in what Matthiessen would call "The American Renaissance." Indeed, Thorp was instrumental in bringing the works of Herman Melville into the American canon, publishing *Representative Selections* of Melville's writings in 1938 and editing *Moby-Dick* for Oxford University Press in 1947.

Like that of Matthiessen, Thorp's dedication to the works of the American Renaissance depended on his immersion in the English Renaissance. Yet Thorp would differ significantly in the kinds of texts from the earlier period that he found valuable. Matthiessen's scholarship on Elizabethan translation, for instance, had focused on such elite works as Sir Thomas Hoby's translation of the *Book of the Courtier* by Baldasare Castiglione and Sir Thomas North's translation of Plutarch. Perhaps not surprisingly, Matthiessen's "American Renaissance" effectively excluded from the canon not only women writers but also such embarrassingly popular authors as Irving, Cooper, Poe, and Longfellow. Thorp, on the other hand, had long championed what he called "realism" and the popular vision. Suspicious of Shakespeare's condescension toward common people, Thorp praised the "social theme" in the works of both Melville and an earlier "water poet," John Taylor. In fact, in his first published article in 1922, Thorp lauded this homespun Elizabethan author as "the neatest example of the popular writer that we could desire."[73] Taylor was in this way more of an American writer than Shakespeare. In a lecture to the Philobiblon Club of Philadelphia in 1945 titled "The Lost Tradition of American Letters," Thorp denied that he had come "to draw the veil and disclose an American Shakespeare hitherto unknown," but went on to suggest that, ironically, an American Shakespeare could not be Shakespearean in social orientation: "Our writers can know what any of their fellows thinks and feels. They are not cut off from the common man, as English writers have often been. Shakespeare was amused by Bottom and Dogberry but in using them he did not care to understand them."[74]

Both Matthiessen and Thorp participated in the construction of an "American Renaissance" canon at approximately the same time, and the coincidence of their endeavors in the period from the late 1920s through the 1940s suggests a larger historical movement that saw champions of American culture first emphasize English culture; yet what they found in the Elizabethan era and what they stressed in the American texts they recovered in light of this Renaissance differed greatly. Thus just as it is wrong to think only of Shakespeare when we define the English Renaissance and its role in the definition of American culture, so is it also wrong to define the English Renaissance narrowly, whether in terms of class or even "genre" of appropriation. As the range of texts and modes of appropriation in the previous paragraphs have suggested, the myth of the Renaissance had many facets, and it appealed in various ways to a variety of artists, scholars, and audiences.

This *copia* of associations is perhaps best illustrated in a quotation of *The Tempest*—a play that critics and teachers have traditionally portrayed as a kind of sermonic "final statement" by Shakespeare—at the close of John Houston's film version of *The Maltese Falcon* (1941). Dashiell Hammett's novel of the same name was originally published in 1929–30 (serialized first in *Black Mask* magazine), and it remains oddly indebted to

Shakespeare for the placement of its narrative in history. As recent editors notice, it is difficult to date the events of the novel, for "Hammett never mentioned the month or year that Sam took Brigid's case."[75] Following William Godschalk, several scholars have pointed out that the only information that anchors the story in time is an otherwise casual passage in which Hammett tells us that Joel Cairo "looked at a theatre-sign in front of him on which George Arliss was shown costumed as Shylock."[76] George Arliss had actually been in San Francisco playing Shylock during two weeks in December of 1928. In this way, Hammett leaves a clue for scholars to follow, one that—producing a kind of "textual effect"—enables literary detectives to use this production of *The Merchant of Venice* to date the action of the novel.

It is in a different manner, however, that Shakespeare helps John Houston's film version of Hammett's story come to a close. Left alone with Sam Spade (Humphrey Bogart) at the end of the film, a slow-witted police detective named Tom Polhaus (Ward Bond) picks up the black statuette and weighs it in his hands, turning to Spade and remarking: "It's heavy. What is it?" Pausing briefly while answering, Spade says: "The, er, stuff that dreams are made of." The "er" in his answer, a temporary hesitation, signals the conscious process of Spade recalling an appropriate reference. Just as Marlowe's fellow character had missed the *Othello* allusion in *Farewell, My Lovely*, however, Polhaus misses the reference—and therefore the meaning—of the enigmatic reply and grunts a monosyllabic query: "Huh?"[77] Spade's allusion to Prospero's "We are such stuff | As dreams are made on" (*Tempest* 4.1.156–57) is already in quotation marks, addressed not to Tom Polhaus but to the audience. Its position at a kind of capping, climactic moment in *The Tempest* may have made it an attractive line with which to close the film: the line, "original" with Houston, appeared in neither Hammett's novel nor two earlier film versions of the story. Using the tag as a moral, Houston brings the narrative into a full, historical circle, for his introductory subtitle to the film had located the source of the Maltese Falcon firmly in the context of Renaissance Europe: "In 1539 the Knight Templars of Malta, paid tribute to Charles V of Spain, by sending him a Golden Falcon encrusted with rarest jewels—but pirates seized the galley carrying this priceless token and the fate of the Maltese Falcon remains a mystery to this day." Here Houston's "historical" background plays on the same awe of wealth and the mystical connections between gold and the riches of fiction that Keynes had posited a little over a decade earlier in his footnote to *A Treatise on Money.*

The elusive Falcon sought so religiously by the characters of Houston's film derives from the dynamism of Renaissance history: kings and tribute, pirates and plunder. If Steven Marcus is right in suggesting an allegorical valence for the Maltese Falcon (originally tribute, then piece of plunder, which became a "mystified object" eventually proved "fake"), a valence in which the statuette "turns out to be and contains within itself the history of capitalism," the history that the Falcon spells out is primarily that of its immediate past: an economic allegory of the 1920s.[78] Glossed in these terms, the layers of gold and gems covered by black enamel suggest the vanished wealth of the previous decades, the feverish pursuit of which engages almost all the story's characters. Thus the film's moral argument takes added seriousness from a historical vantage that Houston possessed in 1941 but that neither Hammett nor Keynes held in the late 1920s. Stressing the Falcon's explicit connections to the Renaissance heritage of the New World, however, one might also construct an interpretation in terms of what this chapter has called the Thirties Renaissance. In such a reading, the Maltese Falcon's influence over the film's characters conveys Depression-era America's preoccupation with Renaissance art, its obsession with retrieving aesthetic artifacts from its storied past. Seen in this light, the black bird encapsulates the riches of America's Renaissance heritage: treasure that, to artists and audiences of the extended 1930s, seemed to lie just under the surface of American life but—like the Falcon—always remained just out of reach.

———

The preceding paragraphs have attempted to demonstrate and account for the ubiquitous nature of Renaissance works, authors, and themes in interwar America. With the advent of mass culture during this period arose a concurrent need to soften the force of what would otherwise seem an oxymoron: How could "mass" and "culture" be combined, especially in relation to such new media as film and radio? How might a definition of culture that had traditionally stressed the elite expand to encompass the demotic? As we have seen, one answer to this problem came through the period's emphasis on works and figures of a prestigious forbear; the English Renaissance brought distinction to a country that felt common and eloquence to a people in search of an articulate voice. To Americans taken with this cultural family romance, perhaps the single most important aspect of the English Renaissance was the "class" it conveyed: stories of intelligent, talented, and well-spoken individuals appealed to audiences who aspired to transcend their ordinary lives through identification with aristocratic characters and settings.

It is precisely the awkward truth of this national fantasy life that calls into question two of the most vigorous critics of the phenomenon that this chapter has described. Walter Benn Michaels, in his indictment of "nativist modernism," and Charlene Avallone, in her critique of the "gendered genealogy" of "renaissance discourse," provide reason for seeing this interwar emphasis on the English Renaissance as alternately racist and sexist. As Michaels argues, during the 1920s and 1930s, a general project he calls "nativist modernism" effectively "invented a new form of racism and produced a new model not only of American identity but of the other identities that would now be available in America. Promoting a conception of identity as both description and responsibility, it made Americanness into a racial inheritance and culture into a set of beliefs and practices dependent on race."[79] In a similar vein, Avallone traces the use of "renaissance discourse" in the critical formation of the American canon, and finds that "the language of renaissance serves to maintain male preeminence . . . through the aesthetics of renaissance excellence."[80] Where Michaels looks at the modernist impulse and sees racism, Avallone sees sexism. And although each of these positions accurately touches on elements of American culture from this period and resonates at times with the preceding argument, neither is supple enough to account for the range of English Renaissance texts, themes, and figures that interested Americans during this period.

Indeed, whether one considers an artist such as Ralph Ellison, who recalled his empowering fantasies of "Renaissance Man," or Katharine Hepburn as a young Eva Lovelace, hopeful that Shakespeare's words will allow her to communicate her innate worth, it is clear that many Americans found in "renaissance discourse" a wealth of aesthetic and intellectual possibilities that temporarily allowed them to become something other than what they were. Surely we can—with Michaels and Avallone—look back on these fantasies with some skepticism. But what remains true about the "project" or myth of the English Renaissance during this period was that it functioned much like a script from the Renaissance itself, a script full of various roles and open to various performers and performance styles. Thus we need to qualify our criticism of this myth with a recognition of the fullness that Americans in the 1920s and 1930s found in it. To Americans of the interwar era, the English Renaissance was most often connected not with race or sex but with distinction, prestige, and "class." These attributes drew Americans to the English Renaissance, and through their quotation of its stories and figures, they worked to invent a usable cultural past.

Afterword

I would like to close this book by considering two quotations—positions, really, taken against the ideas it advances. Each was part of a work published well before the composition of this study and can be said to have been part of the book since its conception. Each addresses questions that the reader of this book may still have in mind. The first comes from *Persecution and the Art of Writing* (1952), by the ever controversial Leo Strauss. In it, Strauss holds that

> The flight to immortality requires an extreme discretion in the selection of one's luggage. A book that requires for its adequate understanding the use, nay, the preservation of all libraries and archives containing information which was useful to its author, hardly deserves being written and being read at all, and it certainly does not deserve surviving its author.[1]

Strauss raises serious questions about the relations among works, readers, and ancillary materials. What kind of book is so involved with its materials that it requires their presence in the reading process? *Shouldn't* books be complete in and of themselves? However arch it may sound, this passage offers a potentially democratic portrait of reading. In contrast to scholars at wealthy institutions blessed with "libraries and archives," that is, the reader whom Strauss describes is expected to have access only to a basic text itself—whether Shakespeare's *Hamlet* or Plato's *Republic*. Strauss imagines someone reading such a text in a state of happy sufficiency, communing or even grappling with the author.

Strauss twice employs the word "use" (once in "useful") and in so doing incidentally asks us to consider the labor involved in reading and interpreting texts. This labor is not attractive to Strauss. Though he admits that authors use books to produce their own, he is no more interested in that use than, say, the patrons of a restaurant would be interested in seeing the parings of the vegetables that had gone into the preparation of their dinners. If writers use books, this use is, to Strauss, less important than the subject and end result. Writers have made these books unnecessary, in fact, by the act of writing itself: they have used other books and libraries so that we do not have to. In Strauss's eyes, immortality is a journey, and the books that get one there are too heavy to be taken along for the flight. Even "adequate understanding" is a destination for which one packs light.

Much hinges on "adequate," of course, and a virtue of Strauss's claim is that it reminds us that the mode of reading suggested in *Quoting Shakespeare* is quite uncommon. Most readers prefer a self-sufficient text, finding such texts adequate, and often for good reason. The more extensive the apparatus connected with a text (footnotes, endnotes, textual notes, bibliography, introductions, et al.), the less whole a text may feel and the more intimidating the act of reading may become. If reading all that supporting material is necessary (one might ask with Strauss), why read the book at all? Likewise, if a book is not complete in itself, by what standards is it really a book? These questions are difficult to answer, in part because they involve erasing comfortable boundaries. It is potentially unsettling, for instance, to say that a book is nothing more and nothing less than a temporarily fixed group of words and phrases borrowed from many thousands of sources and that such a book may similarly be dispersed into countless other works. And surely no one is required to read in accordance with this theory; most readers, in fact, would have little cause to concern themselves over its truth. Nevertheless, it has been the argument of this study that those interested in the relations among books, writers, and the world stand to benefit from seeing books not in isolation but in the context of these books' material sources.

The second quotation I want to consider also satisfies itself as to the sufficiency of texts but differs from Strauss about why. It was first printed in the preface to Annabel Patterson's *Hermogenes and the Renaissance: Seven Ideas of Style* (1970). Patterson quotes an anonymous reader of her manuscript who expressed the following skepticism concerning the assumptions of her book:

> Any "influence study" may at best only argue a case and remain more or less convincing. It must ignore parallel influences and also those innumerable, in-

determinate factors which allow that influence to be exerted. Any study of the influence of a specific rhetorical work confronts the problem that the rhetorical tradition was very extensive, thorough, and inclusive. Further, rhetorical tradition in schools was so thorough that any poet's use of rhetorical devices becomes a subconscious or "natural" activity. Finally, any "influence study" works against itself: the greater the influence, the less likely is any direct influence.[2]

In contrast to the Strauss passage, the quotation above offers an objection regarding methodology and logic rather than decorum. The question is, in part, not whether one should trace a book's compositional paradigms but whether one could. Where Strauss frets about the lack of elegance in relation to an overburdened traveler (one can imagine a suitcase so stuffed with clothing that the ends of shirts and socks jut from its seams), the anonymous reader of Patterson's manuscript addresses a potential paradox of textual making. That is, "the greater the influence, the less likely is any direct influence." This last is perhaps the most serious challenge to the method of reading set out in the preceding chapters. For if this claim is true—that influences may be so powerful that we cannot see them— books are likely to conceal their primary debts.

The rub here, of course, lies in the word "influence." As we have seen throughout this study, it makes all the difference to describe writing as a passive or an active thing. Writers are influenced, of course, and, as the above passage states, the influences upon them are many and elusive. Yet at the risk of pointing out the obvious, writers *write,* choosing their words and topics, committing these choices to paper. And while writers are indeed influenced in these choices, we may also see them as purposeful makers, consciously as well as unconsciously fashioning one set of materials into another. It should be clear by now that I believe that we may often determine what these materials are and where they came from and, further, that this active model of writing can help us learn about the past, its writers, and their books. When phrased in relation to an amorphous "influence," the shapes and structures of a text will indeed be difficult to link to specific formations in the world. To speak not of influence but of resources and material, however, is to use a vocabulary of the practical, with attendant demands of proof and evidence.

It might also be clear that I am skeptical about the usefulness of larger paradigms and categories for certain acts of interpretation, whether phrased as "influence" or "the Elizabethan world picture" or "social energy." Such constructions are invariably post hoc and sometimes seem closer to the rhetoric of advertising than to the language of critical analysis. Too, they are often more useful to explain general movements than to understand how and why individuals came to think and write as they did at specific moments. Instead of following such gleaming abstractions, then, we can benefit from a focus on less tidy, material realities. Because we are verbal and mimetic creatures, the words we produce often carry the residue of their origins. Literature is, accordingly, social, derivative, and messy. To ignore this truth is to risk misunderstanding the texts we read. To follow out its implications is to begin to sense the wealth of relations that connect every work to a host of elements outside its margins.

1. Quoting Shakespeare

1. David Scott Kastan and Peter Stallybrass have referred to a developing genre of criticism in the field as "The New Boredom," in part, Kastan explains, because of this criticism's "greater delight in particularity" and its attention to what Adorno called "mere facts." David Scott Kastan, *Shakespeare After Theory* (New York: Routledge, 1999), 18. However jokingly offered, the phrase captures a larger truth about the desire among critics of early modern drama in the closing years of the century for a more substantial foundation to their arguments.

2. For representative studies that locate such phenomena as quotation, pastiche, collage, and parody at the center of postmodern and twentieth-century aesthetics, see Fredric Jameson, *Postmodernism, or The Logic of Late Capitalism* (Durham NC: Duke University Press, 1991) and Linda Hutcheon, *A Poetics of Postmodernism* (London: Routledge, 1988).

3. The "Hercules" sign first entered critical tradition with George Steevens, who obviously drew on both the name of Shakespeare's playhouse and the following exchange between Hamlet and Rosencrantz:

Hamlet. Do the boys carry it away?

Rosencrantz. Ay, that they do, my lord—Hercules and his load too.

(2.2.360–62)

See The New Arden *Hamlet,* ed. Harold Jenkins (London: Methuen, 1982), Longer Note to 2.2.358, and Richard Dutton, "*Hamlet, An Apology for Actors,* and the Sign of the Globe," *Shakespeare Survey* 41 (1988): 35–43.

4. I am referring, of course, to C. S. Lewis's well-known characterization of the "Golden period of Elizabethan poetry" in *English Literature in the Sixteenth Century, Excluding Drama* (Oxford: Clarendon Press, 1954). And for "the feeling," in later Elizabethan literature, "that anything may happen and anything may be said,

that the mould is, almost, cracking," see Patrick Cruttwell, *The Shakespearean Moment and Its Place in the Poetry of the 17th Century* (New York: Vintage, 1960), 105. On the *copia* of early modern texts generally, see Terence Cave, *The Cornucopian Text: Problems of Writing in the French Renaissance* (Oxford: Clarendon Press, 1979). Richard Halpern explains this *copia* as part of a larger phenomenon of Tudor "style production" in the first chapter of his study, *The Poetics of Primitive Accumulation: English Renaissance Culture and the Genealogy of Capital* (Ithaca: Cornell University Press, 1991); see "A Mint of Phrases: Ideology and Style Production in Tudor England," 19–60.

5. Robert Weimann, "Discourse, Ideology, and the Crisis of Authority in Post-Reformation England," *REAL: The Yearbook of Research in English and American Literature* 5 (1987), 109–40, quote on p. 131. For the cultural implications of the printing revolution, see also Elizabeth L. Eisenstein, *The Printing Press as an Agent of Change: Communications and Cultural Transformations in Early-Modern Europe*, 2 vols. (Cambridge: Cambridge University Press, 1979).

6. [R. Wilson?], *Martine Mar-Sixtus* (London: 1591), A3ᵛ, and Address to the Reader from Florio's *World of Words* (1598), reproduced in appendix 1 of Frances A. Yates, *John Florio: The Life of an Italian in Shakespeare's England* (Cambridge: Cambridge University Press, 1934), 337.

7. On notions of literary originality and indebtedness in early modern English poetic theory, see Harold Ogden White, *Plagiarism and Imitation During the English Renaissance: A Study in Critical Distinctions,* Harvard Studies in English 12 (Cambridge: Harvard University Press, 1935; reprint, New York: Octagon Books, 1965). White's study suggests a shift from explicit to implicit imitation during the Elizabethan and Jacobean eras. In contrast, David Quint's emphasis on the significance of tropes of source and origin in the period leads him to construct an essentially romantic Renaissance, one in which originality prevails: "The Renaissance author emerged as original at the moment when a traditional and authoritative canon was historicized and relativized. And, in order to accommodate him—once innovation became the criterion for admission—the canon had to expand into the future. The impulse to originality came to inform all realms of human thought and discourse, formerly closed, now irreversibly open-ended. What Renaissance poets had begun to learn was learnt over and over again. There could be no return to the source. Originality had become the source of authority." David Quint, *Origin and Originality in Renaissance Literature: Versions of the Source* (New Haven: Yale University Press, 1983), 220. Quint recognizes that what he presents as a transformation to a secular, comparatively modern literary episteme was a dialectical process, and the subject of debate often internal to individual authors. The burden of my argument here, however, is to show that we can benefit from seeing much

literature of the period as less "original" than Quint's paradigm would allow for. On the concept of "citation" in early modern drama, see Elizabeth M. Richmond-Garza, *Forgotten Cites/Sites: Interpretation and the Power of Classical Citation in Renaissance English Tragedy* (New York: Peter Lang, 1994).

8. Compare R. W. Dent on John Webster, whose works, in the view of Dent, feature "a density of borrowings unrivaled in English literature." R. W. Dent, *John Webster's Borrowing* (Berkeley: University of California Press, 1960), 10. The chronicle histories of the late 1580s and early 1590s offer a special challenge to literary historians because of their thorough overlap with other plays of this genre and time. See, for example, the uncanny sharing between *Woodstock* and *Richard II* as explored in the appendix to the edition of *Woodstock* by A. P. Rossiter (London: Chatto and Windus, 1946). See also Eric Sams's exhaustive notes and commentary to *Edmund Ironside* (Aldershot, Hants.: Wildwood House, 1986), which, while they do not persuade me that Shakespeare wrote this play, do establish the common resources behind it and many of Shakespeare's chronicle histories.

9. See *Microcynicon* (London: 1599), B4^r, and *Volpone* 4.1.145–46. For other relevant examples, see *All's Well That Ends Well* 5.3.205, and *Love's Labour's Lost* 2.246–47.

10. A critical use of "quotation" in this sense that anticipates my own came in a 1991 essay on madness and gender in Shakespeare's tragedies by Carol Thomas Neely. Neely analyzes the fragmented mad language of Lear and Ophelia and calls their torrents of borrowed words "quotation," suggesting that their voices are not their own but rather the alienated voices of their cultures. Carol Thomas Neely, "'Documents in Madness': Reading Madness and Gender in Shakespeare's Tragedies and Early Modern Culture," *Shakespeare Quarterly* 42 (1991): 315–38, quote on p. 323. I take up Neely's remarks in chapter 5, below. On "quotation" in *King Lear*, see Paul Hammond, "The Play of Quotation and Commonplace in *King Lear*," in *Toward a Definition of Topos: Approaches to Analogical Reasoning*, ed. Lynette Hunter (London: Macmillan, 1991), 78–129. Hammond analogizes *King Lear* to Montaigne's *Essais* in its "deconstructive play with the rhetorical commonplaces of its sources," 88.

11. See OED, "quote" *v* II 5, a–c. As Stefan Morawski has argued about the word "quotation" (Latin *quot* [interrogative] "What number of? How many?" [OLD]): "Tracking down the etymology of the term we arrive in the court room. A witness is summoned and his evidence is required to be accurate as possible." Morawski, "The Basic Functions of Quotation," in *Sign, Language, Culture*, ed. A. J. Greimas et al. (The Hague: Mouton, 1970), 690–705, quote on p. 690.

12. Walter Benjamin, *Schriften* II, 142–43, 192. In Walter Benjamin, *Illuminations:*

Essays and Reflections, ed. Hannah Arendt (New York: Schocken Books, 1969), 39. For this reference I am indebted to Marjorie Garber, *Shakespeare's Ghost Writers: Literature as Uncanny Causality* (New York: Methuen, 1986), 52. For quotation as an integral part of the modern novel, see Herman Mann, *The Poetics of Quotation in the European Novel,* trans. Theodore Ziolkowski (Princeton: Princeton University Press, 1968).

13. Garber, *Shakespeare's Ghost Writers,* 52.

14. On "the death of the author," see Roland Barthes's 1968 essay of that name in *Image-Music-Text,* trans. Stephen Heath (New York: Hill and Wang, 1977), 142–48, and Michel Foucault, "What is an Author?" in *Language, Counter-Memory, Practice,* trans. Donald F. Bouchard and Sherry Simon, ed. Donald F. Bouchard (Ithaca: Cornell University Press, 1977). Barthes's essay "From Work to Text," also relevant to this theme, is contained in *Image-Music-Text,* 155–64.

15. On the marks for representing quotations, indirect speech, and proverbs in the sixteenth and seventeenth centuries, see M. B. Parkes, *Pause and Effect: An Introduction to the History of Punctuation in the West* (Berkeley: University of California Press, 1993), 58–59; C. J. Mitchell, "Quotation Marks, National Compositorial Habits and False Imprints," *The Library* 5 (1983): 359–84; and G. K. Hunter, "The Marking of *Sententiae* in Elizabethan Printed Plays, Poems, and Romances," *The Library* 5th ser. 6 (1951): 171–88.

16. Ivor Brown, *How Shakespeare Spent the Day* (New York: Hill and Wang, 1963), 163.

17. From Bacon's *Sir Francis Bacon his Apologie* (1604), quoted in *The First and Second Parts of John Hayward's "The Life and Raigne of King Henrie IIII",* ed. John J. Manning, Camden Fourth Series (London: Royal Historical Society, 1991), 42:2.

18. John Marston, "TO THE GENERAL READER," prefaced to the first edition of *Sophonisba,* in *The Selected Plays of John Marston,* ed. MacDonald Jackson and Michael Neill (Cambridge: Cambridge University Press, 1986), lines 3–7.

19. The preceding references are to *Shrew* 3.1.27–45; *Titus* 4.1.14; *As You Like It* 3.5.81–82; *Twelfth Night* 1.5.35; and *Hamlet* 2.2.196–204. The biblical citations come, respectively, in *Henry V* (1.2.98) and *2 Henry IV* (3.2.37).

20. Ann Moss, *Printed Commonplace-Books and the Structuring of Renaissance Thought* (Oxford: Clarendon Press, 1996), vi.

21. Moss, *Printed Commonplace-Books,* viii.

22. Moss, *Printed Commonplace-Books,* 211.

23. Mary Thomas Crane, *Framing Authority: Sayings, Self, and Society in Sixteenth-Century England* (Princeton: Princeton University Press, 1993), 3. On the growth

of the notebook method, see R. R. Bolgar, *The Classical Heritage and Its Beneficiaries* (Cambridge: Cambridge University Press, 1954), 265–75. See also Crane, 201 n.2, for further bibliography. In addition to these studies and others mentioned later in these notes, two other treatments of early modern reading practices have helped me frame some of the claims of this chapter: Lisa Jardine and Anthony Grafton, "'Studied for Action': How Gabriel Harvey Read His Livy," *Past and Present* 129 (1990): 30–79; and Robert C. Evans, *Habits of Mind: Evidence and Effects of Ben Jonson's Reading* (Lewisburg PA: Bucknell University Press, 1995).

24. Crane, *Framing Authority*, 4.

25. See Charles Nicholl, *A Cup of News: The Life of Thomas Nashe* (London: Routledge, 1984), 97 and plate 8.

26. See Nashe in *The foure Letters Confuted* (1592) in Thomas Nashe, *The Works of Thomas Nashe,* ed. R. B. McKerrow (London: Sidgwick and Jackson, 1910), 1:319. On the close relations among the works of Shakespeare and Nashe, see J. J. M. Tobin, "*Hamlet* and *Christ's Teares over Jerusalem,*" *The Aligarh Journal of English Studies* 6 (1981): 158–67; "Nashe and *The Two Gentlemen of Verona,*" *Notes and Queries* 28 (1981): 122–23; "*Macbeth* and *Christ's Teares over Jerusalem,*" *The Aligarh Journal of English Studies* 7 (1982): 72–78; "Nashe and *Richard II,*" *American Notes & Queries* 24 (1985): 5–7; and "Nashe and Shakespeare: Some Further Borrowings," *Notes and Queries* 39 (1992): 309–20. Tobin has identified an extremely close relation among certain passages in these two writers' texts; borrowing from manuscripts prior to publication hints that the authors were on close terms as well.

27. See Claude Lévi-Strauss, *The Savage Mind* (1962; Chicago: University of Chicago Press, 1969), 16–30.

28. See, for example, *Histriomastix* (1599), where Marston speaks of poetasters who "load the stage with stuff | Raked from the rotten embers of stale jests" (3.1). And Massinger in the Prologue of *Believe as You List* (1631): "He dares not boast | His pains, & and care, or what books he hath tossed | & turned to make it up" (13–15). Praising Fletcher in a commendatory poem prefaced to the 1647 Beaumont and Fletcher Folio, Richard Brome held it to the playwright's credit that he did not "trudge | To Wit conventions with Note-book, to glean, | Or steal some Jests to foist into a Scene." Playwrights themselves took pains to redirect this kind of allegation, saying that some audience members came to the playhouses primarily for these verbal souvenirs of their playgoing. Thus Ingenioso, on Gullio in the First Part of *The Return from Parnassus*: "We shall have nothing but pure Shakespeare, and shreds of poetry that he [i.e., Gullio] hath gathered at the theaters." Similarly, Jonson mocks Albius in *Poetaster* (1601) by having him quote and confess: "At your ladyship's service. I got that speech by seeing a play last day, and it did me some

grace now. I see 'tis good to collect sometimes; I'll frequent these plays more than I have done, now I come to be familiar with courtiers" (2.2.90–94). For these references see, respectively, *Histriomastix* in *The Plays of John Marston*, ed. H. Harvey Wood (Edinburgh: Oliver and Boyd, 1939), 3:274; *The Plays and Poems of Philip Massinger*, ed. Philip Edwards and Colin Gibson, vol. 3 (Oxford: Clarendon Press, 1976); Richard Brome, "To the memory of the deceased but ever-living *Author* in these his Poems, Mr. JOHN FLETCHER," prefaced to *Comedies and Tragedies written by Francis Beaumont and John Fletcher, Gentlemen.* (London: 1647), sig. g; and *The Return from Parnassus, Part One*, in *The Three Parnassus Plays (1598–1601)*, ed. J. B. Leishman (London: Ivor Nicholson and Watson, 1949), lines 986–87.

29. Stephen Gosson, *Playes Confuted in Five Actions* (London: 1582), D5ᵛ. The ransacking to which Gosson referred was not only increasingly facilitated by the expansion of printed material but would soon be embodied in the publication of formal collections of these textual fragments. One can see the proliferation of quotations in such collections as *Politeuphuia; Wit's Commonwealth* (1597), *Belvedere; Or, The Garden of the Muses* (1600), and *Wit's Interpreter, the English Parnassus* (1655). By 1655, the date of publication of John Cotgrave's *Wit's Interpreter*, John Bodenham's *Politeuphuia* had gone through seventeen editions. On the popularity of these collections, see Walter J. Ong, "Tudor Writings on Rhetoric, Poetic, and Literary Theory," in *Rhetoric, Romance and Technology: Studies in the Interaction of Expression and Culture* (Ithaca: Cornell University Press, 1971), 48–103.

30. Robert Greene (?), *Greene's Groatsworth of Wit; Bought with a Million of Repentance* (1592), ed. D. Allen Carroll (Binghamton NY: Medieval and Renaissance Texts and Studies, 1994), 85.

31. Thomas Middleton and Thomas Dekker, *The Roaring Girl*, ed. Andor Gomme (London: Ernest Benn, 1976). "To the Comic Play-Readers, Venery and Laughter," lines 1–11.

32. Quoted in *John Webster: A Critical Anthology*, ed. G. K. Hunter and S. K. Hunter (Baltimore: Penguin Books, 1969), 30–31.

33. Leishman, *Three Parnassus Plays*, 294–99.

34. Paul Yachnin, *Stage-Wrights: Shakespeare, Jonson, Middleton, and the Making of Theatrical Value* (Philadelphia: University of Pennsylvania Press, 1997), xi–xv.

35. Vladimir Mayakovsky, *How to Make Verse*, trans. Valentina Coe (Willimantic CT: Curbstone Press, 1985), 29–30.

36. I have discussed Old Historicism at more length in "New Light on the Old Historicism: Shakespeare and the Forms of Historicist Criticism," *Literature and History*, Special Issue: "Shakespeare and History," 3d series. 5, 1 (March 1996): 1–18.

37. Jay Clayton and Eric Rothstein, "Figures in the Corpus: Theories of Influence and Intertextuality," in *Influence and Intertextuality in Literary History*, ed. J. Clayton and E. Rothstein (Madison: University of Wisconsin Press, 1991), 4.

38. Robert S. Miola, "Othello *Furens*," *Shakespeare Quarterly* 41 (1990): 49–69. For recent examples of source study that understand themselves as such—and expand the boundaries of this practice—see Barbara J. Bono, *Literary Transvaluation: From Vergelian Epic to Shakespearean Tragicomedy* (Berkeley: University of California Press, 1984); Claire McEachern, "Fathering Himself: A Source Study of Shakespeare's Feminism," *Shakespeare Quarterly* 39 (1988): 269–90; Robert S. Miola, *Shakespeare and Classical Tragedy: The Influence of Seneca* (Oxford: Oxford University Press, 1992); and Heather James, *Shakespeare's Troy: Drama, Politics, and the Translation of Empire* (Cambridge: Cambridge University Press, 1997). On the relation of "source" to surrounding concepts, see Linda Hutcheon, "Literary Borrowing . . . and Stealing: Plagiarism, Sources, Influences, and Intertexts," *English Studies in Canada* 12 (1986): 229–39. Other illuminating works regarding the concept of "source" and literary revision in relation to the early modern period include White, *Plagiarism and Imitation*; Edwin Haviland Miller, *The Professional Writer in Elizabethan England: A Study of Nondramatic Literature* (Cambridge MA: Harvard University Press, 1959); G. W. Pigman III, "Versions of Imitation in the Renaissance," *Renaissance Quarterly* 33 (1980): 1–32; and Roberta Mullini, *La Scena della Memoria: Intertextualità nel teatro Tudor* (Bologna: Cooperativa Libraria Universitaria Editrice Bologna, 1988).

39. Miola, "Othello *Furens*," 49.

40. For definitions of New Historicism by two critics who work on early modern drama, see Albert H. Tricomi, *Reading Tudor-Stuart Texts through Cultural Historicism* (Gainesville: University Press of Florida, 1996), 1–22; and Edward Pechter, *What Was Shakespeare: Renaissance Plays and Changing Critical Practice* (Ithaca: Cornell University Press, 1995).

41. Stephen Greenblatt, "Shakespeare and the Exorcists," in *Shakespeare and the Question of Theory*, ed. Patricia Parker and Geoffrey Hartman (New York: Methuen, 1985), 163–87, quote on p. 163. Greenblatt's most recent version of this essay was published in *Shakespearean Negotiations: The Circulation of Social Energy in Renaissance England* (Berkeley: University of California Press, 1988), 94–128.

42. Greenblatt, "Shakespeare and the Exorcists," 165. This paragraph is revised in *Shakespearean Negotiations*.

43. T. W. Baldwin, *On the Compositional Genetics of "The Comedy of Errors"* (Urbana: University of Illinois Press, 1965), 1 (my emphasis).

44. Kenneth Muir, "Samuel Harsnett and *King Lear*," *Review of English Studies* 2 (1951): 11–21.

45. Stephen Greenblatt, "*King Lear* and Harsnett's 'Devil-Fiction,'" *Genre* 15 (1982): 239.

46. Louis Adrian Montrose, "*A Midsummer Night's Dream* and the Shaping Fantasies of Elizabethan Culture: Gender, Power, Form," in *Rewriting the Renaissance: The Discourses of Sexual Difference in Early Modern Europe,* ed. Margaret W. Ferguson, Maureen Quilligan, and Nancy J. Vickers (Chicago: University of Chicago Press, 1986), 65–87, quote on p. 69.

47. The phrase "representative anecdote" comes from Kenneth Burke, *A Grammar of Motives* (Cleveland: Meridian Books, 1962); see 59–61, 323–25.

48. Julia Kristeva, *Semiotikè: Recherches pour une sémanalyse* (Paris: Seuil, 1969), 146, cited in and translated by Jonathan Culler, *Structuralist Poetics* (Ithaca: Cornell University Press, 1975), 139. See also Thaïs E. Morgan, "Is There an Intertext in This Text?: Literary and Interdisciplinary Approaches to Intertextuality," *American Journal of Semiotics* 3, no. 4 (1985): 1–40. Morgan writes: "[W]e have both influence, or what I would call the *positive intertextual relation* between two texts—say, Joyce's use of the central episodes from Homer's *Odyssey* to structure the chapters in *Ulysses*—, and inspiration, or the *negative intertextual relation*—here, Joyce's ironic transformation of the epic hero in Bloom. It is important to note that neither influence nor inspiration takes into account a third factor cooperative in both types of intertextual relations: namely, the *intratextual relation* (potentially positive or negative) among earlier and later texts by the same author—for example, how the narrative and value structures in Joyce's *Portrait of the Artist as a Young Man* and *Stephen Hero* affect or are affected by those in *Ulysses*" (3).

49. Kristeva, *Semiotikè*, 139.

50. Montrose, "*A Midsummer Night's Dream*," 87.

51. Richard Helgerson, *Forms of Nationhood: The Elizabethan Writing of England* (Chicago: University of Chicago Press, 1992), 13.

52. Greenblatt, *Shakespearean Negotiations*, 95.

53. The holistic kind of reading to which I am referring is best evidenced perhaps in the "centred spatial text" of G. Wilson Knight and the "poetic" interpretations of Modernist Shakespearean criticism. See Hugh Grady, *The Modernist Shakespeare: Critical Texts in a Material World* (Oxford: Clarendon Press, 1991) and S. Viswanathan, *The Shakespeare Play as Poem: A Critical Tradition in Perspective* (Cambridge: Cambridge University Press, 1980).

54. See Gerald Eades Bentley, *The Profession of Dramatist in Shakespeare's Time,*

1590–1642 (Princeton: Princeton University Press, 1971), 197–234. Bentley says that "the evidence suggests that it would be reasonable to guess that as many as half of the plays by professional dramatists in the period incorporated the writing at some date of more than one man. In the case of the 282 plays mentioned in Henslowe's diary (far and away the most detailed record of authorship that has come down to us) nearly two-thirds are the work of more than one man" (199). On collaboration see also Neil Carson, "Collaborative Playwriting: The Chettle, Dekker, Heywood Syndicate," *Theatre Research International* 14 (1987): 13–23.

55. *Henslowe's Diary,* Part 1, ed. W. W. Greg (London: A. H. Bullen, 1904–8), 1:149.1–4, f. 94. We seem to be more comfortable reading and teaching single-author texts; perhaps for this reason most of the plays in the canon are exceptions to the collaborative rule.

56. W. W. Greg prints a transcript of Alleyn's side in appendix 3 of his edition of the *Henslowe Papers* (London: A. H. Bullen, 1907), 155–71.

57. See, for example, Eric Mallin on "historical inscription" in his *Inscribing the Time: Shakespeare and the End of Elizabethan England* (Berkeley: University of California Press, 1995), 140–66; and Barbara Freedman's discussion of the problems of "occasion" and multiple texts in relation to *The Merry Wives of Windsor* in "Shakespearean Chronology, Ideological Complicity, and Floating Texts: Something is Rotten in Windsor," *Shakespeare Quarterly* 45 (1994): 190–210. See also Kristen Poole, "Saints Alive! Falstaff, Martin Marprelate, and the Staging of Puritanism," *Shakespeare Quarterly* 46 (1995): 47–76, in which Poole demonstrates the continuing influence of the Martin Marprelate controversy, and of the religious and political issues it embodied, on Shakespeare's second tetralogy in the late 1590s.

58. The phrase "point by point" comes from *Eikonoklastes* itself and is quoted by Steven N. Zwicker in *Lines of Authority: Politics and English Literary Culture, 1649–1689* (Ithaca: Cornell University Press, 1993), 38. Zwicker's study is devoted to the politics of polemical responses in the seventeenth century.

59. Thomas Greene, *The Light in Troy: Imitation and Discovery in Renaissance Poetry* (New Haven: Yale University Press, 1982), 45.

60. Studies based on images of literary conflict include Richard Ide's *Possessed with Greatness: The Heroic Tragedies of Chapman and Shakespeare* (Chapel Hill: University of North Carolina Press, 1980); Robert Watson's *Ben Jonson's Parodic Strategy: Literary Imperialism in the Comedies* (Cambridge MA: Harvard University Press, 1987); and R. D. Bedford's *Dialogues with Convention: Readings in Renaissance Poetry* (London: Harvester Wheatsheaf, 1989). Such criticism coincides, of course, with Harold Bloom's theory of the necessary "misreading" of earlier poets, a theory

set out in *The Anxiety of Influence: A Theory of Poetry* (New York: Oxford University Press, 1973) and elaborated in later studies. Bloom summarizes his position in an essay on Shakespeare by saying "poetry depends upon a strong or creative misreading of prior poetic strength." Harold Bloom, *Ruin the Sacred Truths: Poetry and Belief from the Bible to the Present* (Cambridge MA: Harvard University Press, 1989), 53. This "creative misreading" is Bloom's version of "civilized violence"; in Bloom's criticism, it is often as violent, if not more so, than Greene's dialectical *imitatio*. Ide explores the differences between Chapman's and Shakespeare's portrayals of the heroic soldier; their dialogue through this figure, Ide argues, comes in successive statements on the heroic—statements that form what Ide calls a "mutual negative influence." By "negative" here Ide means conflictive, argumentative (Ide, *Possessed with Greatness*, xv). As Watson argues, "Jonson is, in Harold Bloom's terms, a strong poet, because his echoes of his literary rivals function less as servile imitations than as strategic reductions, making the works of those rivals appear as mere incomplete parts of his own complete work" (4). To Watson's study we can join that of James Shapiro, who employs a complex understanding of influence to chart the changing relations among Jonson, Marlowe, and Shakespeare. Shapiro characterizes the chapters of his book as "case studies in influence that illustrate the range of intertextual concerns and strategies that came into play among these rivals." He continues: "If there is one constant throughout these pages it is that rivalry and parody are conceived of as social practices, as ways of leasing and building upon the intellectual and stylistic property of other writers, ways that have much to teach us about our own collaborative enterprise." James Shapiro, *Rival Playwrights: Marlowe, Shakespeare, Jonson,* (New York: Columbia University Press, 1991), viii.

61. It is not surprising, for instance, to find Mary Thomas Crane responding to Greene's emphasis on originality—however mediated through a select tradition—when she challenges his belief that "the work of cataloguing and of rote memory required by this [notebook] method could not in itself produce sensitive understanding and creative imitation." Quoted in Crane, *Framing Authority,* 3; the passage is from Greene's *The Light in Troy,* 318 n.1.

62. See, for example, the critical alternatives mentioned in note 38, above.

63. Michael Baxandall, *Patterns of Intention: On the Historical Explanation of Pictures* (New Haven: Yale University Press, 1985), 58–59. I am indebted to Andrew Weiner for bringing this study and others to my attention.

64. The word "position" does not appear, for instance, in the sonnet sequences of Sidney, Spenser, Drayton, Daniel, or Shakespeare, and while Milton employs it comparatively often in his prose ("THE POSITION," he writes boldly, before the

first chapter of the 1644 *Doctrine and Discipline of Divorce*), it does not grace his English poetry.

65. Richard Bancroft, *Dangerous Positions and Proceedings, Published and Practised Within This Island of Britain, Under Pretence of Reformation* (London: John Wolfe, 1593).

66. Bancroft, *Dangerous Positions*, A2.

67. See *Twelfth Night* 2.5.119; *Troilus and Cressida* 3.3.112; and *Othello* 2.1.236, 3.3.234. In what appears to be a Fletcher scene of *The Two Noble Kinsmen*, it is the painfully pedantic Schoolmaster, Gerrold, who uses the word (3.5.51).

68. Alexander Schmidt, *Shakespeare Lexicon and Quotation Dictionary*, 2 vols. (1902; reprint, New York: Dover, 1971), q.v.

69. See *Tracts Ascribed to Richard Bancroft*, ed. Albert Peel (Cambridge: Cambridge University Press, 1953). Quotation from page xx.

70. See, for example, Crane, *Framing Authority*, who stresses the roots in the humanist energies of the early sixteenth century of what I am arguing came to influence the later 1500s and early 1600s; Brian Vickers, *Francis Bacon and Renaissance Prose* (Cambridge: Cambridge University Press, 1968), esp. chap. 2, "The Aphorism," 60–95; Kenneth Alan Hovey, "'*Mountaigny* Saith Prettily': Bacon's French and the Essay," PMLA 106 (1991): 71–82; Juliet Fleming, "Wounded Walls: Graffiti, Grammatology, and the Age of Shakespeare," *Criticism* 39 (1997): 1–30; and Patricia Fumerton, *Cultural Aesthetics: Renaissance Literature and the Practice of Social Ornament* (Chicago: University of Chicago Press, 1991). On the "new method" of clause-by-clause translation developed from at least 1604 by Joseph Webbe, see Vivian Salmon, "An Ambitious Printing Project of the Early Seventeenth Century," *The Library* n.s. 16 (1961): 190–96. Webbe's scheme was to establish a monopoly on textbooks with works like *Lessons and Exercises Out of Cicero ad Atticum* (1627) and *Pueriles Confabulatiunculae* (1627). Salmon points out that James Shirley, the playwright, was probably one of the first to teach from Webbe's books (191).

71. See, for example, Jonathan Dollimore, *Radical Tragedy: Religion, Ideology, and Power in the Age of Shakespeare* (Brighton, Sussex: Harvester Press, 1984); *Political Shakespeare: New Essays in Cultural Materialism*, ed. Jonathan Dollimore and Alan Sinfield (Ithaca: Cornell University Press, 1985); and Steven Mullaney, *The Place of the Stage: License, Play, and Power in Renaissance England* (Chicago: University of Chicago Press, 1988).

72. See Bryan Reynolds, "The Devil's House, 'or worse': Transversal Power and Antitheatrical Discourse in Early Modern England," *Theatre Journal* 49 (1997): 143–67.

73. Paul Yachnin, "The Powerless Theater," *English Literary Renaissance* 21 (1991): 49–74, quote on p. 51. This essay was incorporated into Yachnin's *Stage-Wrights*, 1–24.

74. In addition to Yachnin's *Stage-Wrights*, a number of "market" studies—and studies that have stressed the routine, entertainment-industry side of playing in early modern London—have suggested that the radical theater described in much cultural materialist and new historicist writing misinterprets the playhouses and their cultural roles. See, for example, Leeds Barrol, *Politics, Plague, and Shakespeare's Theater: The Stuart Years* (Ithaca: Cornell University Press, 1991); William Ingram, *The Business of Playing: The Beginnings of the Adult Professional Theater in Elizabethan London* (Ithaca: Cornell University Press, 1992); James H. Forse, *Art Imitates Business: Commercial and Political Influences in Elizabethan Theatre* (Bowling Green OH: Bowling Green State University Popular Press, 1993); and Lars Engle, *Shakespearean Pragmatism: Market of His Time* (Chicago: University of Chicago Press, 1993).

75. See, for example, Norman Rabkin, *The Common Understanding* (New York: Free Press, 1967) and *Shakespeare and the Problem of Meaning* (Chicago: University of Chicago Press, 1981); Joel Altman, *The Tudor Play of Mind: Rhetorical Inquiry and the Development of Elizabethan Drama* (Berkeley: University of California Press, 1978); E. M. W. Tillyard, *The Elizabethan World Picture: A Study of the Idea of Order in the Age of Shakespeare, Donne and Milton* (London: Chatto and Windus, 1943); and Dollimore, *Radical Tragedy*. In a study with which I became acquainted only after this book was substantially complete, Jonathan Bate discusses the problems that Shakespeare's multiplicity poses for critical binarisms: "The duck-rabbit is a neat icon of aspectuality, but it only has two aspects. Each of Shakespeare's plays has many more than two." Bate, *The Genius of Shakespeare* (Oxford: Oxford University Press, 1998), 327–35, quote on p. 331.

76. See Carolyn Porter, "Are We Being Historical Yet?" *South Atlantic Quarterly* 87, no. 4 (1988): 743–86. Porter points out that "the use of cultural anecdotes is one of the techniques most often remarked upon by the more skeptical members of new historicism's audience" (778, and see her bibliography in note 51, 785). Porter asks: "If anecdotes cannot historicize . . . what is their function in these analyses?" (779).

77. Richard Strier, *Resistant Structures: Particularity, Radicalism, and Renaissance Texts* (Berkeley: University of California Press, 1995), 166–67.

78. Kastan, *Shakespeare After Theory*, 50.

79. Allan Bloom, with Harry V. Jaffa, *Shakespeare's Politics* (New York: Basic Books, 1964), 9–10.

80. As Raymond Williams has argued, "it is with the discovery of patterns of a characteristic kind that any useful cultural analysis begins, and it is with the relationships between these patterns, which sometimes reveal unexpected identities and correspondences in hitherto separately considered activities, sometimes again reveal discontinuities of an unexpected kind, that general cultural analysis is concerned." Williams, "The Analysis of Culture," reprinted in *Culture, Ideology and Social Process: A Reader,* ed. Tony Bennett et al. (London: Batsford, 1981), 43–52, quote on p. 47.

2. Quoting Marlowe's Shepherd

1. Nashe quotes from Sidney's *Astrophil and Stella* in his *Summer's Last Will and Testament* (1592) and refers to Sidney as "a shepherd (that now sleeps in skies)" (lines 1172–3). In *The Works of Thomas Nashe,* ed. R. B. McKerrow, vol. 3.

2. For Marlowe's waning hold on succeeding generations of writers, see Shapiro, *Rival Playwrights.*

3. See Peter J. Seng, *The Vocal Songs in the Plays of Shakespeare* (Cambridge MA: Harvard University Press, 1967), 164; and Frederick Sternfeld and Mary Joiner Chan, "Come live with me and be my love," *Comparative Literature* 22 (1970): 173–87.

4. Here and throughout this chapter I employ the genre terminology of Alastair Fowler in *Kinds of Literature* (Cambridge MA: Harvard University Press, 1982). I have found Fowler's discussion of representational modes and aspects particularly valuable.

5. See, for example, Annabel Patterson, *Pastoral and Ideology: Virgil to Valery* (Berkeley: University of California Press, 1987), esp. 60–192; and Paul J. Alpers, *What is Pastoral?* (Chicago: University of Chicago Press, 1996). On the problematics of the pastoral in the early modern period in England, see Peter Lindenbaum, *Changing Landscapes: Anti-pastoral Sentiment in the English Renaissance* (Athens: University of Georgia Press, 1986). See also Louis Adrian Montrose, "Of Gentleman and Shepherds: The Politics of Elizabethan Pastoral Form," ELH 22 (1982): 5–19. For an account of the Marlovian invitation that differs from my own and grounds it in the tradition of mannerism, see James V. Mirollo, "Postlude: Three Versions of the Pastoral Invitation to Love," chap. 5 in *Mannerism and Renaissance Poetry: Concept, Mode, Inner Design* (New Haven: Yale University Press, 1984), 160–78. More recently, Patrick Cheney has read Marlowe's invitation as an Ovidian response to Spenser's Vergilian practice in "Career Rivalry and the Writing of Counter-Nationhood: Ovid, Spenser, and Philomela in Marlowe's 'The Passionate Shepherd to His Love,'" ELH 65 (1998): 523–55.

6. On "answer" poetry, see E. F. Hart, "The Answer-Poem of the Early Seventeenth Century," RES n.s. 7 (1956): 19–29; and Arthur F. Marotti, *Manuscript, Print, and the English Renaissance Lyric* (Ithaca: Cornell University Press, 1995), 159–71.

7. See R. S. Forsythe's argument in "'The Passionate Shepherd' and English Poetry," PMLA 40 (1925), part 2, 692–742, quote on pp. 701–2. Mention of the poem in Greene's *Menaphon,* for instance, helps form a *terminus ad quem.*

8. Theocritus, *Sixe idillia: That is, Sixe Small, or Petty poems, or Æglogues, Chosen out of the right famous Sicilian Poet Theocritus, and translated into English Verse* (Oxford: 1588).

9. Definitions here from Liddell and Scott's *Greek-English Lexicon.* Readers of modern literary theory are perhaps most familiar with the word *pharmakon* from Derrida's extended essay on "Plato's Pharmacy." See Jacques Derrida, *Disseminations,* trans. Barbara Johnson (Chicago: University of Chicago Press, 1981), 61–171, esp. 70.

10. T. S. Eliot, *Shakespeare and the Stoicism of Seneca* (An address read before the Shakespeare Association, March 18, 1927) (London: Oxford University Press, 1927), 7, 8. The extent to which Othello is actually thinking of Desdemona (rather than of himself) before this speech is, of course, a matter of debate.

11. Helen Vendler, *The Poetry of George Herbert* (Cambridge MA: Harvard University Press, 1975), 18.

12. On the functions of genre in the early modern period in England, see Rosalie Colie, *The Resources of Kind: Genre-Theory in the Renaissance* (Berkeley: University of California Press, 1973); and Stephen Cohen, "New Historicism and Genre: Toward a Historical Formalism," REAL 11 (1995): 405–23.

13. Robert Kimbrough, ed., *Sir Philip Sidney: Selected Prose and Poetry,* 2d ed. (Madison: University of Wisconsin Press, 1983), 127–29.

14. Kimbrough, *Sir Philip Sidney,* 143.

15. Kimbrough, *Sir Philip Sidney,* 158.

16. Compare Gladys Doidge Willcock and Alice Walker in their edition of *The Arte*: "[Puttenham] works out a survey of the Progress of Poesy and relates . . . the smaller kinds . . . to the turning-points in individual existence and the varying moods and passions of men." George Puttenham, *The Arte of English Poesie,* ed. Gladys Doidge Willcock and Alice Walker (Cambridge: Cambridge University Press, 1936), lxiii.

17. Puttenham, *Arte of English Poesie,* 45.

18. Puttenham, *Arte of English Poesie,* 45–52.

19. Puttenham, *Arte of English Poesie,* 53–54.

20. *The Whole Booke of Psalmes: Collected into English Meter, by Thomas Sternhold, John Hopkins, and Others*; printed with the Geneva Bible (London: 1599).

21. On the popularity of the Psalms, see Peter W. M. Blayney, "The Publication of Playbooks," in *A New History of Early English Drama,* ed. John D. Cox and David Scott Kastan (New York: Columbia University Press, 1997), 383–422, quote on p. 388. Blayney notes that, in the twenty-five years beginning in 1583, there were 124 editions published of Sternhold and Hopkins' *The Whole Booke of Psalmes: Collected into English Meter.*

22. *A Treatise made by Athanasius the Great, concerning the use and vertue of the Psalmes.* Undated. STC 885. ("a frag[ment] of an unidentified edition of Sternhold and Hopkins").

23. Izaak Walton, *The Compleat Angler,* ed. Jonquil Bevan (London: J. M. Dent, 1993), 57.

24. Virgil, *Eclogues,* trans. H. Rushton Fairclough (revised edition; Cambridge MA: Harvard University Press, [1965]), 1.63–65.

25. In standard editions, this occurs at lines 738–897. See the edition of the *Metamorphoses* in the Loeb Classical Library, ed. G. Goold, vol. 2 (Cambridge MA: Harvard University Press, 1984).

26. *Shakespeare's Ovid,* trans. Arthur Golding, ed. W. H. D. Rouse (Carbondale: Southern Illinois University Press, 1961).

27. See, for one example of Polyphemus's undirected aggression, Thomas Farnaby's edition of the *Metamorphoses* (Paris: 1637), 72.

28. J. B. Leishman, *The Art of Marvell's Poetry* (London: Minerva Press, 1968), 82, 86, 251–52, 260–67.

29. It sometimes seems as though the suitor has taken a page out of Freud's explication of the dirty joke. See Freud's formulation of the aggressive subtext of such jokes in *Jokes and Their Relation to the Unconscious* (New York: Norton, 1960), 97–102.

30. See Thomas Nabbes, *Hannibal and Scipio: an Historicall Tragedy* (1637), 4.5, in A. H. Bullen, ed. *The Works of Thomas Nabbes* (1882–89; reprint, New York: Benjamin Blom, 1968).

31. On the cultural valences of the "plain" as style, epistemology, and structure of feeling during the early modern era in England, see Kenneth J. E. Graham, *The Performance of Conviction: Plainness and Rhetoric in the Early English Renaissance* (Ithaca: Cornell University Press, 1994).

32. Douglas Peterson, *The English Lyric from Wyatt to Donne* (Princeton: Princeton University Press, 1967), 218.

33. *England's Helicon,* ed. H. E. Rollins (1600; reprint, Cambridge MA: Harvard University Press, 1935), no. 138, 186. The sequence includes nos. 137–39, 184–88.

34. See Eugene R. Cunnar, "Donne's Witty Theory of Atonement in 'The Baite,'" *Studies in English Literature* 29 (1989): 77–98. Cunnar argues that "In shifting the amatory debate from a pastoral to a piscatorial landscape, Donne calls to his reader's attention two traditions of fishing, one sacred and the other profane, that will allow him to challenge and reject Marlowe's false idealism and Ralegh's cynical realism as he seeks to defend ironically reciprocity and mutual sexuality in human love" (78). In my view, the piscatorial tradition is already embedded in the invitational process of Marlowe's lyric and merely made apparent by Donne.

35. *The Dramatic Works and Poems of Shirley,* ed. William Gifford and Alexander Dyce, vol. 1 (London: 1833).

36. It is tempting here to claim that this tendency of the drama is what Bakhtin referred to (in relation to Dostoevsky's poetics) as "polyphony"—despite Bakhtin's pointed and repeated denials that Shakespearean drama (and what seems to us its polyphonic achievement) qualifies for his rubric. Mikhail Bakhtin, *Problems of Dostoevsky's Poetics,* trans. Caryl Emerson (Minneapolis: University of Minnesota Press, 1984). In conjunction with the novel generally, Bakhtin called this *raznorečie,* translated by Caryl Emerson and Michael Holquist as "heteroglossia": "These distinctive links and interrelationships between utterances and languages, this movement of the theme through different languages and speech types, its dispersion into the rivulets and droplets of social heteroglossia, its dialogization— this is the basic distinguishing feature of the stylistics of the novel." *The Dialogic Imagination,* edited by Michael Holquist and translated Emerson and Holquist (Austin: University of Texas Press, 1981), 263. In contrast to Bakhtin, I believe "polyphony" accurately describes the heteroglossic structures of Shakespeare's plays and early modern drama generally. Anatoly Lunacharsky's insightful review of the 1929 edition of *Problems of Dostoevsky's Poetics* is still the most compelling response to the problem of polyphony in Bakhtin's writings. Published also in 1929, the review can be found in Lunacharsky, *On Literature and Art* (Moscow: Progress Publishers, 1973), 79–106.

37. Bakhtin, *Problems,* 252.

38. Georg Lukács, *The Theory of the Novel,* trans. Anna Bostock (Cambridge MA: MIT Press, 1987), 45.

39. The "romance of etymology" supports this view of the formal determinants of the time/dialogue nexus; see Roman Jakobson: "As the etymology of the Latin

term versus itself suggests, verse contains the idea of a regular recurrence, in contradistinction to prose, the etymology of whose Latin term prosa . . . suggests a movement directed forward." In Jakobson, *Verbal Art, Verbal Sign, Verbal Time* (Oxford: Basil Blackwell, 1985), 23. According to the OED, "verse" comes from the Latin *versus,* "a line or row," from the past participle of *vertĕre,* "to turn"; "prose," on the other hand, comes ultimately from *prōvertĕre,* "to turn *forwards*" (my emphasis). The distinction would seem to be one between undifferentiated turning and turning with a direction or goal; hence the related construction *prōsa oratio,* indicating "staightforward discourse."

40. On the dialogical nature of the pastoral lyric in the early modern period in England, see Leishman, *The Art of Marvell's Poetry,* chap. 3, "Pastoral and Semi-Pastoral," 101–92. For an account detailing the perversity of the Elizabethan love sonnet, see Roger Kuin, "Feint/Frenzy: Madness and the Elizabethan Love-Sonnet," *Criticism* 31 (1989): 1–20.

41. R. S. Forsythe cited fourteen instances of oral invitation along the model of "The Passionate Shepherd"—what he called "moving someone to a course of action through an appeal to his desire for luxury, by means of exaggeratedly rich joys and delicacies"—in Marlowe's own plays. Forsythe, "'The Passionate Shepherd' and English Poetry."

42. All references to both parts of *Tamburlaine* are to the Regents edition, ed. John D. Jump (Lincoln: University of Nebraska Press, 1967).

43. See, for example, Harry Levin, *The Overreacher: A Study of Christopher Marlowe* (Cambridge MA: Harvard University Press, 1952); Frank Whigham, *Seizures of the Will in Early Modern England* (Cambridge: Cambridge University Press, 1997), esp. 32, 45, 201; and Dolora A. Wojciehowski, *Old Masters, New Subjects: Early Modern and Poststructuralist Theories of Will* (Stanford CA: Stanford University Press, 1995).

44. *Dido, Queen of Carthage* in *Christopher Marlowe: The Complete Plays,* ed. J. B. Steane (New York: Penguin, 1983). All subsequent references to *Dido* are to this edition.

45. See Barnes's "Sestine 5" in *Parthenophil and Parthenophe: A Critical Edition,* ed. Victor A. Doyno (Carbondale: Southern Illinois University Press, 1971), 127–30. By this point in the collection, Parthenophil is enraged that (in his words) "Parthenophe smiles at my tears" (line 9) and subsequently enters into an unholy alliance with Hecate and a mysterious goat to bring a naked Parthenophe to his secret altar in the woods. I am indebted to Roland Greene for my knowledge of this text.

46. As S. K. Heninger Jr. pointed out to me, Astrophil and Stella appear to grapple in songs 4 and 8. (On this issue see also Nora Fienberg, "The Emergence of

Stella in *Astrophil and Stella,*" *Studies in English Literature* 25 [1985]: 5–19.) That they do so in the songs and not in the sequence proper is precisely my point: many poems incorporate two or more voices, but when they do so, their forms often change, and they become songs, eclogues, debates, even poetic drama. Again, my argument is not that poems—including lyrics—never include dialogue, but rather that, during the early modern era, playwrights came to associate certain *tendencies* with certain modes of literary expression.

47. *Friar Bacon and Friar Bungay,* ed. J. A. Lavin (London: Benn, 1969).

48. *The Plays and Poems of Robert Greene,* ed. J. Churton Collins (1905; reprint, Freeport NY: Books for Libraries, 1970), 1:1,126, lines 1609–20 (act 5, scene 2).

49. *Lust's Dominion; or, The Lascivious Queen,* ed. J. Le Gay Brereton (Louvain: Libraire Universitaire Uystpryst, 1931). This play was originally attributed on its title page to Christopher Marlowe. Scholars have suggested that it may be a collaboration, with John Day, William Haughton, and even John Marston offered as possible coauthors.

50. I am indebted to Marjorie Garber for this observation, passed on in conversation.

51. T. S. Eliot, *Elizabethan Essays* (London: Faber and Faber, 1934), 75.

52. On the Jacobean court and its mythologies, see Graham Parry, *The Golden Age Restor'd: The Culture of the Stuart Court, 1603–42* (New York: St. Martin's Press, 1981); *The Mental World of the Jacobean Court,* ed. Linda Levy Peck (Cambridge: Cambridge University Press, 1991); and Curtis Perry, *The Making of Jacobean Culture: James I and the Renegotiation of Elizabethan Literary Practice* (Cambridge: Cambridge University Press, 1997), esp. 15–49.

53. On Marlowe's contemporary reputation, see Charles Nicholl, *The Reckoning: The Murder of Christopher Marlowe* (London: Jonathan Cape, 1992); and David Riggs's forthcoming biography of Marlowe, which is tentatively titled "Nasty, Brutish and Brilliant: The Life of Christopher Marlowe." I have benefitted from Riggs's research throughout this essay.

54. W. N., *Barley-break: Or A Warning for Wantons* (London: 1607), C3–C3ᵛ.

3. The Agency of Quotation

1. See Ralegh's "The Lie," line 14, in *The Penguin Book of Renaissance Verse, 1509–1659,* ed. David Norbrook and H. R. Woudhuysen (London: Penguin Press, 1992), 116–18. The lines from which this phrase is taken read: "Tell potentates they live | acting by others action, | Not loved unlesse they give, | not strong but by affection" (14–17). Norbrook and Woudhuysen point out (764) that some manu-

script versions of the poem read "acting but others' action," an alternate reading that exactly inverts the one I have quoted but preserves an emphasis on using another to execute one's wishes.

2. On the "lions" and "foxes" of Shakespearean drama and the latters' cunning employment of instrumental reason, see Hugh Grady, *Shakespeare's Universal Wolf: Studies in Early Modern Reification* (Oxford: Clarendon Press, 1996).

3. However comedic in nature, the playwright figure in Shakespeare functions across the lines of genre. Studies by Susan Snyder and Frances Teague, among others, have demonstrated that many of Shakespeare's tragedies have a powerful comedic matrix. Susan Snyder, *The Comic Matrix of Shakespeare's Tragedies: Romeo and Juliet, Hamlet, Othello, and King Lear* (Princeton: Princeton University Press, 1979), and Frances Teague, "*Othello* and New Comedy," *Comparative Drama* 20 (1986): 54–64.

4. William Kerrigan, "The Personal Shakespeare: Three Clues," in *Shakespeare's Personality*, ed. Norman N. Holland, Sidney Homan, and Bernard J. Paris (Berkeley: University of California Press, 1989), 175–90, quote on p. 175.

5. On the thorough infusion of metaphors of playing and theatricality in Shakespeare's works, see Anne Righter (later Anne Barton), *Shakespeare and the Idea of the Play* (London: Chatto and Windus, 1962). For a recent investigation of the phenomenology of playing in Shakespeare, see Meredith Skura, *Shakespeare the Actor and the Purposes of Playing* (Chicago: University of Chicago Press, 1995).

6. Research by Donald Foster suggests verbal evidence for the roles that Shakespeare acted in the reportories of the Lord Chamberlain's Men and the King's Men. See "Shaxicon 1995," *The Shakespeare Newsletter* 45, no. 225 (summer 1995): 25, 30, 32.

7. Greenblatt, *Shakespearean Negotiations*. See esp. chap. 1, "The Circulation of Social Energy," 1–20.

8. Greenblatt, *Shakespearean Negotiations*, 6.

9. Denton J. Snider, *System of Shakespeare's Dramas* (St. Louis: G. I. Jones and Company, 1877), 1:12. A more recent discussion of mediation in Shakespeare's plays—one more indebted to Marx and Lévi-Strauss than to Hegel—is that of Bruce Erlich, "Queenly Shadows: On Mediation in Two Comedies," *Shakespeare Survey* 35 (1982): 65–77.

10. Snider, *System*, 13.

11. Snider, *System*, 40.

12. Cyril Tourneur, *The Atheist's Tragedy*, ed. Brian Morris and Roma Gill (London: Ernest Benn, 1976), 2.4.84–85.

13. A. R. Braunmuller, "'Second Means': Agent and Accessory in Elizabethan Drama," in *The Elizabethan Theater XI*, ed. A. L. Magnusson and C. E. McGee (Port Credit ON: D. Meany, 1990), 177–203. Braunmuller's essay brings legal definitions of agency obtaining in the early modern era to bear on themes and instances of agency in the period's drama.

14. Snider, *System*, 1:42.

15. Manfred Pfister, *The Theory and Analysis of Drama*, trans. John Halliday (Cambridge: Cambridge University Press, 1988), 75. On "production" (as opposed to "creation") as an important trope of poetic theory up to and through the early modern period, see E. N. Tigerstedt, "The Poet as Creator: Origins of a Metaphor," *Comparative Literature Studies* 5 (1968): 455–88.

16. Pfister, *Theory and Analysis*, 75.

17. From Latin *mediāre*, "to be in the middle; to halve; to transact as an intermediary" (OED), the word "mediate" describes the active "in-betweeness" that the producer figure assumes. The OED offers the following among possible definitions: "To occupy an intermediate or middle place or position;" "To act as a mediator or intermediary; to intercede, or intervene for the purpose of reconciling;" "to bring about (a peace, treaty, etc.) by acting as mediator; to procure by intercession." In *2 Henry IV*, King Henry captures several of these senses in his admonition to Clarence to be closer to Hal, so that "noble offices thou mayst effect | Of mediation, after I am dead, | Between his greatness and thy other brethren" (4.4.24–26). Iago uses the word "mediators" in *Othello* (1.1.16) to gloss "Three great ones of the city" whom he (ostensibly) has asked to serve as his go-betweens "In personal suit to make me his lieutenant" (1.1.8–9). For theoretical accounts of "mediation," see the entry in *A Dictionary of Marxist Thought*, ed. Tom Bottomore et al. (Cambridge: Harvard University Press, 1983) and Tamar Yacobi, "Narrative Structure and Fictional Mediation," *Poetics Today* 8 (1987): 335–72.

18. Anthony Giddens, *Central Problems in Social Theory: Action, Structure and Contradiction in Social Analysis* (Berkeley: University of California Press, 1979), 55. In *Making History: Agency, Structure and Change in Social Theory* (Ithaca: Cornell University Press, 1988), Alex Callinicos provides an eloquent synthesis of several theories of agency. See also Perry Anderson, *Arguments within English Marxism* (London: New Left Books, 1980). For a philosophical discussion of agency, see Donald Davidson, *Essays on Actions and Events* (Oxford: Clarendon Press, 1980), esp. chap. 1, "Actions, Reasons, and Causes," 3–19, and chap. 3, "Agency," 43–61. For agency and causality in legal theory, see H. L. A. Hart and A. M. Honoré, *Causation in the Law*, 2d ed. (New York: Clarendon Press, 1985).

19. Bruce Robbins, "The Butler Did It: On Agency in the Novel," *Representations*

6 (1984): 85–97, quote on p. 89. Robbins continues: "My illustration, once again, is the butler who 'does' it, or what might be called more generally the *servus ex machina*: the servant or slave who intervenes with superb and repetitive arbitrariness in plots exclusively dedicated to the destinies of his or her superiors. This device of plot-making antedates Plautus and Menander—the Corinthian messenger and Theban shepherd of *Oedipus Rex*, who first conspire to save Oedipus and then combine to destroy him, offer an interesting example."

20. On the "go between," see the chapter of that title in Stephen Greenblatt's *Marvelous Possessions: The Wonder of the New World* (Chicago: University of Chicago Press, 1991), 119–51.

21. Wayne A. Rebhorn, *Foxes and Lions: Machiavelli's Confidence Men* (Ithaca: Cornell University Press, 1988), 14.

22. Bernard Spivack, *Shakespeare and the Allegory of Evil* (New York: Columbia University Press, 1958), see esp. chap. 2, 28–59.

23. William Hazlitt, "Othello," in *Characters of Shakespear's Plays* (1817), published in Hazlitt, *The Round Table: Characters of Shakespeare's Plays* (London: J. M. Dent, 1960), 207.

24. A. C. Bradley, *Shakespearean Tragedy: Lectures on "Hamlet," "Othello," "King Lear," "Macbeth"* (London: Macmillan, 1904).

25. Sidney R. Homan, "Iago's Aesthetics: Othello and Shakespeare's Portrait of an Artist," *Shakespeare Studies* 5 (1969): 141–58, quote on p. 141; Sigurd Burckhardt, *Shakespearean Meanings* (Princeton: Princeton University Press, 1968), 273.

26. Richard Abrams, "*The Tempest* and the Concept of the Machiavellian Playwright," *English Literary Renaissance* 8 (1978): 43–66, quote on p. 44. On Prospero as magician in the Faustian tradition, see Alvin B. Kernan, *The Playwright as Magician: Shakespeare's Image of the Poet in the English Public Theater* (New Haven: Yale University Press, 1979), esp. chap. 7, "The Playwright as Magician," 146–59. I am particularly indebted to Bernard Knox's important essay, "*The Tempest* and the Ancient Comic Tradition," in *English Institute Essays* (1954), ed. W. K. Wimsatt Jr. (New York: Columbia University Press, 1955), 52–73.

27. Bertrand Evans, *Shakespeare's Comedies* (Oxford: Clarendon Press, 1960).

28. John W. Blanpied, *Time and the Artist in Shakespeare's English Histories* (Newark: University of Delaware Press, 1983), 14.

29. Richard Hillman, *Shakespearean Subversions: The Trickster and the Play-text* (London: Routledge, 1992), 3, 2.

30. An exception to his pattern came in the late 1590s, when, after *The Merchant of Venice*, Shakespeare temporarily tried his hand at the urban comedy genre,

which would shortly begin to dominate the stage. I am thinking here of *The Merry Wives of Windsor* and the agency of Margaret Page and Alice Ford, which Shakespeare would shortly thereafter inflect with (the equally nonaristocratic) Helena in *All's Well That Ends Well.*

31. On the Plautine slave's only temporary power, see Rebhorn, *Foxes and Lions,* 79.

32. Latin text from a facsimile published with an introduction by August Buck (Stuttgart-Bad Cannstatt: Friedrich Frommann Verlag, 1964), 3. The translation here is that of John Rundin, who, having been asked to look over my imperfect attempt, generously (and modestly) provided a much better one—for which, and for permission to use here, I am in his debt. On the "Promethean" aspect of the early modern poet, see Ernst Bloch: "[T]he humanist Scaliger took the word poesy in a literal sense to mean ποιετν [*sic*] in a Promethean sense: the poet is a 'factor,' an 'alter deus.' Accordingly, Scaliger defined the poet not as one who repeats given material but rather as another god who creates and establishes. . . . The comparison of the artist with Prometheus began in 1561, at the time of Faust, when Scaliger's poetics appeared, and it continued through Bacon to Shaftesbury, Klopstock, the *Sturm und Drang* writers, Herder, and the young Goethe. A designation of the will, without a doubt." Ernst Bloch, "The Wish-Landscape Perspective in Aesthetics: The Order of Art Materials According to the Dimension of Their Profundity and Hope" (1959), published under the main heading "Art and Society" in Bloch, *The Utopian Function of Art and Literature: Selected Essays,* trans. Jack Zipes and Frank Mecklenburg (Cambridge MA: MIT Press, 1988), 71–77, quote on p. 76.

33. See Philip Sidney, *An Apology for Poetry,* ed. Forrest G. Robinson (Indianapolis: Bobbs-Merrill, 1970), 12–17; esp. 12 n. 49 and 17 n. 63.

34. Puttenham, *The Arte of English Poesie,* 3.

35. Puttenham, *The Arte of English Poesie,* 6. For a reading of Portia through Puttenham, see Monica J. Hamill, "Poetry, Law, and the Pursuit of Perfection: Portia's Role in *The Merchant of Venice,*" *Studies in English Literature* 18 (1978): 229–43. Quoting Puttenham, Hooker, and Sidney, Hamill argues: "Portia follows in the footsteps of the archetypal poet-lawmakers" (231). It is difficult, however, fully to accept Hamill's conclusions about what she sees as the relatively festive "education" transpiring in this play.

36. Puttenham, *The Arte of English Poesie,* 7.

37. All Latin quotations from Plautus are taken from the edition in the Oxford Classical Texts series, ed. W. M. Lindsay, 2 vols. (1905; Oxford: Oxford University Press, 1980). The translations are my own.

38. George E. Duckworth, *The Nature of Roman Comedy: A Study in Popular Entertainment* (Princeton: Princeton University Press, 1952), 135.

39. Niall W. Slater, *Plautus in Performance: The Theatre of the Mind* (Princeton: Princeton University Press, 1985), 126, 139. With this last description Slater is responding to John Wright, "The Transformations of Pseudolus," *Transactions of the American Philological Association* 105 (1975): 403–16, who calls Pseudolus a theatrical director. To Slater, this term proposes "an anachronistic view of his role that conceals some of the functioning of the creative process" (135 n.22).

40. Such forms the basis of one of my few reservations concerning Robert S. Miola's insightful study, *Shakespeare and Classical Comedy: The Influence of Plautus and Terence* (Oxford: Clarendon Press, 1994).

41. T. W. Baldwin, *Shakspeare's Five-Act Structure* (Urbana: University of Illinois Press, 1947), 665–67, 702–4, 706–7, 713–15; Kenneth Muir, *Shakespeare's Sources: Comedies and Tragedies* (London: Methuen, 1957); Geoffrey Bullough, *Narrative and Dramatic Sources of Shakespeare,* 8 vols. (London: Routledge, 1957–75).

42. Wolfgang Riehle, *Shakespeare, Plautus, and the Humanist Tradition* (Cambridge: D. S. Brewer, 1990), 20. See Riehle's chap. 1, "The Elizabethan Reception of Plautus," 14–43, esp. section 1, "The preference for Plautus over Terence," 14–23. For a detailed bibliography of works dealing with the relationship between Plautus and Shakespeare, see Riehle, 291–93.

43. T. W. Baldwin, *William Shakspere's Small Latine & Lesse Greeke* (Urbana: University of Illinois Press, 1944), 1:436.

44. Timothy J. Moore, *The Theater of Plautus: Playing to the Audience* (Austin: University of Texas Press, 1998), 92–107.

45. Moore, *Theater of Plautus,* 101.

46. Snyder, *Comic Matrix,* 91.

47. Duckworth, *Nature of Roman Comedy,* 339. The translation from *Amphitruo* is Duckworth's.

48. Roscius was often (mis)described by the Elizabethans as a tragic actor; see, for example, Chambers, *The Elizabethan Stage* (Oxford: Clarendon Press, 1923), 1:376–77; 2:297–98.

49. See, for example, Leo Salingar, *Shakespeare and the Traditions of Comedy* (New York: Cambridge University Press, 1974), 278–81, and E. C. Pettet, "Shakespeare's Conception of Poetry," *Essays and Studies* n.s. 3 (London: Wyman and Sons, 1950): 29–46. On the trope of *furor poeticus* generally, see Allan Gilbert, *Literary Criticism: Plato to Dryden* (Detroit: Wayne State University Press, 1962), 8–23.

50. Ovid, *Metamorphoses,* 11.13–14. Latin text from the Loeb edition, 2, ed. and

trans. Frank Justus Miller (1916; Cambridge MA: Harvard University Press, 1984). Golding's translation is reproduced in *Shakespeare's Ovid.*

51. Ovid, *Metamorphoses,* 12.220–21.

52. See also Lear's "Down from the waist they are Centaurs, | Though women all above; | But to the girdle do the gods inherit, | Beneath is all the fiends'" (4.6.124–27).

53. The ultimate sincerity of this gesture might be called into question by Shakespeare's silence over Elizabeth's death in 1603. Then separate publications asked Shakespeare to, in the words of Henry Chettle(?), "remember our Elizabeth." See *The Shakespere Allusion-Book: A Collection of Allusions to Shakespere from 1591 to 1700,* ed. C. M. Ingleby et al., (1909; reprint, Freeport NY: Books for Libraries Press, 1970), 1:123–25.

54. Robert Weimann, *Shakespeare and the Popular Tradition in the Theater: Studies in the Social Dimension of Dramatic Form and Function* (Baltimore: Johns Hopkins University Press, 1978), 74, 79.

55. Evans, *Shakespeare's Comedies,* 46.

56. Evans, *Shakespeare's Comedies,* 67; emphasis in the original. On Portia's dominance in the play, see also Hamill, "Poetry, Law, and the Pursuit of Perfection."

57. Marc Shell, *Money, Language, and Thought: Literary and Philosophic Economies from the Medieval to the Modern Era* (Berkeley: University of California Press, 1982), 69.

58. John Dryden, "Defence of the EPILOGUE: Or, *An Essay on the Dramatique Poetry of the last Age" (The Conquest of Granada II), The Works of John Dryden,* ed. H. T. Swedenberg Jr. (Berkeley: University of California Press, 1956–79), 11:215.

59. Hillman, *Shakespearean Subversions,* 101.

60. Robert Greene(?), *Greene's Groatsworth of Wit,* 85.

4. Quoting the Playhouse

1. For surveys of such criticism, see Meredith Anne Skura, "Discourse and the Individual: The Case of Colonialism in *The Tempest," Shakespeare Quarterly* 40 (1989): 42–69; and Jerry Brotton, "'This Tunis, sir, was Carthage': Contrasting Colonialism in *The Tempest,"* in *Post-Colonial Shakespeares,* ed. Ania Loomba and Martin Orkin (London: Routledge, 1998), 23–42.

2. Skura, "Discourse and the Individual," 52–53.

3. Frances E. Dolan, "The Subordinate('s) Plot: Petty Treason and the Forms of Domestic Rebellion," *Shakespeare Quarterly* 43 (1992): 317–40.

4. Kastan, *Shakespeare After Theory*, chap. 10, "'The Duke of Milan | And his Brave Son': Old Histories and New in *The Tempest*," 183–97, quote on p. 188.

5. Brotton, "'This Tunis, sir,'" 23–42.

6. Jeffrey Knapp, "Distraction in *The Tempest*," chap. 6 in *An Empire Nowhere: England, America, and Literature from "Utopia" to "The Tempest"* (Berkeley: University of California Press, 1992), 220–42. Compare the following: "Part of what causes the rather rigorous exclusion of colonialism in a play so strongly suggesting the issue is, I will maintain, Shakespeare's skeptical mimicry of a brand of imperialism I have associated particularly with Spenser's Fairyland, an antimaterialism holding that the best way to win America is to raise the minds of one's insular nation above the low thought of mere earthly possession" (221).

7. Frank Kermode, ed., *The Tempest*. The Arden Shakespeare (Cambridge MA: Harvard University Press, 1954), xxv–xxvi.

8. Thomas Dekker, *The Shoemakers' Holiday*, ed. D. J. Palmer (London: Ernest Benn, 1975), 6.

9. See *Thomas Platter's Travels in England*, trans. Clare Williams (London: Jonathan Cape, 1937), 170.

10. Thomas Middleton, *Father Hubbard's Tale* (London: 1604), D1^r.

11. E. D. Pendry, ed., *Thomas Dekker: Selected Prose Writings* (Cambridge MA: Harvard University Press, 1968), 99.

12. On the practice of stage sitting, see Irwin Smith, *Shakespeare's Blackfriars Playhouse: Its History and Its Design* (New York: New York University Press, 1964), 148, 220–23, 297–98, 308–11, 330.

13. Robert Weimann, *Playing and Writing in Shakespeare's Theatre*, ed. Helen Higbee and William West (New York: Cambridge University Press, 2000). I am grateful to Robert Weimann for sharing his manuscript with me prior to its publication.

14. Pendry, *Thomas Dekker*, 99; emphasis added.

15. James, *Shakespeare's Troy*, 198–99.

16. Anne Barton, ed. *The Tempest* (London: Penguin, 1968), 153.

17. Kermode, ed. *The Tempest*, 47.

18. Stephen Orgel, ed. *The Tempest* (Oxford: Oxford University Press, 1987), 40–42.

19. Joannes Ravisius Textor, *Epithetorum* (London: 1595), 110.

20. I have characterized this passage as a metatheatrical moment in *Drama and the*

Market in the Age of Shakespeare (Cambridge: Cambridge University Press, 1992), 32–33.

21. See C. W. Wallace, London *Times,* 28 March 1913, 6. Quotations from *London's Love to the Royal Prince Henrie, Meeting Him on the River of Thames, at His Return from Richmonde, with a Worthy Fleete of Her Cittizens, on Thursday the Last of May 1610. With a Briefe Reporte of the Water-Fight and Fire-Workes* (London: 1610), in *The Progresses, Processions, and Magnificent Festivities of King James the First,* ed. John Nichols (London: 1828; reprint, New York: Burt Franklin, 1960–68), 2:319, 321.

22. See Meredith Anne Skura on the role of the directing actor-manager in Shakespeare in her *Shakespeare the Actor,* 47–48, 140–44.

23. On the growing reliance on the visual in Shakespeare, see Gary Schmidgall, *Shakespeare and the Courtly Aesthetic* (Berkeley: University of California Press, 1981).

24. Samuel Daniel, epistle prefaced to *The Vision of the Twelve Goddesses,* line 269. In Alexander B. Grosart, ed., *The Complete Works in Verse and Prose of Samuel Daniel* (1885; reprint, New York: Russell and Russell, 1963), 3:196.

25. Andrew Gurr, *Playgoing in Shakespeare's London* (Cambridge: Cambridge University Press, 1987), 93.

26. Harold Jenkins, ed., The New Arden *Hamlet* (London: Methuen, 1982), note to 3.2.1–35 (Longer Note, 498–99).

27. [Thomas Nashe], *An Almond for a Parrat* (London: 1590), A1. In *The Works of Thomas Nashe,* ed. R. B. McKerrow, 3:341.

28. On Will Kemp's career as clown, see David Wiles, *Shakespeare's Clown: Actor and Text in the Elizabethan Playhouse* (Cambridge: Cambridge University Press, 1987) and Max W. Thomas, "*Kemps Nine Daies Wonder*: Dancing Carnival into Market," PMLA 107 (1992): 511–23. For representative jigs and discussion of Kemp's relation to the jig, see Charles Read Baskervill, *The Elizabethan Jig and Related Song Drama* (Chicago: University of Chicago Press, 1929).

29. On *locus* and *platea,* see Weimann, *Shakespeare and the Popular Tradition,* 74, 79. Kemp's practice appears to have had significant precedent in the medieval and early Tudor theater, where a Vice character might run through and around the audience, talking to spectators and including them in the playworld even as he separated himself from it.

30. Richard Brome from *The Antipodes,* ed. Ann Haaker (Lincoln: University of Nebraska Press, 1966).

31. When Prospero speaks of "The trumpery in my house" (4.1.186), it is soon defined in a stage direction: "*Enter ariel, loaden with glistering apparel, etc. . . .*" Pros-

pero's "house" is thus like a playhouse in containing the "trumpery" and "glistering apparel"—i.e., costumes—central to the business of playing in early modern London. Indeed, it is difficult to exaggerate the importance of apparel to the theatrical industry then. As the research of Ann Rosalind Jones and Peter Stallybrass demonstrates, the theaters of early modern London served as something like extensions of the urban clothing industry. Thus, for example, when in *The Changeling* Isabella asks Lollio for the key to his "wardrobe" to apparel herself as a madwoman—which she does in a brief interval—she could have received the actual key to the *playhouse*'s wardrobe (where a madwoman's costume might well have been found), her project temporarily blurring the boundaries between madhouse and theater (see 4.3.49–102). In much the same way, Prospero manages his house's wardrobe; the "glistering apparel, etc." with which he tantalizes Caliban, Trinculo, and Stephano come from the playhouse's wardrobe. See Ann Rosalind Jones and Peter Stallybrass, *Renaissance Clothing and the Materials of Memory* (New York: Cambridge University Press, 2000).

32. Robert Nares, *A Glossary or Collection of Words, Phrases, Names, and Allusions to Customs, Proverbs, Etc. Which Have Been Thought to Require Illustration in the Works of English Authors, Particularly Shakespeare and His Contemporaries* (London: Gibbings and Company, 1901), vol. 1, "Haydigyes."

33. Will Kemp, *Kemp's nine days' wonder. Performed in a dance from London to Norwich* (London: 1600), reprinted in *Social England Illustrated: A Collection of XVIth Century Tracts, An English Garner*, ed. Edward Arber (Westminster: Archibald Constable, 1903), 139–62, quotes on pp. 141, 143, 144, 147, 150.

34. See C. L. Barber, *Shakespeare's Festive Comedy: A Study of Dramatic Form and Its Relation to Social Custom* (Princeton: Princeton University Press, 1959) and François Laroque, *Shakespeare's Festive World: Elizabethan Seasonal Entertainment and the Professional Stage*, trans. Janet Lloyd (Cambridge: Cambridge University Press, 1991).

35. On Kemp in *Romeo and Juliet*, see Wiles, *Shakespeare's Clown*, 83–94.

36. William Empson, "Honest in *Othello*," chapter 11 of *The Structure of Complex Words* (1951; reprint, Cambridge: Harvard University Press, 1989), 218.

37. On "apprentice frustration" and resulting unrest in early modern London, see Mark Thornton Burnett, "Apprentice Literature and the 'Crisis' of the 1590s," *Yearbook of English Studies* 21 (1991): 27–38.

38. See Mallin, *Inscribing the Time*, chap. 4, "'A twenty years' removed thing': *Twelfth Night*'s Nostalgia," 167–219.

39. My reading of Prospero is akin to that of Clifford Leech, who sees Prospero as evidence of a growing "puritanic strain" in Shakespeare's later plays. See chap. 7,

"*The Tempest*," in Leech, *Shakespeare's Tragedies, and Other Studies in Seventeenth Century Drama* (London: Chatto and Windus, 1950). Leech identifies sentiments uttered by Prospero as Shakespeare's own. And while the conventions of criticism have taught us to be careful about such identifications, Harry Berger Jr.'s response to Leech—"The remark can be changed from a faulty judgment to a useful interpretive insight by substituting 'Prospero' for 'Shakespeare'"—too glibly, in my opinion, separates teller from tale. Berger, "Miraculous Harp: A Reading of Shakespeare's *Tempest*," *Shakespeare Studies* 5 (1970 for 1969): 253–83, 280 n. 3.

40. E. A. J. Honigmann, *Shakespeare's Impact on His Contemporaries* (Totowa NJ: Barnes and Noble, 1982), esp. 7, 9, 11, 22.

5. Quotation and Madwomen's Language

1. Neely, "'Documents in Madness,'" 315–38, 334.

2. Neely, "'Documents in Madness,'" 323.

3. On the sources of the play, see Philip Edwards, "On the Design of *The Two Noble Kinsmen*," REL 5 (1964): 89–105; E. Talbot Donaldson, *The Swan at the Well: Shakespeare Reading Chaucer* (New Haven: Yale University Press, 1985), 50–73; and Ann Thompson, *Shakespeare's Chaucer: A Study in Literary Origins* (New York: Barnes and Noble, 1978), 166–215.

4. See, for example, Linda Charnes, *Notorious Identity: Materializing the Subject in Shakespeare* (Cambridge MA: Harvard University Press, 1993) and Garber, *Shakespeare's Ghost Writers*. For a useful study of the relation of character to rhetoric in Shakespeare's plays and of character criticism generally, see Christy Desmet, *Reading Shakespeare's Characters: Rhetoric, Ethics, and Identity* (Amherst: University of Massachusetts Press, 1992).

5. The Jailer's Daughter has long proved the affective center of the play; from the Restoration to the present, audiences and critics have invariably acknowledged the unexpected force of her role. See, for example, G. Harold Metz, "*The Two Noble Kinsmen* on the Twentieth Century Stage," *Theatre History Studies* 4 (1984): 63–69 and Eugene M. Waith, ed., *The Two Noble Kinsmen* (Oxford: Oxford University Press, 1989), 30–42. Chronicling its stage history from the Restoration, when the Jailer's Daughter was known as "Celania," Waith remarks "In interpreting the play we need to pay attention to the success enjoyed by several actresses in the role of the Jailer's Daughter" (42). Susan Green has described the Jailer's Daughter as both a "locus of the play's illusioning power" and "the play's most potent figure of desire." See Green, "'A mad woman? We are made, boys!': The Jailer's Daughter in *The Two Noble Kinsmen*" in *Shakespeare, Fletcher and "The Two Noble Kinsmen"*, ed. Charles H. Frey (Columbia: University of Missouri Press, 1989), 121–32, quotes on pp. 121, 124.

6. The authorship question in *The Two Noble Kinsmen* has generated a bibliography too lengthy to include here. The best summary of the history of this debate and of the various positions scholars have taken can be found in Will Hamilin, "A Select Bibliographical Guide to *The Two Noble Kinsmen*" in *Shakespeare, Fletcher, and "The Two Noble Kinsmen"*, ed. Frey, 187–204. I base my assignment of 4.3 mainly to Shakespeare on four elements: on Waith's argument (see note to 4.3); on the fact that it, like 2.1, is written in prose; on the use of "troth" (a word favored by Shakespeare), found only in 2.1 and 4.3 of the play; and on the social satire in the "mad" speech of the Jailer's Daughter (4.3.31–56)—the latter being very similar to the kind of mad discourse that Shakespeare employs in *Hamlet* and *King Lear*.

7. On "else," see 3.4.9, 3.4.26, 3.5.77, 4.1.110, 4.1.113; "like a top," 3.4.26, 5.2.50; alliteration, 2.1.22–24, 2.4.20–25, 2.4.27–28, 3.2.8, 3.2.20, 4.1.126–27, 4.1.130–31, 4.3.25–26, 5.2.50, 5.2.67, 5.2.84; "all," 4.1, lines 125, 127, 130, 131, 133, 136.

8. However parodic the Bottom/Titania romance may be, it occurs within a play—and within that play's forest world—where social difference seems (temporarily) less important than desire. On the relations between *Dream* and *Kinsmen*, see Glynne Wickham, "*The Two Noble Kinsmen,* or *A Midsummer Night's Dream, Part II?*" *Elizabethan Theatre* 7 (1980): 167–96.

9. On Shakespeare's absent mothers, see, for example, Mary Beth Rose, "Where are the Mothers in Shakespeare? Options for Gender Representation in the English Renaissance," *Shakespeare Quarterly* 42 (1991): 291–314; Coppélia Kahn, "The Absent Mother in *King Lear*," in *Rewriting the Renaissance: The Discourses of Sexual Difference in Early Modern Europe,* ed. Margaret W. Ferguson, Maureen Quilligan, and Nancy J. Vickers (Chicago: University of Chicago Press, 1986), 33–49; and Stephen Orgel, "Prospero's Wife," in *Rewriting the Renaissance,* 50–64.

10. Michael MacDonald, "Women and Madness in Tudor and Stuart England," *Social Research* 53 (1986): 261–81, quote on p. 280.

11. Maurice Charney and Hanna Charney, "The Language of Madwomen in Shakespeare and His Fellow Dramatists," *Signs* 3 (1977): 451–60, quote on p. 451. On the songs of madwomen in early modern drama in England, see also Joseph T. McCullen Jr. "The Functions of Songs Aroused by Madness in Elizabethan Drama," in *A Tribute to George Coffin Taylor,* ed. Arnold Williams (Chapel Hill: University of North Carolina Press, 1952), 185–96. We perhaps hear Lear acknowledging the gender of one kind of madness in his lines: "O how this mother swells up toward my heart! | *Hysterica passio,* down, thou climbing sorrow, | Thy element's below" (2.4.5–58).

12. William R. Bowden, *The English Dramatic Lyric, 1603–42: A Study in Stuart Dramatic Technique* (New Haven: Yale University Press, 1951), 38 n. 8.

13. So Coleridge, in Collier's report: "The mad scenes of the Jailor's daughter are coarsely imitated from *Hamlet*: those were by Fletcher, and so very inferior, that I wonder how he could so far condescend." And while "coarsely" here has an aesthetic denotation, connotations of morality, even class difference, may exist as well. In *Coleridge's Shakespeare Criticism,* ed. Thomas Middleton Raysor (London: Constable and Co., 1930), 2:32.

14. The passages quoted are from, respectively, 2.4.7, 2.4.26, 3.5.79, 4.1.106, 4.1.129–30, 4.1.132–33, 4.1.137–39, 4.3.37–38, 5.2.51, 5.2.64–65, 5.2.84, 5.2.109.

15. See Anthony Fletcher and John Stevenson, "A Polarised Society?" in *Order and Disorder in Early Modern England,* ed. A. Fletcher and J. Stevenson (Cambridge: Cambridge University Press, 1985), 1–15.

16. R. Malcolm Smuts, *Court Culture and the Origins of a Royalist Tradition in Early Stuart England* (Philadelphia: University of Pennsylvania Press, 1987), 1. See also Parry, *Golden Age Restor'd.*

17. See Leah Marcus, *The Politics of Mirth: Jonson, Herrick, Milton, Marvell, and the Defense of Old Holiday Pastimes* (Chicago: University of Chicago Press, 1986).

18. See Jonson in his *Conversations,* in *Ben Jonson,* 1:134.

19. On the growth and economic importance of London, see F. J. Fisher, *London and the English Economy, 1500–1700,* ed. J. Corfield and N. B. Harte (London: Hambledon Press, 1990), especially "The Development of London as a Centre of Conspicuous Consumption in the Sixteenth and Seventeenth Centuries," 105–18 (orig. pub. 1948) and "London as an 'Engine of Economic Growth,'" 185–98 (orig. pub. 1971); see also E. A. Wrigley, "A Simple Model of London's Importance in Changing English Society and Economy, 1650–1750," *Past and Present* 37 (1967): 44–70, reprinted in Wrigley, *People, Cities and Wealth: The Transformation of Traditional Society* (Oxford: Blackwell, 1987), 133–56. For the influence of London on Jacobean drama, see Brian Gibbons, *Jacobean City Comedy: A Study of Satiric Plays by Jonson, Marston and Middleton,* 2d ed. (New York: Methuen, 1980), and Theodore B. Leinwand, *The City Staged: Jacobean Comedy, 1603–1613* (Madison: University of Wisconsin Press, 1986).

20. Quoted in a different form in Fernand Braudel, *The Wheels of Commerce* (New York: Harper and Row, 1982), 41. For the rapid population growth of London in the late sixteenth and early seventeenth centuries, see E. A. Wrigley and R. S. Schofield, *The Population History of England, 1541–1871: A Reconstruction* (New York: Cambridge University Press, 1989), esp. 531–32.

21. On Shakespeare's deep reliance on imagery drawn from nature, country life, sport, and games, see Caroline F. Spurgeon, *Shakespeare's Imagery and What It Tells*

Us (Cambridge: Cambridge University Press, 1935). I have discussed the influence of London on playwrights' dramatic projects in *Drama and the Market,* 124 n.28. In *Ben Jonson, Dramatist* (Cambridge: Cambridge University Press, 1984), Anne Barton notes that in *The New Inn* (1629), Jonson "abandoned the metropolis which had served him so long in favour of a country setting" redolent of Shakespeare's Elizabethan comedies and Jacobean romances (259). See Barton's remarks on the nostalgic impulse behind this and other late plays by Jonson, 258–84.

22. My use of these terms necessarily calls to mind Perez Zagorin's classic study, *The Court and the Country: The Beginnings of the English Revolution* (New York: Atheneum, 1969), which uses "the Country" to describe a "loose collaboration or alliance of men in the governing class, peers and gentlemen of assured position and often of substantial fortune, alienated for a variety of reasons from the Court" (75). In contrast, however, I employ it in the sense Lawrence Stone provides in defining the Country as "a culture and a style of life," one that could stand for "an experience of the world confined to the shires of England." Stone, *The Causes of the English Revolution 1529–1642* (London: Routledge, 1972), 106. See also Raymond Williams, *The Country and the City* (London: Chatto and Windus, 1973), where "country" and "city" can stand for "the experience of human communities," quote on p. 1.

23. Robert Weimann, "Le Declin de la Scene 'Indivisible' Elisabethaine: Beaumont, Fletcher et Heywood" in *Dramaturgie et Societe* (Paris: Centre National de la Recherche Scientifique, 1968), 2:815–27, quote on p. 825. Weimann's remarks have been borne out in the study by David Wiles, which contrasts Will Kemp, the famous Elizabethan clown, with Robert Armin, the satirical clown who replaced Kemp in the Lord Chamberlain's Men. See Wiles, *Shakespeare's Clown.* Yet in a recent article on Will Kemp, Max W. Thomas argues that by 1600 Kemp himself was not outside the circuit of commercial desire and performance; in his reading, Kemp's famous morris dance from London to Norwich was a phenomenon that moved "toward the commercialization of rural festivity." Thomas, *"Kemps Nine Daies Wonder,"* 514. See also, of course, Weimann's *Shakespeare and the Popular Tradition.*

24. Paul N. Siegel, *Shakespearean Tragedy and the Elizabethan Compromise* (1957; reprint, New York: New York University Press, 1983).

25. Although *Lear* is commonly interpreted as straddling the feudal and modern eras, the play also speaks to a smaller, even generational transition. In *Poets on Fortune's Hill: Studies in Sidney, Shakespeare, Beaumont and Fletcher* (London: Faber and Faber: 1952), J. F. Danby sees 1606 as the first year in a 1606–10 period of transition, with *Lear* something like the former era's last statement (19). For Danby,

the change has a generational cause: "Sidney's *Arcadia* has more in common with Shakespeare's *Lear* and *Pericles* than these have with the plays of Beaumont and Fletcher. Shakespeare and Sidney . . . are somehow members of the same moral community. Beaumont and Fletcher, using the same theatre as Shakespeare, belong to a different world" (17). Shakespeare, born in 1564, also came from a background that—though full of qualifying circumstances—was markedly lower in status than that of Fletcher, born in 1579 and educated at Corpus Christi. It should be noted that a generational shift leads Christopher Hill to call 1614 the turning point in the era; see *Intellectual Origins of the English Revolution* (Oxford: Clarendon Press, 1965), 10–13, 95.

26. See Norman Jones, *God and the Moneylenders: Usury and the Law in Early Modern England* (Oxford: Basil Blackwell, 1989), esp. chap. 7, 175–98.

27. Jones, *God and the Moneylenders*, 179–81.

28. Joseph Angus, ed., *The Works of Thomas Adams* (Edinburgh: J. Nichols, 1861–62), 2:221–53.

29. William Pemberton, *The Godly Merchant, or the Great Gaine* (London: 1613).

30. Jones, *God and the Moneylenders*, 182–86.

31. This last phrase comes from Alexander Welsh, *The City of Dickens* (London: Oxford, 1971) and is quoted by Fredric Jameson in *The Political Unconscious: Narrative as a Socially Symbolic Act* (Ithaca: Cornell University Press, 1981), 186.

32. Brian Vickers, "Rites of Passage in Shakespeare's Prose," *Shakespeare-Jahrbuch* (1986): 45–67, quote on p. 45.

33. See Ann Thompson, "Jailers' Daughters in *The Arcadia* and *The Two Noble Kinsmen*," *Notes and Queries*, n.s. 26 (1979): 140–41.

34. Later commentators frequently indict Fletcher's breaching of decorum of character. See, for example, Richard Flecknoe, who, in *A Short Discourse of the English Stage* (1664), wrote that "*Beaumont* and *Fletcher* were excellent in their kind, but they often err'd against *Decorum*, seldom representing a valiant man without somewhat of the *Braggadocio*, nor an honourable woman without somewhat of *Dol Common* in her." (In *Critical Essays of the Seventeenth Century*, ed. J. E. Spingarn [Oxford: Clarendon Press, 1908], 2:94). During the next decade, Thomas Rymer, commenting on *A King and No King* in *The Tragedies of the Last Age* (1677), stated that "The Characters are all *improbable* and *unproper* in the highest degree, besides that both these, their actions and all the *lines* of the Play run so wide from the Plot, that scarce ought could be imagin'd more contrary." (In *The Critical Works of Thomas Rymer*, ed. Curt A. Zimansky [New Haven: Yale University Press, 1956], 42). Later Rymer would repeat some of these charges against

Othello (in *A Short View of Tragedy*), but there he stresses mainly the improbability of the plot—one more appropriate to farce, he intimates, than formal tragedy.

35. Barber, *Shakespeare's Festive Comedy*, 16.

36. On the "contagion of the marketplace" in *Bartholomew Fair* and Jonson's imagination generally, see Peter Stallybrass and Allon White, *The Politics and Poetics of Transgression* (Ithaca: Cornell University Press, 1986), 59–79.

37. Thomas, *"Kemps Nine Daies Wonder."*

38. Philip Edwards, in his introduction to the text in *A Book of Masques* (Cambridge: Cambridge University Press, 1967), 129.

39. On the layers of calendrical phenomena in *Dream*, see David Wiles, *Shakespeare's Almanac: "A Midsummer Night's Dream," Marriage, and the Elizabethan Calendar* (Rochester NY: D. S. Brewer, 1993).

40. See 2.6.35, 3.2.7, 3.2.25, 2.4.18, 3.2.21, 4.1.110, 4.1.151, 4.3.34, 5.2.49. For the use of such words, see *The English Dialect Dictionary*, ed. Joseph Wright, 6 vols. (London: 1896–1905). The survival of certain words in the North does not prove that they look there for their provenance; that a great number of a character's words are later recorded as dialectal, however, seems to point to a certain geographical inflection. As Eugene Waith indicates in the Oxford edition of the play, the northern dialect form found in the "e'e" for "eyes" in one of the Jailer's Daughter's songs—"And I'll clip my yellow locks an inch below mine e'e" ["eie" Quarto]—is "frequently found in ballads" (note to 3.4.2).

41. See Eduard Faust, *Richard Brome: Ein Beitrag zur Geschichte der englischen Litteratur* (Halle an der Salle: n.p., 1887), 55; Lawrence Babb, *The Elizabethan Malady: A Study of Melancholia in English Literature from 1580 to 1642* (East Lansing: Michigan State College Press, 1951), 166; and *A Critical Edition of Brome's "The Northern Lasse"*, ed. Harvey Fried (New York: Garland, 1980), xxx–xxxi.

42. Her intertextual relations with Ophelia, for example, anchor her to a dramatic story at least as early as 1600/1601. The Jailer's Daughter is also part of a tradition of middle- and lower-class heroines most closely associated with Thomas Heywood (*The Fair Maid of the West* [1604]) and Thomas Dekker (*Patient Grissel* [1600]; with Chettle and Haughton). For an important essay on (later) nostalgia for the Elizabethan period, see Anne Barton, "Harking Back to Elizabeth: Ben Jonson and Caroline Nostalgia," ELH 48 (1981): 706–31 (reprint as chap. 14 in *Ben Jonson, Dramatist*, 300–320).

43. Compare also Hamlet's allusion to the story of Jephthah and his daughter; *Hamlet*, ed. Harold Jenkins (London: Methuen, 1982), 2.2.399–416. See especially Jenkins's "Longer Note" on this story, 475–77. I should note that *The Two Noble*

Kinsmen refers to three other women as daughters (none of them seen): "the tanner's daughter" (2.3.44); "The Lord Steward's daughter" (3.3.29); and "Cicely the sempster's daughter" (3.5.44).

44. *Annals of English Drama* lists *Fair Em* as an anonymous play. In his critical edition (*Fair Em: A Critical Edition* [New York: Garland, 1980]), Standish Henning leans toward Anthony Munday as author.

45. Leah Marcus, *The Politics of Mirth,* 6–7. Marcus draws her concept of "survivalism" from the work of such critics and historians as Raymond Williams, Christopher Hill, and Keith Thomas. The foundational study of the festive base of early modern drama is, of course, Barber's *Shakespeare's Festive Comedy.* See also Michael D. Bristol, *Carnival and Theater: Plebeian Culture and the Structure of Authority in Renaissance England* (New York: Methuen, 1985), and Laroque, *Shakespeare's Festive World.* Laroque's study contains an extensive bibliography of primary and secondary materials on the "festive" in early modern England.

46. Tessa Watt, *Cheap Print and Popular Piety, 1550–1640* (Cambridge: Cambridge University Press, 1991), 6.

47. Natascha Wurzbach, *The Rise of the English Street Ballad 1550–1650,* trans. Gayna Walls (Cambridge: Cambridge University Press, 1990).

48. Wurzbach, *Rise of the English Street Ballad,* 256.

49. Jameson, *Political Unconscious,* 19–20. To be sure, Jameson's "political unconscious" is both overdetermined and vaguely defined. And because it is precisely that which cannot be represented, nowhere does he identify it specifically with a character. In fact, Jameson is much more likely to describe characters as allegorical figures for periods and processes. For example, he calls Heathcliff "the locus of *history*" in *Wuthering Heights* (*Political Unconscious,* 128); and he identifies two authority figures in *Dog Day Afternoon* with, respectively, the local and national (even multinational) power structures of late capitalism (*Signatures of the Visible* [New York: Routledge, Chapman and Hall, 1990], 50). In contrast, I would argue that, in her madness, the Jailer's Daughter exceeds such two-dimensional symbolism by actively staging the cultural forms she represents.

50. Jameson, *Political Unconscious,* 102.

51. See Laroque, *Shakespeare's Festive World,* 122–25. See also E. K. Chambers, *The Mediaeval Stage* (Oxford: Oxford University Press, 1903), 1:195–98.

52. See *Kemp's nine day's wonder,* in Arber, *Social England Illustrated,* 143–58, quotes on pp. 147, 149–50.

53. MacDonald, "Women and Madness," 268.

54. Juliana Schiesari, *The Gendering of Melancholia: Feminism, Psychoanalysis, and*

the Symbolics of Loss in Renaissance Literature (Ithaca: Cornell University Press, 1992), 250.

55. Although apparently arbitrary—in the sense that no language has an essential political or sexual bias—this gendering of speech registers undoubtedly resulted from the institutions where Latin was taught. Walter Ong's insightful argument about Latin education being a "puberty rite" for boys in the early modern period, for instance, suggests that the sexual segregation of the grammar schools, their strict corporeal discipline, insistence upon obedience and imitation, and emphasis on the epic/heroic values of classical literature led to a hardening of the individual student "for the extra-familial world in which he would have to live." Walter J. Ong, "Latin Language Study as a Renaissance Puberty Rite," *Studies in Philology* 56 (1959): 103–24, quote on p. 123. Latin thus came to be perceived as the language of manhood, English remaining the mother tongue. This diglossic structure, William Kerrigan argues, led to the articulation of a bifurcated "linguistic ego" in early modern authors brought up in the "rigid, masculine world" of the grammar school: "As the boy was separated from women, so he was divorced from the mother tongue." William Kerrigan, "The Articulation of the Ego in the English Renaissance" in *The Literary Freud: Mechanisms of Defense and the Poetic Will,* vol. 4 of *Psychiatry and the Humanities,* ed. Joseph H. Smith (New Haven: Yale University Press, 1980), 269.

56. See Phyllis Rackin, *Stages of History: Shakespeare's English Chronicles* (Ithaca: Cornell University Press, 1990), 148. Rackin speaks of the marginal role female characters have in the world of Shakespeare's histories and holds that "the women who do appear are typically defined as opponents and subverters of the historical and historiographic enterprise."

6. A Renaissance of Quotation

1. For a foundational study of the modernist paradigm in critical approaches to Shakespeare, see Grady, *Modernist Shakespeare.* See also Richard Halpern's *Shakespeare Among the Moderns* (Ithaca: Cornell University Press, 1997), which examines, among other issues, the modernist tendency of "historical allegory," in which—for such writers as T. S. Eliot—the past becomes a version of the present.

2. J. M. Keynes, *A Treatise on Money* (New York: Harcourt, Brace, 1930), 2:154 n. 3.

3. It has become a commonplace of economic history that, owing to one of the worst inflationary periods in English history, the 1590s were a time of terrible poverty and hardship for the average English citizen. See Bruster, *Drama and the Market,* 18–19, 122 n.15. On the widespread social discomfort of the 1590s, see the editor's introduction in *The Reign of Elizabeth I: Court and Culture in the Last Decade,* ed. John Guy (Cambridge: Cambridge University Press, 1995).

4. Harry Levin, "English Literature of the Renaissance," in *The Renaissance: A Reconsideration of the Theories and Interpretations of the Age,* ed. Tinsley Helton (Madison: University of Wisconsin Press, 1961), 129. Levin, I should point out, concedes that "commercial prosperity was as much a precondition of the English Renaissance as were its responses to intellectual currents from the continent" (129).

5. On quotation in American modernist poetry, see Elizabeth Gregory, *Quotation and Modern American Poetry: "Imaginary Gardens with Real Toads"* (Houston: Rice University Press, 1996). Gregory points out that "quotation—exact repetition of words from pre-existent texts—proliferates in the work of American modernist poets" (2). See also Leonard Diepeveen, *Changing Voices: The Modern Quoting Poem* (Ann Arbor: University of Michigan Press, 1993).

6. Hugh Kenner, *The Pound Era* (Berkeley: University of California Press, 1971), 439.

7. Malcolm Bradbury and James McFarlane, eds., *Modernism, 1890–1930* (New York: Viking Penguin, 1976), 51.

8. See Walter Benn Michaels, *Our America: Nativism, Modernism, and Pluralism* (Durham NC: Duke University Press, 1995).

9. The incredible popularity of Shakespeare's plays during the era of silent films, for instance, indicates how ready-to-hand Shakespeare was in America in the early years of this century. See Robert Hamilton Ball, *Shakespeare on Silent Film: A Strange Eventful History* (New York: Theatre Arts Books, 1968). The Stage Manager of Thorton Wilder's *Our Town* testifies to this longstanding importance when he confides that, along with the Bible and the Constitution, the residents of Grover's Corners intend to place a copy of Shakespeare's plays into the cornerstone of the town's new bank as a way of telling people "a thousand years from now" a "few simple facts about us." Thorton Wilder, *Our Town* (New York: Coward McCann, 1938), 39, 40. On the history of America's relationship to the Shakespeare myth, see Michael D. Bristol, *Shakespeare's America, America's Shakespeare* (London: Routledge, 1990). Bristol's study begins with the sentence: "Shakespeare is an American institution" (1). See also Marjorie Garber, "Shakespeare as Fetish," *Shakespeare Quarterly* 41 (1990): 242–50.

10. See Lawrence W. Levine, *Highbrow/Lowbrow: The Emergence of Cultural Hierarchy in America* (Cambridge MA: Harvard University Press, 1988). On the role of seventeenth-century texts in nineteenth-century America, I have benefited from Robin Grey's *The Complicity of Imagination: The American Renaissance, Contests of Authority, and Seventeenth-Century English Culture* (Cambridge: Cambridge University Press, 1997). One of the most insightful studies of the "setting up" of

Shakespeare in a different cultural context is that of Michael Dobson, *The Making of the National Poet: Shakespeare, Adaptation and Authorship, 1660–1769* (Oxford: Clarendon Press, 1992).

11. On Tunney's Shakespeare lecture, see "Tunney's Bout with Shakespeare," *Literary Digest* 97, no. 6 (May 12, 1928): 22–23.

12. *Poetry of the English Renaissance 1509–1660*, ed. J. William Hebel and Hoyt H. Hudson (New York: F. S. Crofts, 1929). One can sense the unease associated with their use of the term "Renaissance" in the following justification from their preface: "Having begun with the purpose of illustrating English poetry from the beginning of Henry VIII's reign to the Restoration, in the progress of our work we found a continuous tradition which unified this body of poetry. The animating impulses of this tradition appear to be those which flow from the Renaissance. Thus the title for the volume at which we arrived seems to us exact and adequate" (iii).

13. R. E. Sherwood, "Renaissance in Hollywood," *The American Mercury* 16 (1929): 431–37, quote on pp. 431–32.

14. See Barbara Hogdon, "Katherina Bound; or, Play(K)ating the Strictures of Everyday Life," PMLA 102 (1992): 538–53; see also "Shakespeare 'Pepped Up' by Hollywood," *The Literary Digest* 103 (December 21, 1929): 18–19 and "Shakespeare *via* Hollywood," *Punch* (November 27, 1929): 608.

15. See Rosemary Kegl, "'Wrapping togas over Elizabethan garb': Tabloid Shakespeare at the 1934 Chicago World's Fair," unpublished manuscript. I am indebted to Kegl for bringing this instance to my attention and for sharing her essay with me.

16. Harley Granville-Barker, "Alas, Poor Will!" *The Listener* 17, no. 425 (March 3, 1937): 387–89, 425–26.

17. Alfred Hitchcock, "Much Ado About Nothing?" *The Listener* 17, no. 426 (March 10, 1937): 448–450, quotes on pp. 448, 449.

18. See "Shakespeare on the Air," *American Library Association Bulletin* 31 (1937), 398.

19. See Blevins Davis, *Great Plays: A Drama Guide by Blevins Davis* (New York: Columbia University Press, 1939), 5–6. "'Prestige' drama increased in the 1930s. These programs usually were 'anthologies' offering different stories with new casts each week, sometimes adaptations from other media, but often original radio plays. . . . Prestige series included the *Columbia Workshop* of experimental drama on CBS, started late in 1936, and the more conventional *Lux Radio Theater*, which presented such stars as Helen Hayes, Leslie Howard, and an unknown player named Orson Welles in hour-long versions of current films." Christopher Sterling

and John Kittross, *Stay Tuned: A Concise History of American Broadcasting* (Belmont CA: Wadsworth Publishing, 1978), 166.

20. See Martin F. Norden, *John Barrymore: A Bio-Bibliography* (Westport CT: Greenwood Press, 1995), 142–45.

21. Betty Ann Kane, *The Widening Circle: The Story of the Folger Shakespeare Library and Its Collections* (Washington DC: The Folger Shakespeare Library, 1976), 10.

22. See "The Renaissance Conference at the Huntington Library," *Huntington Library Quarterly* 4 (1941): 133–89.

23. For earlier, scattered examples of this phenomenon, see Anne Ferry, *The Title to the Poem* (Stanford CA: Stanford University Press, 1996), 234–37. Ferry discusses Browning's "Childe Roland to the Dark Tower Came," and Tennyson's "Mariana."

24. In addition to the American writers discussed in what follows, such British authors as Joyce and Yeats were obviously influenced by English Renaissance texts during the first few decades of the twentieth century. Joyce delivered twelve lectures on *Hamlet* in Trieste from 1912 to 1913, for instance, and Shakespeare would continue to be a major part of his works' allusiveness. See William H. Quillian, "Shakespeare in Trieste: Joyce's 1912 *Hamlet* Lectures," *James Joyce Quarterly* 12 (1974–75): 7–63; William M. Schutte, *Joyce and Shakespeare: A Study in the Meaning of Ulysses* (New Haven: Yale University Press, 1957); Vincent Cheng, *Shakespeare and Joyce: A Study of Finnegans Wake* (University Park: University of Maryland Press, 1984); and Halpern, *Shakespeare Among the Moderns.* On Yeats's Renaissance reading, see T. McAlindon, "Yeats and the English Renaissance," PMLA 82 (1967): 157–69. McAlindon suggests a strong link between Yeats's re-reading of Elizabethan and Jacobean literature during the early teens and the "defiant adoption of an aristocratic outlook" in his poetry (157).

25. Robinson published his poem in *The Drama* 5 (November 1915): 543–54; and Frost's "Out, Out—" appeared in *McClure's*, July 1916.

26. James Torrens, "T. S. Eliot and Shakespeare: 'This Music Crept By,'" *Bucknell Review* 29 (1971): 77–96, quote on p. 77; for Eliot's critical engagement with Shakespeare, see also Charles Warren, *T. S. Eliot on Shakespeare* (Ann Arbor MI: UMI Research Press, 1987).

27. Freud, "Family Romances," in *The Standard Edition of the Complete Psychological Works of Sigmund Freud,* trans. James Strachey et al. (London: Hogarth Press, 1959), 9:237–41.

28. Thomas Wolfe, *Look Homeward, Angel: A Story of the Buried Life* (New York: Charles Scribner's Sons, 1957), 352. A Joycean potpourri of allusions to canonical texts, *Look Homeward, Angel* makes considerable reference, explicit and implicit,

to Shakespeare. Wolfe seemed to take special delight in recording the budding bardolatry of a young Eugene, who, celebrating the Shakespeare tercentenary in 1916, "tore the Chandos portrait from the pages of the *Independent* and nailed it to the calcimined wall of the back-room. Then, still full of the great echoing paean of Ben Jonson's, he scrawled below it in large trembling letters: 'My Shakespeare, rise!' The large plump face—'as damned silly a head as ever I looked at'—stared baldly at him with goggle eyes, the goatee pointed ripe with hayseed vanity. But, lit by the presence, Eugene plunged back into the essay littered across his table." The essay to which Eugene returned, like the essay to which Wolfe himself returned in the incident he "fictionalized" here, bore the title "Shakespeare the Man" and eventually won both Eugene and Thomas Wolfe the prize medal of the *Independent Magazine*'s Shakespeare Tercentenary essay contest. *Look Homeward*, 307. Wolfe would worship Shakespeare—literally—all his life. In an interview printed in Boston's *Evening Transcript*, September 26, 1931, Wolfe included both Shakespeare and John Donne in a list of three works and authors (the other being the Bible) that he read "all the time." Shakespeare came in for particular notice: "It seems to me that Shakespeare in his vast understanding of humanity was a sort of god. I imagine that he was one with this insatiable capacity to live. By that I don't mean that he wanted long life, but simply that while life was with him he demanded that it be full." *Thomas Wolfe Interviewed*, ed. Aldo Magi and Richard Walser (Baton Rouge: Louisiana State University Press, 1985), 19.

29. George F. Whicher, "Shakespeare for America," *The Atlantic Monthly* (June 1931): 759–68, quote on p. 766.

30. One might contrast Susan Baker's rendering of the "expanded equation or metonymic cluster" underlying the citation of Shakespeare in twentieth-century detective fiction: "Shakespeare equals good taste equals social superiority equals intellectual superiority equals moral superiority." Baker, "Shakespearean Authority in the Classic Detective Story," *Shakespeare Quarterly* 46 (1997): 424–48, quote on p. 445. My understanding stresses the role of social class over morality. Given the nature of detective fiction, however, morality seems much more likely to have been involved in the calculus of citation. See also Baker's "Comic Material: 'Shakespeare' in the Classic Detective Story," in *Acting Funny: Comic Theory and Practice in Shakespeare's Plays*, ed. Francis Teague (Rutherford NJ: Farleigh Dickinson University Press, 1994), 164–79.

31. On the "American" nature of certain Elizabethan styles, one might witness C. S. Lewis's description of Nashe's *Pierce Penilesse*: "Its appeal is almost entirely to that taste for happy extravagance in language and triumphant impudence of tone, which the Elizabethans have, perhaps, bequeathed rather to their American than to their English descendants." *English Literature*, 412.

32. Elizabeth Carney, "Experiencing Shakespeare through the Radio Theater Party," *English Journal* 27 (February, 1938): 133–36, quote on pp. 134–35.

33. Joan Shelley Rubin, *The Making of Middlebrow Culture* (Chapel Hill: University of North Carolina Press, 1992). Rubin's fascinating history of the popularization of "great" books during the 1920s and 1930s provides a valuable background for some of the claims I make here.

34. To Habermas, a legitimation crisis is primarily political, resulting "from a need for legitimation that arises from changes in the political system (even when normative structures remain unchanged) and that cannot be met by the existing supply of legitimation." Jürgen Habermas, *Legitimation Crisis,* trans. Thomas McCarthy (Boston: Beacon Press, 1975), 48. What one might call the cultural legitimation crisis of the 1930s arose from a pervasive social and economic uncertainty, taking shape from the resulting attempts to understand, interpret—even create—value. For a study that relies on crisis-theory in relation to the influential but relatively short-lived Federal Theatre Project (1935–39), see Lauren Kruger, *The National Stage: Theatre and Cultural Legitimation in England, France, and America* (Chicago: University of Chicago Press, 1992).

35. See Michael Bristol's explanation for this apparent paradox in *Shakespeare's America,* where he discusses the figure of Shakespeare in Emerson's *Representative Men* (123–30). Bristol suggests that Shakespeare functions in part "as a screen memory used to rationalize a chronic ambivalence towards both the practice of democracy and archaic forms of authority and the absolutist state" (123).

36. Ralph Ellison, *Shadow and Act* (New York: Random House, 1964), 7.

37. Ellison, *Shadow and Act,* 5.

38. As David Levering Lewis points out, the phrase "Harlem Renaissance" developed from an article in the New York *Herald Tribune,* May 7, 1925, titled "A Negro Renaissance." Lewis, *When Harlem Was in Vogue* (New York: Alfred A. Knopf, 1981), 116 and note.

39. Because no screenplay for the film has been published, dialogue from *Morning Glory* is taken from the film itself. *Morning Glory,* dir. Lowell Sherman, screenplay by H. J. Green. (RKO, 1933).

40. A number of ironies, to say the least, attend the split between popular and aristocratic in American culture. In *Shakespeare's Ghost Writers,* Marjorie Garber points out that Charlie Chaplin, ostensibly the source of *Morning Glory's* comedic *Hamlet,* himself held anything but common or populist views on Shakespeare. "I'm not concerned with who wrote the works of Shakespeare," he stated in his autobiography, "but I hardly think it was the Stratford boy. Whoever wrote them had an aristocratic attitude." Garber goes on to suggest that it seems significant

that "Authorship of the autobiography is on the title page attributed to *Sir* Charles Spencer Chaplin." Garber's study attributes this kind of comment to what she sees as a typically American, "ambivalent fascination with aristocracy" (9, 8). *Hamlet* and Hamlet would assume a recurring role in Chaplin's life and aesthetic: see, for example, Charles J. Maland, *Chaplin and American Culture: The Evolution of a Star Image* (Princeton: Princeton University Press, 1989), 63, 110, 180, 241, 356.

41. Lewis, *When Harlem Was in Vogue,* 116 and note.

42. Langston Hughes, *The Big Sea* (New York: Knopf, 1940), 228.

43. Hughes, *Big Sea,* 223.

44. Langston Hughes, *Shakespeare in Harlem,* with drawings by E. McKnight Kauffer (New York: Knopf, 1942), preface.

45. Hughes, *Shakespeare in Harlem,* 111.

46. Edmund Wilson, *The Thirties,* ed. Leon Edel (New York: Farrar, Straus and Giroux, 1980), 334. "Abracadabra" is one of the words that Shakespeare does *not* use.

47. Robert Kimball, ed., *Cole* (New York: Holt, Rinehart and Winston, 1971), 59.

48. Porter's Shakespeare satire wasn't confined to the 1930s: while at Yale in 1913 he wrote a lyric called "A Member of the Yale Elizabethan Club," where he says: "I convert New Haven | To the bard of Avon, | And a highbrow must I be; | For I give support | To the latest college sporto, | Tea by the quart | And editions by the quarto. | Good Gadzooks! But I love those books" (Kimball, *Cole,* 23). For *Kiss Me, Kate,* the 1948 adaptation of *The Taming of the Shrew,* Porter wrote "Brush Up Your Shakespeare," an impish song arguing that the best way for men to seduce women is with a knowledge of Shakespeare; its lyrics can be summed up with the following: "Brush up your Shakespeare, | And the women you will wow. | Better mention 'The Merchant of Venice' | When her sweet pound o' flesh you would menace" (Kimball, *Cole,* 220–21).

49. Kimball, *Cole,* 124. Later versions of this lyric substitute "Ascot bonnet" for "Bendel bonnet."

50. As Roland Marchand points out in *Advertising the American Dream: Making Way for Modernity, 1920–1940* (Berkeley: University of California Press, 1985), a history of the rise of advertising in America in the early twentieth century, "Some copywriters proudly compared the purposes and challenges of their craft to the labors of Shakespeare, Stevenson, and Dickens. They fondly quoted Aldous Huxley's statement that 'the advertisement is one of the most difficult of modern literary forms. . . . The problem presented by the sonnet is child's play compared with the problem of the advertisement'" (26).

51. Stanley Cavell, *Pursuits of Happiness: The Hollywood Comedy of Remarriage* (Cambridge MA: Harvard University Press, 1981), 1.

52. Cavell, *Pursuits of Happiness,* 142.

53. Cavell, *Pursuits of Happiness,* 144.

54. Cavell, *Pursuits of Happiness,* 143; cf. *Midsummer Night's Dream* 2.1.166–82.

55. Cavell, *Pursuits of Happiness,* 144.

56. Philip Barry, *The Philadelphia Story* (New York: Coward-McCann, 1940), 115, 141, 116.

57. George Lyman Kittredge, *Shakspere: An Address* (Cambridge MA: Harvard University Press, 1924), 9.

58. Cavell, *Pursuits of Happiness,* 19.

59. Raymond Chandler, *The Big Sleep* (New York: Vintage, 1976), 1. On "Shakespeare" in the genre of detective fiction, see Baker, "Shakespearean Authority." Baker's archaeology of Shakespearean citations and thematics in this genre indicates a *terminus ab quo* during the late 1920s and early 1930s, with such works as Josephine Tey's *The Man in the Queue* (New York: E. P. Dutton and Co., 1929) and Ross Barnaby's *Drury Lane's Last Case: The Tragedy of 1599* (New York: Viking, 1933). Baker also notes the relevance of Paul McGuire's *A Funeral in Eden* (New York: Grosset and Dunlap, 1938), Josephine Bell's *Curtain Call for a Corpse* (New York: Macmillan, 1939), and Michael Innes's provocatively titled *A Comedy of Terrors* (1940; reprinted in *Appleby Intervenes: Three Tales from Scotland Yard* [New York: Dodd, Mead, 1965]).

60. Quoted in Jerry Speir, *Raymond Chandler* (New York: Frederick Ungar, 1981), 30.

61. Speir, *Raymond Chandler,* 30.

62. On the relation of noir themes to those of Elizabethan revenge tragedy, see Linda Charnes, "Disremember Me: Shakespeare, Paranoia, and the Logic of Mass Culture," *Shakespeare Quarterly* 48 (1997): 1–16.

63. Raymond Chandler, *Farewell, My Lovely* (New York: Vintage, 1988), 174.

64. Robert Parker, *Perchance to Dream: A Sequel to Raymond Chandler's "The Big Sleep"* (New York: Putnam, 1990); Colin Dexter, *The Wench is Dead* (New York: St. Martin, 1990).

65. Leslie J. Hotson, *The Death of Christopher Marlowe* (Cambridge MA: Harvard University Press, 1925), 25.

66. Samuel A. Tannenbaum, *The Assassination of Christopher Marlowe (A New View)* (New York: Tenny Press, 1928), 63–67.

67. Letter to Edgar Carter, June 3, 1957, in *Selected Letters of Raymond Chandler,* ed. Frank MacShane (New York: Columbia University Press, 1981), 452.

68. Quoted in Eric Bentley, ed., *Thirty Years of Treason* (New York: Viking, 1971), 25.

69. Bentley, *Thirty Years,* 25.

70. Martin Dies, quoted in "Maps Wide Inquiry Into Propaganda," *The New York Times,* June 19, 1938, 26.

71. *Concise Dictionary of American Biography,* 3d ed. (New York: Scribner, 1980).

72. F. O. Matthiessen, *American Renaissance: Art and Expression in the Age of Emerson and Whitman* (New York: Oxford University Press, 1941), vii.

73. Willard Thorp, "John Taylor, Water Poet," *Texas Review* 8 (1922): 32–41, quote on p. 32.

74. Willard Thorp, *The Lost Tradition of American Letters* (Philadelphia: Privately Printed for the Philobiblon Club, 1945), 1, 23.

75. Dashiell Hammett, *The Maltese Falcon* (San Francisco: North Point Press, 1987).

76. Hammett, *Maltese Falcon,* 280.

77. Dialogue in Richard J. Anobile, ed., *The Maltese Falcon* (film transcript) (New York: Avon Books, 1974), 253.

78. Steven Marcus, ed., *The Continental Op* (New York: Vintage, 1974), xxiv–xxv.

79. Michaels, *Our America,* 141.

80. Charlene Avallone, "What American Renaissance? The Gendered Genealogy of a Critical Discourse," PMLA 112 (1997): 1102–20, quote on p. 1102.

Afterword

1. Leo Strauss, *Persecution and the Art of Writing* (Chicago: University of Chicago Press, 1952), 160.

2. Annabel Patterson, *Hermogenes and the Renaissance: Seven Ideas of Style* (Princeton: Princeton University Press, 1970), xi.

INDEX

Abrams, Richard, 96, 97, 233 n.26

Adams, Thomas, 156, 244 n.28

agency, 232 n.13 n.18, 232–33 n.19; consequences of literary models of, 94; defined, 93–94; in drama, 90–92; Marlowe and, 76–79, 85–87; Shakespeare and, 8–9, 90, 92–95, 97–98, 103–16

Alleyn, Edward, 37, 221 n.56

Alpers, Paul J., 225 n.5

Altman, Joel, 45, 224 n.75

Anders, H. R. D., 31

Anderson, Maxwell, 11, 176, 178, 179, 180, 181, 182

Anderson, Perry, 232 n.18

Appian (of Alexandria), 20

Aristotle, 33, 100

Arliss, George, 205

Armin, Robert, 243 n.23

Armstrong, Louis, 179

Athanasius the Great, Saint, 66–68, 227 n.22

The Atheist's Tragedy, 92, 231 n.12

Avallone, Charlene, 207, 255 n.80

Babb, Lawrence, 245 n.41

Bacon, Francis, 19, 156, 216 n.17, 223 n.70, 234 n.32

Baker, George Pierce, 202

Baker, Susan, 251 n.30, 254 n.59

Bakhtin, Mikhail, 74, 75, 228 n.36

Baldwin, T. W., 30, 103, 219 n.43, 235 n.41 n.43

Ball, Robert Hamilton, 248 n.9

ballads and ballad singing, 147, 151–53, 161–62, 164, 172

Bancroft, Richard, 41–43, 46, 223 n.65 n.69

Bankhead, Tallulah, 178

Barber, C. L., 138, 158, 161, 239 n.34

Barley-break, 86, 230 n.54

Barnaby, Ross, 254 n.59

Barnes, Barnabe, 79, 229 n.45; *Parthenophil and Parthenophe*, 79, 229 n.45

Barrol, Leeds, 224 n.74

Barry, Philip, 11, 180, 181, 193–95, 202, 254 n.56; *The Philadelphia Story*, 193–98

Barrymore, John, 178

Barthes, Roland, 91, 216 n.14

Barton, Anne (Righter), 231 n.5, 237 n.16, 243 n.21, 245 n.42

Baskervill, Charles Read, 238 n.28

Baxandall, Michael, 40, 222 n.63

Beaumont, Francis, 24, 155, 159, 217–18 n.28, 243–44 n.25, 244 n.34; *The Knight of the Burning Pestle*, 45